W9-BBW-075

INDIA'S STRATEGIC FUTURE

Also by Ross Babbage

A COAST TOO LONG: Defending Australia beyond the 1990s
GEOGRAPHIC INFORMATION SYSTEMS: Defence Applications
(*coeditor with Desmond Ball*)
RETHINKING AUSTRALIA'S DEFENCE
SHOULD AUSTRALIA PLAN TO DEFEND CHRISTMAS AND
   COCOS ISLANDS?
THE SOVIETS IN THE PACIFIC IN THE 1990s (*editor*)
THE STRATEGIC SIGNIFICANCE OF TORRES STRAIT

Also by Sandy Gordon

BUSINESSMEN AND POLITICS: Rising Nationalism and a
   Modernising Economy in Bombay, 1918–33

India's Strategic Future

Regional State or Global Power?

Edited by

Ross Babbage

and

Sandy Gordon

Foreword by Senator the Honourable Robert Ray

St. Martin's Press   New York

First published in the United States of America in 1992

Printed in Great Britain

ISBN 0–312–07494-8

Library of Congress Cataloging-in-Publication Data
India's strategic future : regional state or global power? / edited by
Ross Babbage and Sandy Gordon.
p. cm.
ISBN 0–312–07494-8
1. India—Defenses. 2. India—Foreign relations—1984–
I. Babbage, Ross, 1949–   . II. Gordon, Sandy.
UA840.I49 1992
355'.033054—dc20   91–28575
                                                         CIP

Contents

Acknowledgements

This book was only possible because of the sustained efforts of a very capable team.

The contributing authors not only gave freely of their time and considerable expertise in researching and drafting their texts but travelled, in most cases, very long distances to have their papers reviewed at a conference in Canberra in April 1990. Editorial comments and suggestions followed and through all of this the team of contributors remained cheerful and committed to the task of producing the best possible product.

Professor Desmond Ball, Head of the Strategic and Defence Studies Centre, lent strong support to the project and marshalled much of the administrative assistance required for its success.

Helen Wilson masterminded the conference administration and much of the correspondence with authors. Nearly all difficulties were resolved effectively by her before they came to our attention. Jena Hamilton produced the index. Elza Sullivan provided extensive and very high quality word processing support. Marlene Arney, Tina Lynam and Karen Smith contributed substantial secretarial support.

A much larger group of people, many with extensive qualifications and experience in the field, gave freely of their time in contributing insights.

We are very grateful for the substantial contributions made by this large and diverse group of people.

ROSS BABBAGE
SANDY GORDON

Notes on the Contributors

Gregory Austin holds a BA from the University of Queensland and a Masters of International Law from the Australian National University. He is a strategic analyst specialising in Soviet involvement in the Asia-Pacific region. He has worked for the Australian Defence Department for a number of years, for the Australian Consulate in Hong Kong, and as Secretary of the Senate Foreign Affairs, Defence and Trade Committee. He is completing a PhD on Soviet military strategy for small wars.

Ross Babbage holds a BEc. and an MEc. from the University of Sydney and a PhD from the Australian National University. He was formerly Deputy Head of Strategic and Defence Studies Centre at the Australian National University. He has held several senior positions in the Australian Public Service. He is currently Chief General Manager, Consulting Division, Australian Defence Industries Ltd. His published works include *Rethinking Australia's Defence, Should Australia Plan to Defend Christmas and Cocos Islands?, The Soviets in the Pacific in the 1990s* (editor), *Geographic Information Systems: Defence Applications* (joint editor) and *A Coast Too Long: Defending Australia Beyond the 1990s.*

Sandy Gordon holds a BA from the University of Sydney, and MA and PhD degrees from Cambridge University. He served in the Office of National Assessments, the Australian International Development Assistance Bureau and the Department of Employment, Education and Training, where he was Executive Director of the Asian Studies Council. He is currently a Visiting Fellow at the Strategic and Defence Studies Centre, Australian National University. His publications include *Businessmen and Politics: Rising Nationalism and a Modernising Economy in Bombay, 1918-33.*

A. Hasnan Habib (Lt Gen. Rtd) is Special Advisor to Professor Dr Diplom Ing B. J. Habibie, Indonesian Minister of State for Research and Technology and Chairman of the Agency for the Assessment and Application of Technology. In 1973 he became Chief of Staff responsible for Strategic Planning and Administration of the Department of Defence and Security with the rank of Lieutenant General. He served as Ambassador to Thailand (1978–82) and USA (1982–85). He was elected an Executive Director of the IMF in 1982. General Habib has also served as a Member of the People's Consultative Assembly in 1966–68, and again in 1977–80.

Manoj Joshi holds a PhD degree from Jawaharlal Nehru University, New Delhi. He is a special correspondent for *The Hindu*, based in New Delhi. He has written extensively on Indian defence, security and political issues and is closely familiar with the processes of defence decision-making in India. His books include *New Perspectives on America and South Asia* (joint editor).

Gary Klintworth holds a BA, and LLB and Masters of International Law degrees from the Australian National University. He is a Senior Research Fellow in the North East Asia Program, Research School of Pacific Studies, Australian National University. He has studied strategic, political and economic issues concerning China, Japan, the Koreas, Taiwan, Hong Kong and Indochina as well as great power involvement in the Asia/Pacific region since 1971 in the Joint Intelligence Organisation, in the Australian Consulate, Hong Kong, and at the Strategic and Defence Studies Centre, Australian National University. His publications include *China's Modernisation and the Strategic Implications for the Asia/Pacific Region*, *Vietnam's Intervention in Cambodia in International Law* and *China's Crisis: The International Implications* (editor).

Amin Saikal holds BA and PhD degrees from the Australian National University. He is Reader in Political Science at the Australian National University. He has been a visiting fellow at Princeton University, Cambridge University and at the Institute of Development Studies, University of Sussex. He has also been a Rockefeller Foundation Fellow in International Relations from 1983 to 1988. His publications include *The Rise and Fall of the Shah*, T*he Afghanistan Conflict: Gorbachev's Options*, *The Soviet Withdrawal from Afghanistan* (joint editor), and *Refugees in the Modern World* (editor).

Raju G. C. Thomas holds a BSc (Econ) from the London School of Economics, an MA in International Relations from the University of Southern California and a PhD in Political Science from the University of California, Los Angeles. He is Professor of Political Science at Marquette University at Milwaukee, USA. He has held Postdoctoral Research Fellowships at Harvard University, the University of

California, Los Angeles and the Massachusetts Institute of Technology. His publications include *Indian Security Policy*, *The Defence of India: A Budgetary Perspective*, *The Great Power Triangle and Asian Security* (editor), and *Energy and Security Among the Nuclear Threshold Countries* (joint editor).

Foreword

This chance to give an Australian perspective on Indian Ocean strategic developments comes at an opportune time. There has been much recent media attention on changes in what is loosely called the Indian Ocean region, most notably on the buildup of Indian military forces. While it is indubitably true that major strategic changes are occurring, much of the comment has been ill-informed and lacks the type of sustained analysis that the issues deserve. This book will hopefully provide more substance and rigour to a field which is clearly attracting increasing attention.

The first and perhaps most fundamental point to make when talking about the Indian Ocean is that it is not a distinct geopolitical region. Unlike the north Atlantic or north Pacific there is no commonality linking the various rim countries. In fact it is more accurate to view the Indian Ocean as a medium that separates rather than one that binds. This is partly due to the size of the Indian Ocean, which covers several distinct strategic regions. In particular major international strategic interests are focused in the north west, and the Gulf, and in the north east, and the Straits of Malacca. Indeed in as much as there is a focus of Indian Ocean strategic geography, it lies across the span of the Ocean's northern boundary from the Red Sea to the Malacca Strait. This is an arc that encompasses a number of actual and potential conflict zones including the Gulf area, Afghanistan, the Pakistan/India border and Cambodia.

Of course strategic perceptions are related to geographic position. For Australia our position means that the strategic impact of events that occur on the Indian Ocean's northern span is most acutely focused in the Southeast Asian region. Our relations with Malaysia and Singapore under the Five Power Defence Arrangements, for example, mean that Australia must pay close attention to their interests and concerns there. Consequently events outside our area of direct military interest do indirectly impact on Australia's defence through their effect on these nations.

Thus the Indian Ocean exemplifies the dynamics of Australia's security. Australia's region is not characterised by military threat, but rather by a large number of independent countries and the increasing complexity of interactions between them. Having said that, it is important that we are clear about the rationale behind Australian security interests in the Indian Ocean and, at the practical level, the rationale for increasing Indian Ocean maritime deployments and west coast naval and air basing.

Australia's increased naval involvement in the ocean is related, simply and directly, to the defence of Australia. The shift in strategic focus to include the Indian Ocean seaboard is not a reflection of the increase in other countries' activities in the Indian Ocean or of any perceived development of threat from the Indian Ocean. Our interest in the region is based on our wish to protect our interests there. This interest has been developed through the 1970s and early 1980s when it became increasingly clear that more balance was needed in our naval basing. The 1987 White Paper, which was the culmination of the move in thinking towards true defence self reliance, finally set out our goals for west coast development.

The White Paper is a total approach, covering as it does the issues of strategic and tactical environment, warning time, contingency levels, and force structure, as well as the implications of these on personnel, defence support and industry policies. Consequently the White Paper provides both a strategic framework in which to place naval operations as well as a practical approach to operating from the west coast. The areas of direct military interest which are defined in the White Paper dictate the necessity of west coast basing:

> Basic facts of our geographic location indicate that conventional military attack against Australia would most likely be directed against the northern part of the mainland, its maritime approaches or offshore territories.

The approach here is quite clear; the criterion we consider is geography. Put in these terms our increased involvement in the Indian Ocean region makes sense. We are not reacting to any particular threat, but rather appropriately using the forces that we have and are developing to provide a fundamental level of defence capability – while at the same time seeking to work cooperatively with regional nations to maintain regional stability.

The priority we give to the self-reliant defence of Australia must be seen in the full context. We must be sensitive to wider developments which have implications for our security and that of our neighbours.

Since the British withdrawal to west of Suez in the early 1970s the main external military forces in the Indian Ocean have been United States, Soviet and French naval elements. Most attention has been focused on the Gulf, where the United States has been committed to protecting western access to oil supplies for a decade. Recently, however, both United States and Soviet deployments in the region have decreased. In the case of the Soviet Union this reduction in forces is probably due to a combination of a move to a 'Defence of the Soviet Homeland Doctrine' and financial constraints. For the United States, the lessening of tension in the Gulf region following the end of the Iran–Iraq War, as well as the Soviet withdrawal from Afghanistan, have probably been the main factors in the decrease in their forces. The likelihood of cuts to United States defence expenditure in general in coming years may also result in further reductions in deployments.

The current Soviet preoccupation with the progress of political and economic reforms at home and in Europe and their endeavours to establish a more balanced and acceptable international image, not simply based on military power projection, should mean that the region will remain a low priority for Moscow. We should not, however, rule out the possibility that Soviet naval units might return to the Gulf area in the event of a serious crisis involving Soviet interests.

The French presence is likely to continue at current levels.

These developments should be seen in concert with the increase in regional military forces, in particular of course, Indian forces. And while not wishing to encroach on later speakers' territory, it would be useful now to look at the broad picture of India's military buildup.

Over the last decade India has undertaken a sustained buildup of its naval forces. Considerable resources have continued to be directed towards the army and air force but India has now developed a genuine 'blue water' capability which enables it to project significant maritime power across the northern Indian Ocean. The Indian navy is now the largest regional force in the Indian Ocean. Recent significant acquisitions have included a second small aircraft carrier, a nuclear powered submarine leased from the Soviet Union and the purchase of modern conventional submarines from the Soviet Union and West Germany. India is also developing new naval bases in the south of the sub-continent and upgrading its facilities in the Andaman Islands. Despite this maritime buildup, India's overall strategic preoccupation, and the rationale for its major force development program, remains the security of its borders with both China and Pakistan. India is not, and will not be in the foreseeable future, in a position to turn its back on those potential threats, to undertake a major military campaign remote from the Indian mainland. Furthermore the nature and scope of the Indian maritime program suggest that it is not directed to any specific operational objective. From an Indian perspective the present naval buildup is both reasonable and necessary. The emphasis has been on the modernisation or replacement of ageing vessels, the strengthening of India's ability to defend its more immediate maritime approaches, and the early acquisition of several major platforms which have considerable symbolic importance. Less emphasis appears to be being given to the acquisition of sophisticated munitions or the development of war stocks to support a protracted conflict.

The ability of the Indian navy and air force to project power beyond the Andaman Sea is of importance for countries in Southeast Asia. Malaysia, Thailand, Indonesia and Singapore are all known to be concerned at the implications of India's expanding power projection capability – an expansion that coincides with the more robust Chinese naval presence in the South China Sea. This may well cause our ASEAN neighbours to consider further naval buildups of their own.

However, India's power projection capabilities are limited. Clearly there is no intention to use its growing military force to threaten Australian security interests or our international trade routes. Indeed, India regards Australia as a legitimate Indian Ocean power and a friendly state whose influence contributes to regional stability.

The increasing concerns of our neighbours in Southeast Asia about India's military potential are at this stage essentially embryonic. They reflect longer term concerns rather than immediate perceptions of threat. In practical terms, they mean that the countries of Southeast Asia are now paying rather more attention to India's strategic orientation and trends in India's force structure development. They will be watching carefully for any signs that India has aspirations to exercise strategic influence outside the subcontinent and the maritime surrounds in the northern Indian Ocean.

This longer term concern about the maritime ambitions of India (and China) will probably be an additional factor in priorities for military capability development in Southeast Asia. There is already a trend towards the development of maritime capabilities in place of the large land forces that reflected post-independence concerns with internal security. That trend has been influenced primarily by concerns about protecting off-shore resources, but it will be reinforced by concerns about the maritime capabilities and intentions of China and India.

There are implications for Australia which we need to consider. Australia has traditionally emphasised maritime capabilities in our force structure because our security circumstances and geography require them. At one level the emergence of significant regional maritime capabilities will tend to erode the capability advantage we have traditionally enjoyed. Yet at another – and arguably more important level – an increasing regional interest in the maritime theatre will offer greater scope for Australia to participate in efforts to promote regional security. In addition to their practical contribution to defence self-reliance, our bases on the west coast will greatly facilitate our regional defence cooperative activities. Naval deployments to Southeast Asia from the west will take only about half the transit time required from Sydney.

Australia has for some years been conducting extensive maritime surveillance operations in the region in support of its own and broader western security interests. Cooperation in this area is now becoming increasingly attractive at the regional level. We are maintaining a program of continuous rotational deployment of P3C long-range maritime patrol aircraft through Butterworth. Malaysia's and our own surveillance provide a valuable contribution to regional surveillance efforts by monitoring the busy seaways of the South China Sea and the Straits of Malacca. We have also established arrangements to rotate F/A-18 and F-111 aircraft through Butterworth.

These activities are very different to earlier allied-dominated security initiatives like SEATO, and to the material aid projects appropriate when our neighbours in Southeast Asia were initially developing their military capabilities. We can expect further developments in regional defence cooperation through the 1990s. It will not be Australia's role to dictate the nature and scope of that cooperation. Rather, through discussion and experiment we will find areas where increased cooperation will serve mutual security interests. A positive approach to regional defence cooperation can make a major contribution to a safer future for Australia and all the countries of our region. A common interest in maritime defence will be central to this.

It is only in the last few years that the strategic significance of the Indian Ocean has been fully incorporated into our defence strategy. In that process it has gained an importance recognised by the establishment of a major fleet base at Cockburn Sound and air bases at Tindal and Curtin. Furthermore, Indian Ocean developments give credence to our increasing emphasis on using naval forces (including maritime air elements) to enhance regional defence cooperation. Consequently, for Australia, Indian Ocean issues should be viewed in the context of their effect on Southeast Asian regional coherence and stability. An understanding of those issues and a commitment to a comprehensive regional response are both key elements in our defence outlook.

SENATOR THE HONOURABLE ROBERT RAY
Australian Minister for Defence

Acronyms

ATV	Advanced Technology Vessel
ASAT	Anti-Satellite Weapon
ASEAN	Association of South-East Asian Nations
AWACS	Airborne Warning and Control System
BJP	Bharatiya Janata Party
CAVCTS	Combined Acceleration Vibration Test System
CCPA	(Indian) Cabinet Committee on Political Affairs
CIA	Central Intelligence Agency
CPI	Cost Price Index
CENTO	Central Treaty Organisation
DPS	(Indian) Defence Planning Staff
DRDO	(Indian) Defence Research and Development Organisation
EC	European Community
ECC	Emergency Committee of the (Indian) Cabinet
EEZ	Exclusive Economic Zone
FBIS	Foreign Broadcasting Information Service
FRG	Federal Republic of Germany
GDP	Gross Domestic Product
GNP	Gross National Product
IAF	Indian Air Force
ICBM	Inter-Continental Ballistic Missile
IGMDP	(Indian) Integrated Guided Missile Development Program
INS	Indian Naval Ship
IRBM	Intermediate Range Ballistic Missile
ISI	Inter-Services Intelligence Directorate (of Pakistan)
JIC	(Indian) Joint Intelligence Committee
KOPKAMTIB	(Indonesian) Commander for the Restoration of Order and Security
LCA	Light Combat Aircraft
MBB	Mutual Bombs-in-the-Basement
MBT	Main Battle Tank
MIRV	Multiple Independently Targeted Re-entry Vehicle
MNB	Mutual Nuclear Brinkmanship

NCDS	National Centre for Development Studies, Australian National University
NAM	Nonaligned Movement
NASA	National Aeronautical and Space Agency
NPT	Non-Proliferation Treaty
OECD	Organisation for Economic Cooperation and Development
PDPA	People's Democratic Party of Afghanistan
PLA	(Chinese) People's Liberation Army
PLO	Palestine Liberation Organisation
PMO	(Indian) Prime Minister's Office
POK	Pakistan Occupied Kashmir
POL	Petroleum, Oil and Lubricants
PRCN	People's Republic of China Navy
RAPID	Reorganised Army Plains Infantry Divisions
RAW	Research and Analysis Wing
RCD	Regional Cooperation for Development
RSS	Rashtriya Swayamsevak Sangh
SAARC	South Asian Association for Regional Cooperation
SALT	Strategic Arms Limitation Talks
SDRs	Special Drawing Rights
SEATO	South-East Asian Treaty Organisation
SIPRI	Stockholm International Peace Research Institute
SLV	Space Launch Vehicle
SPG	(Indian) Strategic Policy Group
SSBN	Ballistic Missile Firing Nuclear Powered Submarine
SSN	Nuclear-Powered (attack) Submarine
START	Strategic Arms Reduction Talks
TOW	Tube-launched, Optically-tracked, Wire-guided anti-tank missile
VHP	Vishwa Hindu Parishad
ZOPFAN	Zone of Peace, Freedom and Neutrality

1 Introduction
Ross Babbage

The 1970s, 1980s, and early 1990s have seen significant growth in India's military capabilities. All major elements of India's armed forces have been expanded and substantially modernised. India's Navy has grown to become easily the most powerful of the Indian Ocean littoral states. It now boasts two aircraft carriers, twenty-six destroyers and frigates, one nuclear-powered and sixteen conventionally-powered submarines, and numerous support and smaller vessels. Moreover, New Delhi has tested an intermediate-range ballistic missile and has pressed ahead with a range of nuclear programs. In recent years India has also used its armed forces to intervene in the off-shore countries of the Maldives and Sri Lanka.

These developments have stimulated considerable comment in the Indian Ocean region and further afield. But India's rise to prominence has not simply been a consequence of the country's growing strength. It has also been spurred by the concurrence of India's rise with a broader re-ordering of the global balance of power.

There has been a marked decline in the relative strength of the two superpowers, especially the Soviet Union. The Soviet politburo is now heavily occupied with the difficult challenges of restructuring the domestic economic and political system and of simply holding the USSR together. It continues to modernise its strategic nuclear forces, but defence expenditure overall has been cut and conventional military forces are being reduced. When combined with the collapse of communism in Eastern Europe, Soviet strategic influence is clearly receding. One consequence is that the USSR will be a much less influential actor in South Asia through the 1990s and it will certainly be a less useful partner for India.

The United States is experiencing a rather less dramatic reduction in relative power. Washington is reducing its military capabilities in response to the receding Soviet threat, but the American economy remains generally robust and easily the largest in the world.

It is in the context of this retreat of the superpowers that we are seeing the rise of a new set of highly competitive major powers. Most prominent among these emerging powers are a more unified Europe,

1

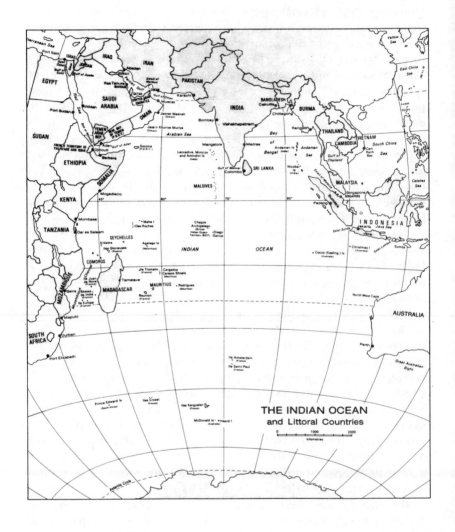

THE INDIAN OCEAN
and Littoral Countries

Japan, China and India. In this rapidly changing global order, India's rise has implications far beyond the South Asian region.

In early 1989, several researchers at the Australian National University held informal discussions on these issues and concluded that substantial research needed to be conducted into India's strategic future. It was agreed that many issues deserved examination. A central theme was the motivation for India's military build up. Is India's sustained defence effort really just a bi-product of its impressive rate of economic growth? Does it rather reflect an Indian aspiration to great power status? How much is India's military development an effort to deter major power intervention in the region, or are New Delhi's driving concerns more those of strengthening coastal defences, providing enhanced security for India's vast exclusive economic zone and enhancing security for the country's long and very important sea lines of communication? What are likely to be India's military priorities in the future? In particular, is New Delhi likely to strive hard to build longer range force projection capabilities?

An important related question is why India is committed to the sustained development of nuclear and long-range ballistic missile systems? Are these capabilities viewed as essential hallmarks of a major power, or does the Indian government believe that such systems are required to deter China, Pakistan and the larger nuclear powers?

If it can be assumed that India is likely to try to sustain its pace of strategic development, questions arise about the country's economic, technological, industrial, educational, social and political strength to pursue these objectives. What are the prospects for the Indian economy in the 1990s and beyond? Will the social and political diversity that has given rise to serious tensions and local violence in several parts of the country generate more taxing internal security demands in the period ahead? And what about the quality and cohesiveness of India's military units? Does increasing use of the army to maintain domestic law and order suggest the possibility of greater influence and broader roles for the armed forces in the future?

A wider set of important questions concerns how India might use its increased military strength. Do the military operations in the Maldives and Sri Lanka portend active military adventures further afield in the late 1990s, or have the difficulties of the Sri Lankan deployment reinforced the long-standing caution of the Indian military establishment? In what ways are India's relationships likely to change with the major global powers? How valuable will Moscow be to New Delhi as a security partner in the 1990s? Will the gradual long term reduction in the American military presence in the Indian Ocean encourage a more rapid warming of the political, security and economic ties with Washington? And how relaxed is China likely to be about India's increasing conventional and nuclear capabilities?

The approaches of India's more immediate neighbours will also be important through the 1990s. How, for instance, will Pakistan, Afghanistan and the Persian Gulf states respond to a more powerful and potentially more assertive India? And what are the perceptions of the major Southeast Asian governments, especially Indonesia, Malaysia, Singapore and Thailand? Are these relationships likely to be subjected to increased tensions in the 1990s and beyond?

In order to address this extraordinarily wide range of important issues, the Strategic and Defence Studies Centre at the Australian National University decided to commission papers from acknowledged experts in relevant fields. These people were assembled in Canberra in April 1990 to deliver their papers and test their views before an audience of some 150 senior officials, diplomats, servicemen, business people and academics. This provided a valuable opportunity to refine views and revise chapters for this volume.

In Chapter 2, Sandy Gordon discusses the economic, technological, social and political foundations of India's security development focusing, in particular, on the country's underlying strengths and weaknesses and its capacity to sustain the pace of its military development. Raju Thomas considers the long-term trends in India's defence development in Chapter 3. He analyses closely how India's military forces have expanded and the capabilities New Delhi is likely to possess in the first decades in the twenty-first century. Manoj Joshi, in Chapter 4, looks very closely at the motivations of India's security planners and the complex and rather messy decision-making processes employed in Indian force development. In Chapter 5, Amin Saikal considers the implications of India's strategic development and its broader security policies for Pakistan, Afghanistan and the Persian Gulf states.

China's future relationship with India is discussed by Gary Klintworth in Chapter 6. He considers, in particular, the prospects for renewed tensions on their common border and Chinese perceptions of India's growing nuclear and ballistic missile capabilities. Greg Austin takes a hard look in Chapter 7 at the place of India in Moscow's perceptions in 1990s. He looks closely at the role of peripheral international theatres, such as South Asia, when the Soviet Union is so preoccupied with domestic, economic and political restructuring.

During the 1965 Indo–Pakistan war, the Indonesian Government offered military assistance to Pakistan. More recently, a number of ministers from the ASEAN countries have expressed concern about India's military buildup, its nuclear capabilities and its expanding military facilities in the Andaman and Nicobar Islands. In Chapter 8, General Hasnan Habib discusses the basis of these concerns and proposes measures for preventing the development of new regional tensions.

The regional interests of major Western powers in the Indian Ocean region are analysed in Chapter 9. Particular focus is on the changing regional role of the United States, the prospects for closer Indian–Western political, economic and security relations and the serious complicating factor of threatened regional nuclear proliferation.

The threads of argument of the various chapters are drawn together in Chapter 10. There Sandy Gordon underlines the many factors for change in India's strategic circumstances, both domestic and international, and ponders the nature and speed of India's expanding influence.

In brief, this book explores New Delhi's rapidly changing strategic role. The political, economic and strategic influence of India is clearly on the rise, and the implications for regional relationships and the border global order are profound.

2 Domestic Foundations of India's Security Policy
Sandy Gordon

A country's security policy evolves by way of a constant dialogue between domestic and external factors. This is particularly so for a democratic and heterogeneous nation such as India that exists within 'turbulent frontiers'.[1] The nature of the dialogue and the rules that govern it will change with time and it is impossible in a chapter such as this to convey the picture in its full complexity. What I will seek to do instead is describe a number of paradigms that provide the framework within which the dialogue on security policy has been conducted at various times since India became independent. I will then draw on these paradigms to see how security policy might unfold in future.[2]

THE EVOLUTION OF INDIA'S SECURITY PERCEPTIONS

The post-colonial era (1947–62): the 'old' Congress world view

The long anti-colonial struggle left the Congress party with a hybrid security policy. It was a policy that was shaped both by the nature of the predominantly non-violent struggle and by British colonial attitudes to security. The two made uneasy bedfellows. Generally, this innate tension was resolved through application of the Gandhian doctrine of non-violent conflict resolution in India's dealings on the world stage and adherence to the colonial inheritance in its actions on the subcontinent.

Under the British, the security of the Indian possession was thought to be dependent on a sphere of infuence up to and around the natural barriers of the Hindu Kush and Himalayas.[3] To give effect to such a policy, the British created a system of buffer states in Persia, Afghanistan, Nepal, Tibet, Sikkim and Bhutan. Within these states they would not interfere, provided no other power did so.[4]

There emerged in 1947, however, a number of newly independent nations within the natural frontiers of the subcontinent. This post-

6

colonial settlement was not only to engender a highly problematic physical security environment, but also a series of ethnic and religious anomalies that trouble the security of the subcontinent to this day. These are relevant to the present work in as much as the problems they produced have become closely enmeshed in the domestic politics of all the nations on the subcontinent.

One major anomaly in the post-colonial settlement was the fact that many Hindus and Muslims found themselves on the 'wrong' side of the border at independence. Hindus from what was then the Pakistani province of East Bengal streamed into the Indian state of West Bengal, contributing considerably to the social and political problems of a state that was already in economic decline. In Kashmir, when the Hindu ruler opted to transfer to India, Muslims found themselves in India when they would have preferred to be in Pakistan. In 1947 and 1948, Pakistan supported an attack of tribals on Indian Kashmir, and the state has remained divided, hotly contested and the single greatest source of tension between India and Pakistan since. The Indian tribal peoples in the North-East felt alienated from the rest of India and mounted a series of insurgencies that have continued to this day, at times with covert support from China. The Muslims of East Bengal felt exploited by Pakistan's Western wing and fought a civil war, to emerge as Bangladesh in 1971, triggering mass migrations into India.

The continuing infiltration of people from Bangladesh into India has caused considerable unrest in India's Eastern states and Assam. Similarly, Nepalis seeking to escape the deteriorating economic conditions in that country continue to spread into the hills and plains of India, contributing to demands for independence in India's own hill tracts, where the people are of the same ethnic background. In Sri Lanka, the Tamils in the North were increasingly forced to the margins of political and economic life. From 1979, they conducted a guerrilla campaign seeking to establish an independent Tamil state. They were encouraged and assisted from the Indian state of Tamil Nadu, where the Tamil population had itself mounted an independence campaign in the 1960s. And in the Indian state of Punjab, Sikhs who were conducting a violent campaign for an independent *Khalistan* appeared to pass with ease across the border into Pakistani Punjab.

The way in which border problems tended to interact with India's domestic political problems strongly reinforced in independent India those aspects of colonial strategy that held that the only viable defence was a subcontinental one and that no outside power should interfere in the affairs of South Asia. As Nehru said of Nepal, 'Much as we stand for the independence of Nepal we cannot allow anything to go wrong in Nepal or permit that barrier [the Himalayas] to be . . .weakened, because that would be a risk to our own security.'[5]

The precept of a subcontinental defence zone has been accepted as part of the prevailing paradigm with very little political challenge within India right up to the last few years of Rajiv Gandhi's government. Nehru's remark could as well have been made by Curzon or Indira Gandhi and could apply equally to Bhutan or Sikkim as Nepal. A recent example of India's sensitivity to 'outside' interference in South Asia may be found in the accord with Sri Lanka.[6]

But if Congress security doctrine embraced some elements of imperial policy, it was equally a reaction to the long anti-colonial struggle. A number of important elements in the doctrine derive from that struggle and subsequently came to assume wide political acceptance within India. These beliefs were contested only fitfully by the right wing of the Congress led by Vallabhbhai Patel.

First, the Gandhian doctrine of non-violent struggle subsequently came to be regarded as important in the international arena. As Jawaharlal Nehru remarked, 'He [Gandhi] taught us the doctrine of non-violence, not as a passive submission to evil, but as an active and positive instrument for the solution of international differences.'[7] As a corollary, the Congress party came to believe that the new nations of Africa and Asia were, to use Nehru's term, a 'moral make-weight to restore the balance in the world'.[8] The European former colonial powers, on the other hand, were thought to be tainted by war and the colonial experience.[9] Early graduation of the leading colonial powers to the nuclear club reinforced the view that right was on the side of the former colonies. Defence, it was held, would be conducted from the moral high ground. In this period, defence spending never rose above 2% of GNP.

This emphasis on the moral found practical expression in collective security through the United Nations, the adoption of the principles of *Panchsheela* (five principals governing the conduct of foreign relations based on mutual respect and non-interference) and the Nonaligned Movement. Despite opposition from Patel and his followers, the Chinese invasion of Tibet was glossed over and finally accepted officially in 1954, as were Chinese incursions into territory claimed by India in 1959. By this time, however, the public and parliament were starting to turn against Nehru on the issue of China. Public opinion had entered the security equation in a major way for the first time.[10]

As befitted a nation that emphasised moral suasion and collective security as well as one that had its colonial status underwritten by the military, the Congress leadership consciously downgraded the army's position administratively and socially.[11] The Service chiefs were made responsible to the Defence Minister. Senior military ranks were lowered in the order of precedence.[12] The position of Commander-in-Chief was abolished in 1947 because the Congress party felt that the power of the army would be reduced if the Chief of Army Staff was only 'first among equals'. It has never since been reinstated, to the detriment of defence planning in India.

A second factor emanating from the freedom struggle was the belief that India was colonised in the first place because it had been weakened by the British through a deliberate policy of 'divide and rule'. The Indian nationalists countered the British argument that India was even more diverse than Europe with the theory that the peoples of South Asia had a cultural unity. For instance, in 1945 Nehru visited Colombo and spoke of Ceylon being 'culturally, socially and linguistically as much a part of India as any province'.[13] Such a view necessitated a secular state and the secular nature of India was enshrined in the Constitution. In the military, the policy followed by the British of recruiting from the ranks of the 'martial races' such as Sikhs and Rajputs was stopped in the belief that the army, as much as any other institution, should become the proving ground of a secular India.[14]

The Congress belief in a secular India meant that the creation of Pakistan was only accepted grudgingly as the product of the British policy of divide and rule.[15] Similarly, the defence of Kashmir became embedded in the Indian security paradigm in part because any threat to Indian Kashmir was seen as a threat to the concept of a secular India.

A third aspect of nationalist belief was that India had once been a nation of great wealth and high technology which had rivalled and even surpassed Europe. Paradoxically, this India had been conquered as a result of its technological backwardness, particularly in the area of sea power.[16] This myth of a golden past underwrote intellectually the boycott and *swadeshi* ('home-grown') movements that had constituted powerful weapons against the British in the hands of the nationalists.[17]

Consequently, independent India came into being with a strong urge to make up lost ground in technology and, more importantly, to do it through its own independent means. This desire to achieve security through independence became central to both the economic and security strategies adopted by India. It brings with it a suspicion of any power upon which India might become over-dependent. When Khrushchev reportedly said to Nehru: 'If you ever require any help, just whistle', Nehru supposedly replied: 'Mr General Secretary, I have learned a lot of things in my life, but I have not learned to whistle.'[18]

The desire for complete independence was evident in Congress policy early on. It took several forms. First, there was a drive to achieve indigenous production wherever possible. Then there was the pressing desire to leap-frog in technology, to catch up at the leading edge and never to be left behind again. As a leading official in the defence industries has written: '. . . the entire defence planning in India centres round . . . her becoming self-reliant in weapons and systems.'[19]

In pursuit of the goal of self-reliance, in 1955 India began its drive to develop an independent nuclear industry. The Defence Research and Development Organisation was established in 1958 to provide an indigenous design facility. A space research program was commenced in the 1970s to provide for civilian and military needs. Technical education was made the subject of major investment, to the extent that India now has a pool of nearly 4 million technically trained people, the third largest in the world after the United States and the Soviet Union. Under the Ministry of Defence Production, large numbers of factories were built in order to produce military equipment. Another aspect of the desire for complete independence is the policy of seeking diversity in the purchase of arms so as not to become over-reliant on any one source. This policy is manifest in the wide variety of equipment now in use in the armed forces.[20]

And finally, India's poverty and the vacillating or negative role of big businessmen and large landlords in the freedom struggle convinced Nehru and the majority of Congress leaders that India should have a substantially planned, socialist economy.[21] Nehru had travelled to Russia as a young man and was attracted to some of the ideas he found there, particularly economic planning.[22] This belief in a planned, mixed economy reinforced the role of the state in defence research and production. To this day the government sector dominates defence production in India. It can also be argued that when India began to move towards the Soviet Union after 1962, it did so from a position of sympathy and understanding; but it is not a point that can be taken too far because Nehru and the Congress were avowedly socialist and not communist[23] and because, as we shall see, other factors were important in defining the Soviet tilt.

The first shock to the Congress security edifice was applied by the unexpected attack and victory by a smaller Chinese force in 1962. In

Nehru's words, the defeat forced an 'agonising reappraisal of India's foreign policy.'[24] Feeling was so strong in India following the war that the parliament passed an act that no government could ever sacrifice Indian land in negotiation with China. India felt betrayed not only in relation to China, but also in relation to the benign world view paradigm that it had adopted after independence, for China was an Asian nation and not one of the colonising powers. By the 1965 war with Pakistan, defence spending as a percentage of GNP had doubled, and it was never again to fall much below 3% of GNP. This depth of feeling in India has affected the relationship with China to this day, making it more difficult for any Indian government to give up territory in negotiations with China. The Chinese on their part profess not to admit public opinion as a real factor in India's position.[25]

One further important change was precipitated by the war with China. The Congress government came out of the war badly. It had been shown up as being naive, poorly prepared and badly coordinated. From then on it began to lose some of the prestige it had inherited from the independence struggle.[26] Yet it still had intact the general goodwill of the Indian people, its pyramid-type structure which had enabled it to reach the farthest corners of the land and its reputation as the best chance for a secular Indian state.

Congress on the defensive: the 'weak–strong' paradigm (1962–1989)

Shortly after Indira Gandhi assumed office in 1966, the Congress edifice began to crumble. Following the national elections in 1967, Congress became reliant on a coalition with the pro-Moscow Communist Party of India (CPI). In her desire to assert her authority over the Congress old guard 'Syndicate', Mrs Gandhi had cut the bonds that linked Congress to its political grass-roots.[27] It was never again to rule India in the virtually uncontested way that it had done under Nehru.

As India's regional circumstances changed following the 1962 war and as Congress' political circumstances became more difficult, so too did the party adopt a different attitude to security issues in a number of important respects.

First, while retaining the full rhetoric associated with nonalignment that had been evident in the earlier years, it developed a stronger tilt towards the Soviet Union. Mrs Gandhi's reliance on the support of the Communists in parliament was paralleled by a growing radicalism in her domestic policy designed to cut the ground from under the Syndicate. While these developments facilitated the relationship with the Soviet Union, that relationship was more the result of other factors such as India's increasing reliance on Soviet arms, the United States' support for Pakistan during the 1971 war and a geopolitical reality under which the Soviet Union was exceptionally well-placed to apply pressure on China in its dispute with India. Moreover, by 1971 Mrs Gandhi was no longer reliant on the Communists in parliament, and when in 1975 she used the provisions of the Constitution in order to declare a state of emergency, they increasingly opposed her authoritarianism. By 1982 the CPI had decided to 'trot behind Indira Gandhi on the foreign trail and snap at her on the home turf.'[28]

Far more than the pre-1962 period, Congress was now required to operate within a combative political milieu. It is not surprising, therefore, that security policy was more hotly contested. Centre-left politics was still dominant in India, but increasingly the political right began to challenge the Congress security framework, and especially the pro-Soviet tilt.

By the time of the Emergency (1975-77), a disparate array of political parties had serious differences with the thrust of the Congress security policy. Some of these coalesced into the Janata party, led by a former Congress stalwart, Morarji Desai. This party was comprised of disgruntled former Congressmen, the Jana Sangh (later the Bharatiya Janata Party-BJP) and a peasant party based in the North led by Charan Singh. The BJP was supported by the Rashtriya Swayamsevak Sangh (RSS), which characterised itself as a Hindu social organisation but which had the backing of a large cadre and engaged in political activities

When Desai led the Janata party to power in 1977, he undertook to return India to 'genuine nonaligned status'. He also sought to mend fences with India's neighbours on the subcontinent and with China. He pledged that India would not develop nuclear weapons, which he felt to be abhorrent. He sought to undermine the power of the military by turning it into a force that was more closely aligned with development efforts.[29] In effect, he sought to swing the pendulum back from the more forthright foreign policy adopted by Mrs Gandhi to something that was nearer to the ideals of Mahatma Gandhi.

The Desai government, however, quickly found that in the security 'dialogue' external reality prevailed over domestic political ideology. Cheap Soviet arms appeared to be integral to India's security policy. In Pakistan, Bhutto's government was ousted by the military. When the

Indian Foreign Minister, A.B. Vajpayee, went to Beijing in 1979 in an attempt to open up a dialogue, China launched an attack on Vietnam at the very time he was there. Mrs Gandhi was thus able to portray the Janata foreign and security policy as weak, anti-national and naive. For example, in the 1980 election campaign she levelled the scathing accusation against Janata that India had been so weakened that 'even Bhutan' was pushing it around.[30] The stage was set in the Janata years for a politically acceptable swing of the pendulum back to a more forthright policy under the new Indira government in 1980.

As India became more politicised and the task of governing more complex, there was another important shift in the concept of security. This has been described by Raju Thomas as the widening of the concept of security from a concern with external factors to a concern also with internal threats to national integrity. This shift reflected the growing role of the security forces in the maintenance of law and order and the political integrity of the country.[31]

The most important role of the military in the political process was provided by its veiled presence in the wings of the political stage. As Stephen Cohen has argued, the military presence gives the civil authority a power that it could not otherwise sustain.[32] Cohen's point has since been given added weight by the crises in the Punjab and Kashmir.

Yet the use of the military in 'nation building' is a double-edged sword. The more the military is exposed in support of the civil authority, the more its effect is dissipated and the greater the threat that it will choose to participate in the political process either directly or indirectly. As General Sinha has quipped, any government that resorts to the military too often might finish inside the tiger like the 'young lady of Niger . . .'[33] Like their colonial predecessors, governments in independent India have understood the need for restraint. Nevertheless, with growing politicisation and erosion of the social fabric, the military has perforce been required to intervene in support of the civil authority more and more frequently. In the four years to 1987, for example, it was called out 369 times, mostly to restore law and order.[34]

The military is one of the more isolated institutions in India, generally confined to separate schools, colleges and cantonment areas.[35] Nevertheless, there have recently been a number of disturbing incidents which together suggest that some of the current difficulties in Indian society might be starting to rub off on it.[36] For example, 'Operation Bluestar' in the Punjab in 1984, in which the army raided the Golden Temple, precipitated a mutiny amongst a small percentage of Sikh soldiers. This was, however, a mutiny of one aggrieved minority within the military and to that extent was atypical. Perhaps more serious was the fact that during prolonged fighting between castes in Gujarat in 1974 and again in 1984, the government was shocked to find that the introduction of the military had little, if any, effect.[37]

But it is not just within the serving ranks that we should look for signs of unrest. The Indian army is a peasant army. It dispels into the countryside a constant stream of retiring soldiers who are literate, skilled and trained in the use of arms. The effect is multiplied many times by virtue of the fact that recruiting is still heavily biased in favour of the states in the North-West.[38] From the government's perspective, the influx of ex-soldiers into the countryside has both positive and negative effects. The positive effects through the infusion of new skills, ideas and money in the form of pensions are incalculable.[39] Farmers, however, have a growing sense of grievance.[40] Some observers have expressed alarm at the existence of disaffected peasant groups trained in the use of arms[41] such as the organisation led by a Jat ex-soldier, Mahendra Singh Tikait, which has many ex-soldiers in its ranks.[42]

Another factor that contributed considerably to the sense of alienation in the ranks of the military was the intervention in Sri Lanka in 1987. The army suffered considerable hardship and loss in the campaign. But worse in the opinion of some, it was treated with indifference or criticism at home. This left a sense of bitterness, so much so that one military journal asserted that 'We can . . . do without a lot of dovish cooing and crooning from the official media. We cannot send our troops to war on slogans of peace.'[43] Such feelings would be exacerbated by scandals such as Bofors and a general belief in the military that political standards are declining.[44] The military leadership itself recognises that morale is low, as indicated by the famous 'Sundarji Letter'.[45] Any government will in future need to consider more carefully when and how to use the military if it wishes to intervene in the region.[46]

The growing problems relating to internal security outlined above contributed to another change in the nature of the security debate. This development involved a fundamental shift in the way the Congress party used security issues for internal political purposes. It is important enough to be characterised as a shift in the security paradigm.

Lloyd and Suzanna Rudolph have characterised India as the 'weak–strong' state.[47] They were not referring specifically to security policy, but the description is apt for the type of message about security that the Congress party under Indira Gandhi and later under Rajiv sought to convey in circumstances in which fissiparous tendencies were becoming ever more pronounced, and in which the hold of the Congress on power was ever more tenuous. At one extreme in this paradoxical view of security, India was held to be threatened by a shadowy 'foreign hand' (sometimes identified as the United States or CIA) that played on its internal divisions in order to make it collapse from within. By the time of the Emergency in 1975, external factors were used by Mrs Gandhi as an explanation of India's deteriorating internal position.[48] Implicit and sometimes explicit in the argument was the view that Congress was the only party capable of maintaining India's integrity against powerful outside forces, and that those parties advocating more autonomy for the regions were 'anti-national'.[49]

With the decision of the Reagan administration to provide 40 F-16 fighter aircraft to Pakistan in 1981, Mrs Gandhi was accused of whipping up a 'war psychosis'.[50] In that year she was asserting that there were dangers 'all round us'. At the same time, she was charging the opposition with spreading disunity and threatening 'national integration'.[51] During the 1989 national election, Rajiv Gandhi also played heavily on the theme of the threat to national unity, including by outside forces. Extensive newspaper advertising prior to the election portrayed India as a vulnerable, partly dismembered doll.

On the other side of the equation, India was lauded by Congress as a resurgent power. Its achievements on the international stage and in science and technology were highlighted and equated with the Congress party. For example, as early as 1974 the explosion of a nuclear device had been used by Mrs Gandhi to provide a much-needed boost to her waning fortunes.[52]

Under Rajiv, the government-controlled electronic media ran a series of advertisements in the run-up to the 1989 election. These extolled India as a great nation, one that was active as a peace keeper in the region, capable of launching the *Agni* rocket and building nuclear power stations.[53] The Minister for Information and Broadcasting, K.K. Tewari, gave an interview to the *Illustrated Weekly of India* in which he argued that the time had come for India to find its own role and assert its worth; but at the same time he described it as threatened by dissention and outside forces. It is a classic example of the 'weak–strong' paradox.[54]

The use by the Congress party of external factors in domestic political play in the general sense of a reference to an 'outside threat' or 'foreign hand' did not necessarily carry over into the formulation of actual policy. As Leo Rose has remarked, relations with neighbours 'are both too important and too specific to be handled by slogan-mongering.'[55] To an extent, all countries in South Asia recognise the domestic constraints within which their neighbours have to operate. For example, India recognised that Zulfikar Ali Bhutto had to mount an unparalleled round of invective against it in order to ward off the threat from his own military, just as his daughter attempted to do in respect of Kashmir early in 1990. As we shall see, even the use by Mrs Gandhi of the United States as public 'whipping boy' was not carried over fully into official relations and certainly not into people-to-people relations.

But the relationship between outside events and internal perceptions is not always one of mere shadow-boxing for domestic purposes. In view of the somewhat arbitrary nature of the post-colonial carve-up, cross-border strife affects relationships between India's different ethnic and religious groups in a way that is all too real. An obvious example is to be found in the flow of 10 million refugees into West Bengal at the time of the 1971 civil war in Pakistan. More recently, delivery of supplies by air to the Sri Lankan Tamil population at the time of the goods embargo from the South was due in part to fears on the part of the Union Government that there would be a strong adverse reaction from India's own Tamil population if nothing was done and that a new refugee situation might develop on India's shores.[56] In the Punjab, where the Sikh guerrillas were using Pakistan as a source of arms and a place of refuge, cross-border activity became such an issue between India and Pakistan that Rajiv Gandhi said that Pakistan's attitude towards its suppression was a 'litmus test' of the relationship as a whole.[57] And in 1990, alleged cross–border support for insurgents in Indian Kashmir has brought India and Pakistan to the brink of war.

The rise of a 'Hindu' Nation

We have seen that a tenet of the post-independence Congress was the belief that India should be a secular state. However, throughout the 1970s and particularly in the early 1980s the tension between Hindus and Muslims worsened considerably. Once out of office, the successor of the Jana Sangh, the BJP, became more radical in its approach to the issue of the Muslim minority. It led a virulent attack on Congress against the flow of Gulf money into India. According to the BJP and

RSS, these funds were used to foster fundamentalist Islam and draw ex-untouchable converts into the Muslim fold.[58] Such accusations by the opposition fed the growing feeling on the part of Hindus against Muslims and a vicious circle of hatred and recrimination was set in train. For example, the numbers of clashes between the two communities rose from 238 in 1975 to 500 in 1983.[59]

The growing division between Hindus and Muslims presented Mrs Gandhi with a considerable difficulty. With the 1979 oil shock, India found itself in the uncomfortable position of importing over 50% of its crude oil,[60] most of it from the Persian Gulf. Increasingly, the foreign exchange required to do this was covered by remittances from Indian guest workers in the Gulf. India's position was further complicated by the fact that Pakistan under Bhutto had discovered its links with a resurgent and wealthy Muslim world. Zia ul-Haq continued the trend towards Islam, while at the same time developing the relationship with the United States – a balancing act that required considerable skill. In the context of Pakistan's nuclear program, India became suspicious that Pakistan was using Middle East money to finance an 'Islamic' bomb.

What *was* known was that Pakistan had developed a security relationship with Saudi Arabia involving the stationing of two armoured brigades on Saudi soil. While this was aimed more at Islamic fundamentalism in the Gulf itself than at India, India feared that the Saudis would provide a *quid pro quo* for Pakistan's assistance in the form of finance for acquisition of arms or direct military support in the event of a war between India and Pakistan.[61] Pakistan, moreover, was inclined to use the growing relationship with the oil-rich Gulf states to India's detriment. One lever it could use was the widening rift between Hindus and Muslims in India itself. During the Hindu–Muslim riots in Aligarh in 1979, for example, Pakistan called on the Gulf states to apply pressure on India. When, in 1979, India sought financial assistance from Saudi Arabia for the Rajasthan Canal, Pakistan attempted to intervene, arguing that the canal was a strategic threat.

Given India's dependence on Gulf oil and remittances, growing unrest between Hindus and Muslims in India and the potential that Pakistan would be pushed into a closer embrace with other Islamic nations, Mrs Gandhi had to proceed with great caution. It was a situation she handled with consummate skill. At home, the government attempted to defuse the issue of foreign funds by passing an act requiring the registration of all money entering the country. Abroad, Mrs Gandhi made common cause with the Islamic world by being strongly critical of United States support for Israel. In 1982, she sent a series of diplomatic missions to the Middle East. She also visited Saudi Arabia and argued for even-handed treatment between India and Pakistan.[62] At the same time, India made a concerted effort to reduce its reliance on imported oil, eventually managing to reduce imports to only 33% of its needs.[63]

With the passing of the oil crisis of the early 1980s, the Congress (I) party became more partisan on communal issues. While at the official level it scrupulously maintained its secular stance, after 1980 a subtle Hindu symbolism entered into its use of the media and became associated with its claim to greatness for the Indian nation.[64] In part, this shift resulted from the fact that India's neighbours now see themselves in less compromising terms as Islamic nations (Bangladesh declared itself an Islamic nation in 1988) in competition with a larger Hindu nation, notwithstanding India's claims to secular status.[65] But in part also it was a result of the Congress party's need to cultivate the support of the growing middle class in circumstances in which it was suffering long-term political decline.[66] The Congress also needed to counter the growing influence of the Hindu-based parties. The increasing tendency on the part of the Congress party to associate India with Hinduism, albeit in an indirect way, has, in turn, fed into the over-all communal situation.[6]

II OUTLOOK FOR THE 1990S

The political dimension

India's view of its place in the world has since independence been a vacillating one. On the one hand, we have noted the fundamentally benign world view espoused by Mahatma Gandhi and Jawaharlal Nehru. On the other, we have observed the view that India exists in a threatening world, with the threat emanating both from without and within. A related belief is that India should pursue greatness and security through military and technologically based strength. The former world view has tended to reflect socialist, secular and nonaligned concerns; the latter, particularly in recent years, is underwritten by the belief in India as a Hindu nation, one that ought to be an expression of Hindu genius.

Of these two positions, the one that favours a stronger and more pro-active India has been dominant for most of the period. With the possible exceptions of Indira Gandhi and Lal Bahadur Shastri (who was not in office for long enough for the pattern to be repeated), every Indian prime minister commenced office with good intentions in foreign and security policy.[68] Every prime minister saw those good intentions shattered, particularly by events in India's immediate sphere of South Asia. The way in which the turbulent conditions around India have interacted with the nation's increasingly difficult internal security situation has been at the core of the problem. This process has reinforced New Delhi's wider concern to ensure that the 'natural' frontiers of the subcontinent should not be breached by any outside power. We have seen this to be the case for Nehru, for Morarji Desai and for Rajiv Gandhi. It certainly proved to be the case for V. P. Singh.

Singh came to power determined to reduce defence expenditure and conduct good-neighbourly relations in South Asia.[69] He signalled his moderate position strongly in both foreign and domestic policy.[70] His position reflected a view in the electorate that Rajiv Gandhi's foreign policy had been 'adventurist'. It also reflected a debate that has emerged only recently about the dimensions of India's defence budget. Before 1988, the defence budget passed virtually unchallenged in the parliamentary and public arenas.[71]

In some respects, Singh's successors will in the 1990s operate in more favourable circumstances in the conduct of foreign and security policy than governments in the 1980s. The superpower conflict, which had become so deeply entangled in the affairs of the subcontinent, has been largely defused, at least for the time being. Even should the Cold War be resumed, it is unlikely that either power would seek or would be capable of achieving the same kind of strategic role in South Asia to which it aspired previously. Moreover, a China which feels rejected by the West is seeking friends from whatever quarter it can. It is ready and willing to discuss better relations in all areas short of significant concessions on the border.[72]

But in other respects, Indian governments will be as deeply ensnared in the imperatives of the immediate neighbourhood as were their predecessors. Given the intrinsically unstable nature of the post-colonial settlement in South Asia, there are bound to be other problems similar to those encountered recently between India and Sri Lanka and India and Nepal. Just as they did in colonial and post-colonial times, problems of the neighbourhood are likely to spill across India's borders and affect its domestic politics. Moreover, however much India might wish to stand aside from the difficulties of its neighbours, its comparative size will make it difficult for it to do so.

But as part of the 'dialogue' with the external world, the Sri Lanka experience has probably made India more cautious about how it puts its subcontinental security policy into practice, if only to ensure that the military, upon which governments have become ever more dependent, is not further alienated.

In fact, V. P. Singh's government encountered difficulties of precisely the kind described above in relations with Pakistan over the state of Jammu and Kashmir. In that state, internal unrest amongst the predominantly Muslim population of the Srinagar Valley destroyed tentative moves between India and Pakistan to improve relations. The fact that Singh's room to manoeuvre in handling the Kashmir crisis was restricted by the vital role of the BJP in support of his minority government raises important questions about the policies of and long-term prospects for the BJP.

The BJP took a tough line on foreign policy issues in general and on Kashmir in particular when compared to Singh's Janata Dal party. It wishes to have the provisions of the Constitution that give Jammu and Kashmir special status removed and was a supporter of hard-line Governor Jagmohan, who had to be removed by Singh. The party at times supported the RSS and its associated 'intellectual' wing, the Vishwa Hindu Parishad (VHP) in their challenge to Singh's resolutely secular stance.[73] It advocates nuclear weapons for India and was critical of Rajiv Gandhi's moves to improve relations with China.[74] It was also critical of his modernisation drive, is generally suspicious of foreign influences and is a strong advocate of the use of indigenous languages, and especially Hindi, rather than English.

In analysing how far the views of a party like the BJP might actually come to affect India's foreign policy in the 1990s, we need to consider a number of issues. First, how likely is the party either to assume office in its own right or to position itself so as seriously to affect foreign and security policy, for example on the issue of nuclear weapons? Secondly, even should the BJP acquire office or significant influence over policy, might it not then moderate its views, just as its predecessor, the Jana Sangh, did when in office as part of the Janata party?

Although the BJP and associated organisations such as the RSS and VHP are far better organised than the parties at the centre of politics and currently have much greater electoral appeal than the Communists, it could prove difficult for the BJP to achieve the kind of political reach that would enable it to govern in its own right. The growth in popularity of the BJP has not been as rapid as the rise from two to 88 seats between the 1984 and 1989 elections would suggest. As long ago as 1977, its predecessor, the Jana Sangh, commanded over 80 seats. Furthermore, given the diffuse nature of the Hindu religion and the great variety of regional variations it contains, it may well prove difficult for confessional politics to obtain a broad national following *in a form that would have a significant impact on India's foreign and security policy.* By way of illustration, the Muslim vote is significant in one-fifth of electorates. Should Hindu confessional politics become a serious threat, Muslims would likely vote for the dominant centre-oriented party. Centrist politicians would likely close ranks against the BJP. These forces at the centre of politics commanded 75% of votes at the last elections compared with the 12% commanded by the BJP.[75] Similarly, the record would suggest that the South, which commands 25% of parliamentary seats, has consistently voted for Congress during those times when the secular nationalist perception of India has been under serious threat by the so-called 'cow belt' parties.[76]

The one factor more than any other that would assist the BJP in taking power nationally would be a serious loss of credibility by all the parties at the centre of politics because of a perception on the part of the electorate that none of them is capable of solving India's problems. Unlike the situation under Janata, the BJP maintained its separate identity from Singh's Janata Dal party. The party was therefore not on this occasion to be tarred with the brush of the Janata Dal collapse.

Even should the BJP assume office in its own right, the necessities of governing India's 100 million strong Muslim community and of maintaining support of the countless other elements outside the mainstream of Hinduism might well force a modification of the current strong stand on religious and foreign policy issues. A BJP government would, however, be more forthright in its pursuit of India's power and position in the region than would one of the centre-oriented parties. It would, for example, probably move fairly quickly to adopt openly nuclear weapons.

Even though it may prove difficult for the BJP to win power in its own right, the RSS and VHP may well continue to create friction between Hindus and Muslims. Parties at the centre (and this applies particularly to the Congress (I) party), may also choose further to emphasise the Hindu character of India in order to counter the influence of the RSS and BJP.[77] Should a further deterioration in Hindu–Muslim relations occur, it would make any solid improvement in relations between India and Pakistan more difficult to achieve. It could also make other Islamic countries, especially those in Southwest Asia, more wary of India. There may even be an inclination on the part of these countries to 'gang up' on India to counter its growing military influence.[78]

But provided that centre-oriented governments continue to hold power, such governments would try to moderate any negative perceptions on the part of Pakistan's Islamic neighbours, just as V. P. Singh worked to mitigate any negative effects of the current problems in Kashmir,[79] and just as Indira Gandhi mounted a successful diplomatic offensive to mend relations with Islamic nations in 1980. To understand why this is so, it is necessary to introduce an important distinction.

While the predominant security paradigm no longer reflects the views of Mahatma Gandhi or Nehru, it does not necessarily embrace the more extreme chauvinism and revisionism espoused by some in the RSS and VHP. What it represents, rather, is the aspirations of an Indian middle class that is growing in importance, confidence and wealth. For this group, the desired future is that of an increasingly confident, predominantly Hindu and technically advanced and independent nation that will continue to carry considerable weight in South Asia and increasingly exercise influence in the Indian Ocean region and the world. What such people want is recognition of India's rightful place as a respected Hindu nation, rather than the creation of a nation that would seek to dominate its neighbours in order to impose a Hindu hegemony. At this stage, it is a question of asserting Hindu rights, both at home and abroad, rather than asserting Hindu dominance.

India, moreover, still has a strong dependence on the countries of the Gulf in terms of its oil requirements and security interests in general. Its dependence on imported oil is again growing.[80] Under a centre-oriented government it would not wish in any way to create a situation in which the oil-rich states were persuaded to bankroll Pakistan in its quest for strategic parity in the subcontinent. India, rather, is likely to seek to do all in its power to ensure smooth relations with Gulf countries and to counteract any attempts to isolate it in Southwest Asia.

To the outside observer it might appear that India is a country in political crisis. With separatist movements flourishing in the Punjab, Kashmir and the North-East, with ever increasing demands of middle and lower caste groupings for a slice of the development action, with governments at the centre and in the states falling with monotonous regularity and with ever-increasing involvement of the armed forces in the maintenance of law and order, one might well ask where it will all end.

While it is undeniably the case that the tensions surrounding the Indian state have increased and will probably continue to do so, this process will not lead automatically to disintegration of India. The physical, political and constitutional instruments at the disposal of the central government would appear to be too great for this to happen. Nor is the centre likely to fall from within. Despite increasing political instability at the centre, what we have witnessed over time is a kind of circulation of elites, combined with at least some flexibility on the part of the political system to draft new members into the elite group. Indeed, one could conclude that the Indian political system should so far be noted more for its resilience than for its atrification.

The economic dimension of power

We observed earlier the strong desire to achieve as independent a stance as possible in technology, arms supply and the economy generally. We saw also that the system involved a high degree of state intervention. In the context of an India that will continue to ascribe a reasonably high value on security, we must ask whether the set of beliefs that emphasises independence in arms production can be sustained economically and technically.

The drive to indigenise the arms industry in India is as strong as ever. In earlier days it was motivated largely by fear of over-dependence. Today the desire to save foreign exchange in the light of India's falling rupee and deteriorating balance of payments position[81] and also to provide the basis for eventual great power status are also important. Furthermore, the military forces and the arms and related industries now provide a significant number of jobs in the formal employment sector[82] and the arms industries are deeply rooted in the bureaucracy. The industry therefore has an important domestic constituency. It is most unlikely that India will in the 1990s turn away from a policy of attempting to achieve indigenisation, notwithstanding the fact that its experience to date has been at best mixed.[83]

Prospects for a viable industry capable of manufacturing almost entire weapons systems will depend on two factors. The first is the shape of and strength of the economy that emerges in the 1990s, for it is economic growth rather than a marked rise in defence expenditure as a percentage of GNP that has contributed most to the growth of Indian defence spending in real terms.

Recent years have seen a structural change in India's economy in favour of the industrial, service and finance sectors.[84] It is these sectors and the process of liberalisation that has contributed to their growth[85] that have fuelled the higher growth of the Indian economy.[86] But the continued high growth in the industrial sector in the 1990s is dependent on a massive investment of Rs 900 bn. (about A$ 90 bn.) in the energy sector during the Eighth Five Year Plan and significant continuing investment in other areas of infrastructure, especially communications.[87] Such investment will not prove possible if any government gives way to pressures from the rural lobby to divert resources to that sector. Performance to date, however, indicates that no government is likely to seek to dismantle the liberalisation measures that since 1975 have contributed to the Indian economy's achievement of a higher growth path or to succumb to the rural lobby.[88] Should the current trend towards a more liberal economy be maintained, there is a reasonable chance that over the decade India will maintain the current underlying economic growth rate of about 5% of GNP. But with growing current account and budget deficits, India will need to return to what the World Bank has called its traditional 'macroeconomic stability',[89] and this process could trigger a period of slower growth in the early years of the decade.

Continuing reasonable growth in the economy will itself do much to neutralise the emerging 'guns or butter' debate in India because defence will be, proportionately, an ever decreasing burden. It can be seen from Figure 2.1 that any cut in defence expenditure as a percentage of GNP down to, for example, 3.5% from the current rate of just under 4%, would not result in a real cut in defence spending over time. On the contrary, India can maintain a more powerful armed forces while at the same time cutting defence spending both as a percentage of GNP and also of total government spending.[90] Even should defence spending be lowered to 3% of GNP, a comparatively low rate in relation to some of India's neighbours,[91] the same would still hold true.

The second factor that will govern the effectiveness of the Indian drive towards indigenisation of the arms industry is the degree to which the government will open up the industry to the private sector. Although India's ability to produce less sophisticated items such as rifles and trucks is not in question, there are growing doubts about its ability to produce sophisticated weapons systems such as state-of-the-art fighter aircraft and battle tanks.[92] In recognition of the set-backs in the industry, there is a general feeling that the private sector should be

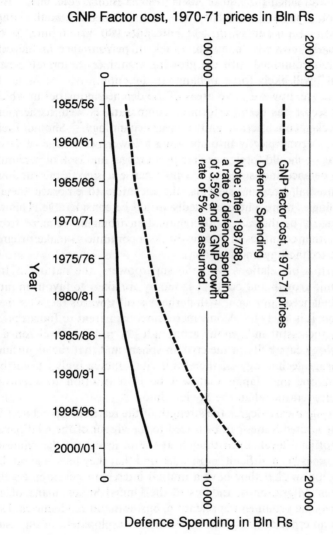

GNP Factor cost, 1970-71 prices in Bln Rs

Figure 2.1 GNP at factor cost and defence spending 1955/56–2000/01, 1970/71 prices

- - - - GNP factor cost, 1970-71 prices

——— Defence Spending

Note: after 1987/88, a rate of defence spending of 3.5% and a GNP growth rate of 5% are assumed.

Year

1955/56
1960/61
1965/66
1970/71
1975/76
1980/81
1985/86
1990/91
1995/96
2000/01

Defence Spending in Bln Rs

Sources: Economic Survey, 88/89, table 1.1; ISS, *Military Balance*, 87–88, 88/89.

more closely involved in the defence industries. Despite a number of official pronouncements to that effect,[93] to date little has been done to involve the private sector more closely. Given the fact that governments are placing most of their resources into the task of sheer survival, it is unlikely that there will be a substantial change in direction in favour of private enterprise for some time to come. Eventually, however, continuing lack of performance in the defence industries combined with the growing vigour of the private sector in general[94] will likely force a change in direction.

There are, however, two areas of the defence industries in which the public sector has been performing comparatively well, namely missile and rocket construction and nuclear technology.[95] Should India be squeezed economically into spending a lower percentage of GNP on defence, or should foreign exchange shortages and lack of performance in the defence industries as a whole cause a significant rundown in conventional weapons systems, the incentive to embrace these new technologies more whole-heartedly would be considerable. This would particularly be the case if the regional environment remains troubled and if other countries in Southwest Asia continue to make progress in missile technology and rocketry.

In terms of relations with the superpowers, the nature of India's economic growth and political economy are likely to favour in future a more balanced approach, with perhaps a tilt towards the West in years to come. It is likely to become increasingly apparent to Indian planners that a successful indigenous arms industry must be built on a high technology capability in the civilian sphere and that the acquisition of dual-usage technology is, therefore, vital. Increasingly, it will be the US, Europe and Japan that will be in a position to supply such technology rather than the Soviet Union.[96]

To a significant degree the strength of the relationship between India and the United States can be traced to the vigour of the relationship at the unofficial level. Even though at the official level the relationship has at times been difficult, both sides find that they have a great deal to build on now that they have a mutual interest in developing stronger relations. Migration of Indians to the United States, many of whom have become prominent in scientific, business and academic circles, has played an especially important role in the development of the relationship.[97]

While it is questionable whether the Soviet Union will continue to be well-placed to provide the heavily subsidised arms packages it has in the past, it will likely continue to be important to New Delhi as a potential counterweight to a possible loose Islamic alliance against India. As was noted above, such an alliance could emerge should relations between Hindus and Muslims further deteriorate. This factor, combined with an important residual arms relationship,[98] will mean that it is unlikely that India and the Soviet Union will reach the point of a sudden or obvious break in relations.

III CONCLUSION

India's attitude to its security has been shaped above all by the way in which the 'turbulent frontiers' left over from the colonial period have interacted with an increasingly difficult domestic political environment. India's difficulties in finding a settled state within its own neighbourhood have driven it away from a belief in the early post-independence security paradigm towards one that would see the world as a more dangerous place, and that consequently places greater emphasis on defence in the overall allocation of resources.

The movement away from a more secure world view has occurred in the context of a lessening of the influence of the Congress (I) party and a growing feeling on the part of the Hindu majority that India must find its place in the world as a Hindu nation.

India may from time to time fluctuate back towards the earlier, more benign world view, just as it did in the early days of the National Front government. An important factor in such shifts will be competition for resources between the needs of development and those of security. But over the longer term, such competition is not likely seriously to affect the capacity of the armed forces or stop the slow accretion of power on the part of India. Indian governments are increasingly dependent on the armed forces to maintain law and order. This dependence should shape both the overall commitment of resources to the military and the way in which India chooses to intervene in the neighbourhood: it will do so henceforth with considerably more caution. Other factors that will tend to favour continuing growth of Indian military power are the underlying strength and growing sophistication of the Indian economy, the growing perception on the part of many influential Indians that India must find its place in the world through economic and political power rather than through moral and spiritual means, and the difficult circumstances that are likely to continue to exist in India's neighbourhood.

The effect of the last of these factors is likely to be paradoxical. While a difficult neighbourhood environment and a growing role for the military in the maintenance of law and order will militate towards an increasing allocation of resources to security, they will also act to restrain the use of military power outside the South Asian sphere. India will not feel confident in the exercise of its power further afield while it faces such difficult circumstances in its own immediate surrounds.

For all that the Indian security paradigm has shifted to a more forthright approach, the moral and democratic streams still run strongly through the Indian nation. India, moreover, is a country that is still struggling to find its own place in terms of its polity and its relations with its neighbours. For these reasons, India should remain for many years a 'status quo' nation, especially with respect to its behaviour towards the wider Indian Ocean region.

NOTES

1. The phrase belongs to John S. Galbraith and is quoted by Ashley J. Tellis. See Tellis' paper, 'Securing the Barrack: the Logic, Structure and Objectives of India's Naval Expansion', in R. Bruce (Ed.), *The Modern Indian Navy and the Indian Ocean*, Perth, 1989, p. 7.
2. While I have placed predominant paradigms in specific time frames, in reality the edges were far more blurred than suggested here, with some elements of a particular structure of beliefs persisting long after the predominant paradigm had disappeared.
3. Pran Chopra, 'Security, Sovereignty, and India-Sri Lanka Relations' in S. Kumar (Ed.) *Yearbook on India's Foreign Policy 1987/1988*, New Delhi, 1988, p. 107.
4. Tellis, *op. cit.*, pp. 7–12.
5. Quoted in O. P. Singh, *Strategic Sikkim*, New Delhi, 1985, p. 37.
6. Under the accord, Sri Lanka undertook that 'Trincomalee or any other ports in Sri Lanka will not be made available for military use by any country *in any manner prejudicial to India's interest*' [Emphasis added]. Quoted in V. Suryanarayan, 'India–Sri Lanka Accord and the prospects for security in South Asia', in K. P. Misra and V. D. Chopra (Eds.), *South Asia-Pacific Region Emerging Trends*, New Delhi, 1988, p. 132.
7. J. Nehru, *India's Foreign Policy: Selected Speeches*, New Delhi, 1961, p. 128.
8. Quoted in P. Gupte, *India: The Challenge of Change*, London, 1989, p. 317.

9. Nehru, *op. cit.*, p. 3 and p. 23.
10. Y. Vertzberger, *Misperceptions in Foreign Policy Making: The Sino–Indian Conflict, 1959–1962*, Boulder, Colorado, 1984, p. 65.
11. H. Rizvi, 'Civil–Military Relations and National Stability in South Asia', *Pakistan Horizon*, XLII, No. 2, April, 1989, p. 64.
12. S. Cohen, *The Indian Army: Its Contribution to the Development of a Nation*, Berkeley, 1971, pp. 71–2.
13. Quoted from B. Warriawalla, in *Illustrated Weekly of India*, 11–17 June, 1989.
14. Cohen, *The Indian Army*, p. 190.
15. Nehru, *op. cit.*, p. 456: 'We did not accept it [Pakistan] at any time on the basis of the two nation theory.'
16. For a contemporary expression of this view see Jasjit Singh, 'Indian Ocean and Indian Security', in S. Kumar (Ed.), *Yearbook on India's Foreign Policy, 1987/88*, New Delhi, 1988, p. 133.
17. These views were expounded originally by Dadabhai Naoroji and R. C. Dutt. See R. C. Dutt, *The Economic History of India in the Victorian Age*, London, 1956, and D. Naoroji, *Poverty and Un-British Rule in India*, London, 1901.
18. Evidence of Admiral Nayyer to the United States Global Strategy Council Forum, p. 38 (transcript prepared in Washington and dated 9 October, 1989).
19. V. S. Arunachalam, 'Defence, Technology and Development: an Indian Experience', conference on *Implications of the New Technology for Australian Regional Security*, SDSC, Canberra, November, 1989, p. 2.
20. The armed forces from time to time complain about this diversity and maintain it is inefficient. Indian Defence Review Research Team, 'Weapons and Equipment State: are we getting our money's worth', *Indian Defence Review*, July, 1988, p. 141.
21. D. Norman (Ed.), *Nehru: The First Sixty Years*, Vol. 1, London, 1965, p. 55.
22. Nehru, *op. cit.*, p. 58.
23. *Ibid.*
24. Noor A. Hussain, 'India's Regional Policy: Strategic and Security Dimensions', in S. Cohen (Ed.), *The Security of South Asia, American and Asian perspectives*, University of Illinois Press, Urbana, c. 1987, p. 31.
25. See Giri Deshinkar's report of his visit to China as a member if an Indian delegation, *Times of India*, 13 December, 1989.
26. Vertzberger, *op. cit.*, p. xvi.
27. The decline of Congress in this period has been documented *inter alia* by L. & S. Rudolph, *In Pursuit of Lakshmi: The Political Economy of the Indian State*, Chicago, 1987; R. Jeffrey, *What's Happening to India?*, London, 1986; and F. Frankel, *India's Political Economy, 1947–1977*, Princeton, 1978.
28. Ravindra Nath in the *Indian Express*, 9 April, 1982.
29. The Janata Government also attempted to remove English as the basic language of the officer corps and to suppress British traditions. See Maj. K. C. Praval, *The Indian Army After Independence*, New Delhi, 1987, p. 604.

30. *Economic and Political Weekly*, XVIII, 9 April, 1983, No. 15, p. 558.
31. R. Thomas, *Indian Security Policy*, Princeton, 1986, p. 7.
32. Cohen, *The Indian Army*, p. 196.
33. See Sinha writing in the Indian *Defence Review*, January, 1987, p. 32.
34. *Ibid.*
35. Rudolph and Rudolph, *op. cit.*, p. 87.
36. Sinha, *op. cit.*, p. 32.
37. See Frankel, *op. cit.* pp. 523–8, for the situation in 1974.
38. In the district of Meerut alone a total of 2.3 million persons are either ex-servicemen or associated with servicemen through family. Lt. Colonel Shyam Singh, 'Peasant Agitation and Internal Security', *Indian Defence Review*, July, 1988, p. 134.
39. Jeffrey, *op. cit.*, p. 30 refers to the benefits of returning ex-*jawans* in the Punjab. The returning soldier factor may have contributed considerably to the 'green revolution' in the Indian North-West, the region in which the agricultural revolution has been most successful.
40. C. Lenneberg, 'Sharad Joshi and the Farmers: The Middle Peasant Lives', *Pacific Affairs*, Vol. 61, Fall 1988, No. 3, p. 451.
41. Singh, *op. cit.*, p. 134.
42. *Ibid.*
43. Indian Defence Review Research Team, *Indian Defence Review*, July, 1988, p. 40.
44. See for example Maj. Gen. E. Habibulla, *The Sinews of Indian Defence*, New Delhi, 1981, p. 213.
45. When General Sundarji took over as Army Chief of Staff, he wrote a letter to all his officers. The letter dealt fundamentally with issues relating to the poor morale in the forces. Many officers evidently felt that the letter failed to come to grips with the basic issues. See *Indian Defence Review*, July, 1986, p. 217, anonymous letter referring to the Sundarji letter.
46. These problems have not been lost on governments. Under the Fourth Pay Commission, pay and pensions have been improved considerably. Ex-military have been inducted into the 500,000-strong paramilitary forces. The crack National security Guard was formed in part for this purpose in 1985. See J. Masselos, 'India: a power on the move', *Current Affairs Bulletin*, Vol. 64, March, 1988, No. 10, p. 26, for this last point.
47. L. & S. Rudolph, *op. cit.*, p. 1.
48. Frankel, *op. cit.*, pp. 527–8.
49. Jeffrey, *op. cit.*, p. 157.
50. *Patriot*, 15 August, 1981.
51. Report of a speech by Mrs Gandhi at Lucknow, *Statesman*, 21 December, 1981.
52. P. Galbraith, 'Nuclear Proliferation in South Asia: Containing the Threat', report to the United States Senate *Committee on Foreign Relations*, Washington, 1988, p. 2.
53. Report on a public interest advertisement on Doordarshan TV, *Times of India*, 22 July, 1989.
54. Tewari saw it as the media's role to create this new self-image. *Illustrated Weekly of India*, 28 May, 1989.

55. Leo Rose, 'India's Regional Policy: Non Military Dimensions' in S. Cohen, *The Security of South Asia*, p. 4.

56. Pran Chopra maintains that the growing feeling on the part of Indian Tamils prompted New Delhi to shift its thinking from the view that the ethnic problem was Sri Lanka's alone to one in which India had a say. Chopra, *op. cit.*, p. 111.

57. Quoted in *Defense and Foreign Affairs*, December, 1988, p. 17.

58. Foreign Broadcasting Information Service, *South-East Asia Report*, No. 1044, 4 September, 1981, p. 188; *Times of India*, 24 February, 1982. See also Walter K. Anderson and Shridhar D. Damle, *The Brotherhood in Saffron: The Rashtriya Swayamsevak Sangh and Hindu Revivalism*, Westview Press, Boulder, Colarado, 1987, p. 135.

59. Y. K. Malik and D. K. Vajpeyi, 'The Rise of Hindu Militancy: India's Secular Democracy at Risk', *Asian Survey*, Vol. xxix, March 1989, No. 3, p. 318.

60. Tata Services Limited, *Statistical Outline of India, 1988–89*, Bombay, 1988, p. 67.

61. Thomas, *op. cit.*, p. 39.

62. *The Hindu*, 9 April, 1982.

63. Tata Services, *op. cit.*

64. B. Wariavwalla, *op.cit.*, p. 17; Malik and Vajpeyi, *op. cit.*, p. 320; Jeffrey, *op. cit.*, p. 157.

65. Malik and Vajpeyi, *Ibid.*, p. 321; Cohen, *The Indian Army*, p. 191.

66. Malik and Vajpeyi, *Ibid*, p. 320.

67. *Ibid*, pp. 320–1.

68. Statement by former Foreign Secretary, Eric Gonzalves, at a conference on South Asia, La Trobe University, Melbourne, 8 December, 1989.

69. Sarah Sargent, *Australian Financial Review*, 4 December, 1989.

70. For example, he appointed India's first Muslim Home Minister.

71. S. Gupta and P. Guha, 'Heading for a Crisis', *India Today*, 28 February, 1989.

72. Deshinkar, *op. cit.*

73. Editorial, *Times of India*, 14 December, 1989.

74. Bhabani Sen Gupta, *Illustrated Weekly of India*, XXIV, No. 3, 21 January, 1989, p. 120.

75. *India Today*, 31 August, 1990, pp. 33–4.

76. In 1977, when Mrs Gandhi was ousted, she received a solid vote from the South, as did Rajiv in the 1989 election.

77. The Congress (I) recently sponsored its own consecration ceremony at Ayodhya using a leading religious figure as proxy, with the objective of embarrassing the NF government. See *Sunday*, 20–26 May, 1990 and *India Today*, 31 May, 1990.

78. There are already indications that this is occurring with respect to inter-communal unrest in Kashmir. See a report in *The Canberra Times*, 30 January, 1990. Dr Robin Jeffrey pointed out on the ABC Program *Asia-Pacific* on 10 February, 1990, that in the context of the deteriorating Kashmir dispute Iran had offered moral support to Pakistan and that India had in turn sought a statement of support from the Soviet Union, which itself has problems with its Muslim minority. Iran did, in fact,

cancel a scheduled visit by the Indian Foreign Minister in response to the situation in Kahsmir.

79. *Canberra Times*, 30 January, 1990.

80. The Singh government recently banned the sale of petrol on Sundays in an attempt to reduce the rapid rise in the consumption of petroleum products that has accompanied India's economic growth and contributed significantly to the balance of payments problem.

81. Gupta and Guha report that the falling value of the rupee alone contributed a Rs14 bn. rise in defence spending in 1988–89. Gupta and Guha, *op. cit.* Between 1986–87 and 1988–89, India's foreign exchange reserves (excluding gold and SDRs) fell from Rs 76.45 bn. to Rs 62.8 bn, Department of Foreign Affairs and Trade, submission to Senate Standing Committee on Foreign Affairs, Defence and Trade, *Enquiry into Relations with India,* June, 1989, Annex B.

82. The armed services, paramilitary, defence, space and nuclear industries together employ approximately 2 million people, which is almost one quarter of those employed in the formal factory sector and 8% of those employed in the total formal sector. Figures derived from Thomas, *Indian Security Policy*, pp. 224–5 and Tata Services, *op. cit.*, p. 81 and p. 135.

83. See Amin Gupta, 'India's Mixed Performance', *Defense and Diplomacy*, Vol. 7, May, 1989, No. 5, pp. 44–52.

84. See D. P. Chaudhri, *Recent Trends in the Indian Economy*, Working Paper No. 88/2, NCDS, Canberra, 1988, Table 2, p. 4.

85. Within these sectors, some sub-sectors such as machine tools and electronics have performed exceptionally well. See for example, *Annual Report* of the Department of Electronics, as reported in the *Times of India*, 23 May, 1990. The electronics sector grew by 31% and exports of electronics by 63% in 1989. In the past two years exports of engineering products have doubled. See *India Today*, 15 August, 1990, p. 42.

86. Chaudhri, *op. cit.*, p. 1.

87. See Economist Intelligence Unit, *India, Nepal Country Report*, No. 2, 1989 (quarterly, London), p. 23 for the requirements of the energy sector. The same publication (p. 27) points out that India also faces a 'crisis' in road transport in the next decade.

88. The 1990 Budget lowered company tax from 50% to 40%. There is no evidence to date that the government is seeking to reverse the liberalisation measures introduced in 1985. If anything, liberalisation will continue at a steady rather than a dramatic pace. See *Asiaweek*, 25 May, 1990.

89. World Bank, *India: Recent Developments and Medium-Term Issues*, Vol. 1, 1988, p. ii.

90. For a further exposition of the argument that Indian defence expenditure is not overly burdensome, see R. Thomas in R. Bruce (Ed.), *op. cit.*, pp. 103–5.

91. The ISS *Strategic Balance 1988/89* reports a rate of expenditure for Pakistan of 6.5% for 1986 (p. 226). In reality the rate would be higher because a significant amount of Pakistan's expenditure is not reported. The same document reports China as having a rate of 2.6% for the same year; but again, this would be a serious underestimation. India's defence

spending is also under-reported, but is on the whole more transparent than Pakistan's or China's. Ravi Rikhye estimates that India's rate of expenditure could be as high as 5% of GNP. See 'Indian Defence Budget: Fact and Fantasy', *Economic and Political Weekly*, April 29, 1989, p. 907.

92.   See James Clad, 'Power amid Poverty', *Far Eastern Econonic Review*, 7 June 1990, pp. 47–51 and R.G. Matthews, 'The Development of India's Defence-Industrial Base', *The Journal of Strategic Studies*, Vol. 12, December, 1989, No. 4, pp. 405–29.

93.   For example, statement of Minister of State for Defence Ramanna, as in Clad, *Ibid.*, p. 47.

94.   Interestingly, the growth in the private sector continues apace, notwithstanding the problems relating to macroeconomic management and the performance of the public sector. See 'Bulls on the Rampage', *India Today*, 15 August, 1990, pp. 93–4 and 'The Stock Market Boom', *Frontline*, 18–31 August, 1990, p. 109.

95.   See Hormuz P. Mama, 'India's New Tactical Missiles', *International Defence Review*, No. 7, 1989, pp. 963–4.

96.   In the defence industries, India is already developing an interesting relationship with the US. Former Defence Minister Pant, during a visit to the US in 1989, showed interest in acquiring a number of technologies in relation to India's Light Combat Aircraft project. The project will involve extensive US assistance in the areas of avionics and engine design. The US reportedly reacted positively to Pant's request for assistance with high-strength fibre technology. It also reportedly reacted positively to his request for sophisticated underwater technology and a number of other technologies. See Sandananda Mukherjee in *Jane's Defence Weekly*, 28 October, 1989, p. 912. See also Mohammed Ayoob, 'India in South Asia: the Quest for Regional Predominance', in *World Policy Journal*, Vol. VII, Winter, 1989–90, No. 1, p. 113

97.   Many Indians who migrate to the US retain close links with India. Many more receive their advanced education in the US and then return to India. Such links are of considerable value in the development of India's more sophisticated technologies. For example, Abdul Kalam, who was in charge of the *Agni* rocket program, and five other scientists spent some time studying at NASA. See an article by John Fialka in the *Wall Street Journal*, 6 July, 1989. An example of the significance of this type of interchange may be seen in the report of the National Science Foundation, *Indian Scientific Strengths: Selected Opportunities for Indo–US Cooperation*, Washington DC, 1987. The report advocated closer links in a number of important areas in science and technology. Its members included a number of US Indians prominent in scientific and business circles. There are currently over 400,000 skilled Indians living abroad. Of these, 20% are highly skilled scientists. Reported in a recent study of the Centre for Planning Research and Action, New Delhi.

98.   The heart of the Indian Air Force is comprised of MiG 21s and MiG 29s These aircraft are still being manufactured under licence from the Soviet Union, with Soviet assistance. Similarly, the Indian Navy is still acquiring Soviet *Kilo* class submarines, which will constitute the bulk

of the Indian submarine force. A high level Indo–Soviet joint defence group recently undertook a comprehensive review of the security environment in the region and decided on steps further to expand cooperation in the field of defence. Source – *Pacific Defence Reporter*, May, 1990, p. 31.

3 The Growth of Indian Military Power: From Sufficient Defence to Nuclear Deterrence
Raju G. C. Thomas

I THE SOURCES OF INDIA'S MILITARY BUILDUP

Is the ongoing Indian arms buildup justified? Or is there, indeed, a significant disproportionate increase in India's military capabilities over previous decades? Critics claim that there is an excessive growth that is destabilising the region. The Government of India and its supporters insist that such claims are without basis.[1]

According to the first perspective, the rationale of India's strategic planning and weapons procurement policies over the last decade exhibits a sizeable gap between the level of threat to India and the level of military capabilities being acquired by the Indian government. There have been no major wars on the subcontinent since the third and last Indo–Pakistani war of December 1971. This was the longest period of peace that India has experienced since its first war with Pakistan in 1947–48. In between, India also fought two other major wars: the first in 1962 against China, and the second in 1965 against Pakistan. To be sure, the prospects of war with Pakistan over the Kashmir issue appear real in the early 1990s as militants in that state resort to armed violence to achieve independence from India or accession to Pakistan. However, those who perceive an Indian military preponderance in the South Asian and greater Indian Ocean regions would argue that such a war is not likely to occur in the present military circumstances, and if it occurred, that it would be decisive in India's favour.

From the second perspective, especially that of the Government of India, there is no significant relative increase in India's military growth. Indeed, from 1987 to 1988, there was a marginal decrease in annual budgetary allocations to the Indian Ministry of Defence.

Overall, defence spending was maintained at between 3 and 4 per cent of the Indian gross national product (GNP) during the 1980s, the same as in the earlier two decades since the war with China was fought in 1962.[2] This compares to around 6 to 7 per cent in Pakistan, South Korea, Taiwan and the United States. Similarly, compared to India's military expenditure of $10 *per capita* in 1988, Pakistan spent $26 *per capita*, Egypt $61, South Korea $147, Taiwan $192, Iraq $433, Israel $821, and the United States $1,061.

These figures notwithstanding, the growth of the Indian economy at an average rate of about 5 per cent of the GNP since 1979 (and at almost 9 per cent in 1988), means that despite a steady annual allocation of 3 to 4 percent of the GNP to defence since 1962, the absolute amounts allocated since 1979 are greater than during the previous decades of war and turbulence.[3] A prosperous economy automatically induces a generous defence allocation even if the percentage of the GNP that is allocated remains approximately the same. This trend may be more readily seen in the relatively large annual increases in resource allocations to Indian defence over the previous year, despite the steady state in the economic burden of defence relative to the GNP. For example, after taking inflation into consideration, there was an increase of 27.3 per cent in defence allocations from 1985 to 1986, and of 21.1 per cent from 1986 to 1987.[4]

Although there was a decrease in allocation by 3.6 per cent from 1987 to 1988, this does not take into account the cost of Indian military operations between 1987 and 1989 in Sri Lanka, in the Siachen Glacier, and in the Maldives. It also does not include the increased foreign exchange component of overseas weapons purchases which is provided by the Ministry of Finance, some of the defence research and development that is also undertaken by the Department of Science and Technology, and the allocations to the Departments of Atomic Energy and Space, much of which carry military applications.[5]

The Indian arms buildup during the era of crisis and wars before 1972 was significantly less than the arms buildup during the era of peace since 1972. India has achieved regional military superiority in South Asia and, through its naval expansion and its missile development programs, its military reach is being extended steadily towards the Middle East, Central and Southeast Asia, and in the general arc of the Indian Ocean region as far southeast and southwest as Australia and South Africa.

Supporters of the continuing Indian military buildup may argue that the era of relative peace in South Asia is the result of India's military dominance – the familiar 'peace through strength' argument so often propounded by various American presidents since the Second World War. True, India and Pakistan have clashed repeatedly over the Siachen Glacier in Kashmir since the mid-1980s, and nearly 50,000 Indian troops were deployed in Sri Lanka to fight the Tamil guerrilla insurgency.[6] But, unlike the wars of the past, these two military campaigns in the 1980s did not involve full-scale deployments. They did not create the earlier type of crisis environment in Indian domestic politics, although there was occasional criticism by the political opposition against the government's policies; and, they did not stretch India's relations with the neighbouring states to the diplomatic breaking point as during the major wars with Pakistan and China in the past. The perception of India as the 'regional bully', especially following its partial economic blockade of Nepal in 1989, did not mean that India was being seriously threatened by any of its smaller neighbours.

Under such circumstances, opponents may argue that India is not so much responding to a changing strategic environment, as creating that change through its military buildup as other states become compelled to respond to the growth of Indian military power. This is the reverse of conditions from the 1950s to the early 1960s, and from the mid 1970s to the mid 1980s. During the first period, India was responding to the American arming of Pakistan under the SEATO and CENTO defence pacts. During the second period, India was beginning to respond to the arms buildup by the oil-rich Muslim states of the Middle East, and to the large-scale movement of naval forces of the United States, the Soviet Union and France into the Indian Ocean. The second reactive military buildup generated some political debate in India on the diplomatic and military policies needed to deal with the increasing militarisation of the extended Indian strategic environment that included the Middle East, Southeast Asia and the Indian Ocean.

Herein lies one clue in explaining current Indian military policy that may be familiar in other like situations. To a certain extent, what may be perceived as an unjustified arms buildup by one state may be due to time gaps that occur between initial threat perceptions and delayed military responses because of political, economic and technological constraints within a country. Subsequently, similar counter responses occur among other affected states, producing periodic time-delayed action-reaction arms spirals. The net result will be the occurrence of cyclical military imbalances between two or more states when viewed on a long-term time scale. What is unique in the present arms buildup on the subcontinent, especially under the earlier administration of Prime Minister Rajiv Gandhi from 1984 to 1989, is that India is leading the arms buildup rather than essentially reacting to one.

There may be other domestic explanations for the Indian military buildup. Once an upward military momentum is generated within a country, it may be difficult to reverse that trend because of committed investments in manpower and technology that are assigned to the development of a particular weapons system, or because of vested interests that become established in powerful civilian and military bureaucracies once funds and personnel are assigned. Such conditions tend to generate a military momentum of their own that may be unrelated to the external threat environment.

Finally, the Indian military buildup may also be explained by the various decision-maker's political image of the state in international society. One of the problems with Indian leaders and policy-makers since the death of Prime Minister Jawaharlal Nehru in 1964, is the feeling that India does not get enough respect, especially compared to China, with which it sees itself as essentially equal in size, population and economic development. Instead, India is constantly equated with Pakistan, a nation at one time one-fifth its size in population and capabilities, and only one-eighth its size since the creation of Bangladesh in December 1971.

Whatever the reasons and causes for the Indian military expansion, there are a variety of consequences that India will have to face in the 1990s. Indian naval expansion has already triggered a Pakistani naval expansion and set off alarms as far off as Australia. A major Indo–Pakistani arms race in combat aircraft began shortly after the Soviet invasion of Afghanistan in 1979, when Pakistan was offered forty American F-16 fighters. India responded in kind, and the arms race in combat aircraft continues apace even after the Soviet withdrawal from Afghanistan in 1989. Similarly, the development of the Indian missile program and the prospect of an Indian nuclear weapons program will aggravate and reformulate the Sino-Indian and Indo–Pakistani military balances as India's two traditional adversaries respond to the new situation. The general growth of Indian air and sealift capabilities will affect the military balances in the Middle East and Southeast Asia.

The rest of this chapter will examine India's general military strategy and doctrine, the nature of the regional conventional military balance, and the latent nuclear and ballistic missile arms race in the region.

II MILITARY STRATEGY AND DOCTRINE

Military strategy and doctrine must be related to the objectives of a nation's foreign policy, to the nature of external threats that are perceived, and to the military capabilities of potential adversaries. During more than forty years after Indian independence in 1947, the cornerstones of India's foreign policy were built around the principles of 'nonalignment' and 'peaceful coexistence'.

These two principles carried much security relevance during the Cold War. Shortly after independence in 1947, Prime Minister Jawaharlal Nehru had argued that peace and security were not just obtained through military buildups and alliance systems, but also through skillful diplomatic policies and efforts to forge friendships with other countries, especially those with different political and economic systems. Joining a Western-sponsored military alliance, according to Nehru, would reduce India's security – not increase it – by embroiling the country in East–West conflict issues. These views were embodied in Nehru's twin foreign policy pillars of nonalignment and *panchsheel*. (*Panchsheel* are the five principles of peaceful coexistence that were embodied in the Sino–Indian Treaty of 1954 on Tibet and subsequently reiterated at the nonaligned conference at Bandung in Indonesia.) Thus, nonalignment was expected to keep India out of East–West arms races and conflicts; and *panchsheel* would be the basis of good relations between India and the communist states.

There were, nevertheless, security complications for India. Pakistan's entry into the American-sponsored SEATO and CENTO alliance systems compelled India to turn to Western Europe for offsetting weapon systems in tanks and aircraft. Subsequently, the Tibetan rebellion of 1959 and the Sino–Indian war of 1962 brought into question the effectiveness of *panchsheel*. The overt declaration of the Sino–Soviet rift in 1963 produced closer Indo–Soviet military cooperation, thus raising doubts in some Western circles about India's commitment to nonalignment. Sino–American rapprochement, commencing with President Nixon's visit to China in February 1972, and the Soviet invasion of Afghanistan in December 1979, further consolidated India's military dependency on the Soviet Union and, thereby, increased that of Pakistan on the United States. India became entwined in the Cold War in spite of efforts to avoid it.

Nonalignment and *panchsheel* are almost obsolete today in the aftermath of Gorbachev's introduction of *glasnost* and *perestroika* in the Soviet Union, and the subsequent revolutions against communist dictatorships in Eastern Europe in 1989–90. However, one of the legacies of the Cold War on the subcontinent is the continuation of the Indo–Pakistani arms race. The United States continues to be the major supplier of arms to Pakistan, and the Soviet Union to India. It is important to note that the root causes of the Indo–Pakistani arms race in the past lay not with ideological conflict issues that paralleled those between the Western and Communist bloc countries, but with religious antagonism, territorial claims and other political differences between the two sides. These causes have not yet been fully resolved on the subcontinent. In particular, the Kashmir issue that lay dormant since the creation of Bangladesh in December 1971, resurfaced during 1989.[7] Simmering discontent during much of that year finally led to a violent separatist movement in early 1990. The revival of this emotional Indo–Pakistani issue in the 1990s may reverse the greater cooperation that had prevailed between the two countries since the Simla Agreement was signed by Prime Ministers Zulfikar Ali Bhutto and Indira Gandhi in 1973.[8] The crisis of 1990 suggests that Indo–Pakistani wars of 1947–48 and 1965 over Kashmir could happen again.

Similarly, despite considerable improvement in ties between India and China throughout the 1980s, territorial differences and lingering Indian doubts about harsh Chinese policies in Tibet, continue to make India wary of its larger neighbour. The Chinese crackdown on Tibetan nationalists and militants between 1987 and 1989 is an indication that the Sino-Indian border controversy may heat up again.[9] After all, the roots of the Sino-Indian war of 1962 may be found in the Chinese occupation of Tibet in 1950 and the subsequent Tibetan revolt of 1959.[10] Moreover, the Chinese military buildup, especially in nuclear weapons and delivery systems, continues to remind India of the unexpected Sino-Indian war of 1962 and the need to keep open its nuclear weapons option. Hence much of Indian military strategy and the intended deployment of forces continue to be premised on the earlier threat analyses based on Sino-Pakistani military capabilities.

To this established and more concrete threat environment was added new strategic concerns in the 1970s. These included the arms buildup among the oil rich states of the Middle East following the 1973 Arab–Israeli war, the movement of the superpower navies into the Indian Ocean following the withdrawal of British forces east of Suez, and the Sino-Vietnamese war of 1979 that resembled India's own experience in 1962.[11] Concerns about the arms buildup in the Middle East arose from Pakistan's military links with some of these countries such as Saudi Arabia, Libya and the United Arab Emirates. India's objections to entry of the superpower navies into the Indian Ocean stemmed in part from the experience of 1971, when the American nuclear-powered carrier *Enterprise* entered the Bay of Bengal in a show of force against India during the Indo–Pakistani war. The war in Indochina demonstrated China's continuing willingness to engage in border wars to teach neighbouring military powers a lesson.

The degree to which India should respond to these developments, or even their degree of relevance, was never very clear. However, by the early 1980s there emerged a distinction between a *minimalist* strategic policy based on the traditional Sino-Pakistani threat perspective, and a *maximalist* strategic policy based on an extended strategic perspective that would encompass the Middle East, the Indian Ocean and Southeast Asia.

By the late 1980s, controversy among the littoral states over the issue of maintaining the Indian Ocean as a 'zone of peace' had subsided, as had conflict issues in the Persian Gulf and Indochina. The intrusion of the superpower navies did not seem as threatening as it had seemed initially. The Iran-Iraq war which began in 1981, had ended in 1989. Similarly, Vietnam's occupation of Cambodia, which had added to the tensions between the Soviet Union and the United States, was terminated in 1989 when Vietnam withdrew its forces. The threat of another Sino-Vietnamese war had also receded. Nevertheless, the need to watch the wider strategic environment – the *maximalist* perspective – had become apparent. However, there was uncertainty and controversy on how (or even whether) to deal with it in terms of military capabilities.

The earlier *minimalist* strategic response to the traditional threat perspective was the ability to fight 'one-and-a-half wars' (see Table 3.1). India needed sufficient military capability to fight a full scale war with Pakistan, and a border holding operation on the ground against China until superpower diplomatic or military intervention could be obtained. In contrast, the newer *maximalist* extended threat environment seemed to indicate the need for military preparedness for 'three full and three half wars' that would make India an Asian, if not a global military power.

The first extra 'full war' capability of the future is likely to be built on nuclear weapons and missile delivery systems that would deter future Chinese conventional and nuclear threats to India. The Chinese nuclear threat problem had been left unresolved since 1964, partly because India did not have sufficient resources and capabilities to address it, and partly because the threat was perceived to be low much of the time. In the 1990s, an Indian decision to 'go nuclear' may be based on the ability to produce intermediate range delivery systems so as to possess an independent nuclear deterrent against China. The decision may be triggered more specifically by the outcome of negotiations to renew the Non-Proliferation Treaty in 1995, although it could also come earlier based on Pakistan's nuclear policies and programs.

The second additional full war capability would revolve around the growth of Indian naval power that may be deployed in an extended arc of the Indian Ocean. The purpose here would be the more vague demonstration of 'sea power' befitting a large peninsular and maritime country like India located in the strategic centre of the arc of the Indian Ocean littoral. This larger capability was expected to make foreign great power naval intervention less likely in the conflicts of the region by raising the political stakes and the military threshold of such intervention.

The first additional new 'half war' capability would allow India to engage in military interventions around the subcontinent as exemplified in the two cases of Indian military intervention in the Maldives in 1988, and in Sri Lanka for an extended period from 1987 to 1990. This objective called for short range sealift and airlift capabilities. The second extra half-war capability would facilitate the more specific need to defend the maritime economic zone and the rapidly increasing sea-borne trade of India.

In examining Table 3.1, three points should be kept in mind. First, the growth in Indian military capabilities suggests a long-erm *movement* from the minimum to the maximum war-fighting capabilities rather than a deliberate short-term *policy* to reach the maximum. The movement portrays a steady accumulation of new capabilities, often under different administrations, as new problems arise thereby propelling India from one level to the next. Thus the flight testing of the *Agni* IRBM in 1989 and India's three year military intervention in Sri Lanka from 1987 to early 1990 may be perceived as landmarks demonstrating that India had achieved a two-full and two-half war capability.

Second, most of these roles overlap and do not necessarily imply the raising and deployment of specially designated forces for each of the war objectives. India's military capabilities do not have to be tripled to meet the contingencies of three full and three half wars. Perhaps only a 50 to 75 per cent increase in forces may be necessary to reach the *maximalist* posture. For example, military interventions in the vicinity

Table 3.1   India's war-making capabilities

A. *The Traditional Power Posture, 1963–1971*
(The *Minimalist* Perspective)

'One-Full-and-One-Half War' Capability
Single Full War: War against Pakistan on land, air and sea
Single Half War: Land-based border war against China

B. *The Transitional Power Posture, 1972–1988*

'One-Full-and-Three-Half War' Capability
Single Full War: War against Pakistan on land, air and sea
First Half War: Land-based border war against China
Second Half War: Latent Nuclear Weapons Capability
Third Half War: Proximate Island Interventionism

C. *The Extended Power Posture, 1989–1995*

'Two-Full-and-Two-Half War' Capability
First Full War: War against Pakistan on land, air and sea
Second Full War: Latent Nuclear Weapons and IRBMs
First Half War: Land-based border war against China
Second Half War: Proximate Island Interventionism

D. *The Asian/Great Power Posture, 1996–2000*
(The *Maximalist* Perspective)

'Three-Full-and-Three-Half War' Capability
First Full War: War against Pakistan on land, air and sea
Second Full War: Nuclear Weapons with IRBM/ICBMs
Third Full War: Naval Power in the Indian Ocean
First Half War: Land-based border war against China
Second Half War: Proximate Island Interventionism
Third Half War: Defence of Maritime Zone

---

of the Indian peninsula do not require extra forces. Existing regiments of the army, and current air and sealift capabilities, may be sufficient to undertake such tasks. It is quite likely, nevertheless, that India's experiences in the Maldives and Sri Lanka may have resulted in a review leading to marginal upward adjustments to existing capabilities to undertake more such tasks in the future. Similarly, efforts to acquire a naval blue water capability would enable India also to defend its extended maritime frontiers. No special separate forces are necessary for the narrower objective of the third half-war capability, although such a position would assume that the necessity of fighting each of the full and half wars will not occur simultaneously.

Third, the *maximalist* war fighting posture may not come about. The Indian military capability projected by the year 2000 is based on subjective assessments of past and present capabilities and trends. However, the decade of the 1990s may prove to be one of great uncertainties. The present political turmoil in the communist bloc countries suggesting revolutionary changes in global strategic relationships and military capabilities may also generate similar politics in the South Asian region producing newer political relationships and downward trends in military procurements.

This expanded Indian military perspective also implied a shift from a basically defensive posture (the *minimalist* posture) to a conventional as well as nuclear deterrent posture (the *maximalist* posture), especially with reference to the traditional Sino–Pakistani threat (see Table 3.2). Conventional deterrence would be directed at Pakistan and would require Indian military superiority. Nuclear deterrence would be directed at both China and a potentially nuclear Pakistan. It would be based on an assured nuclear retaliatory strike capability should either of these two traditional adversaries threaten to attack India with nuclear weapons. The expanded military posture would also add the ability to deal with security problems in a limited way further afield in the Middle East, Indian Ocean and Southeast Asia – at least to the extent that they may directly or indirectly impinge on Indian security.

This grander (perhaps grandiose) strategy will, no doubt, be hotly denied by Indian government officials. Indeed, the *maximalist* perspective has not been established as the most desirable policy, let alone fully realized through the buildup of military capabilities. India's current war capabilities and implicit military doctrines have reached the level of 'C' in both Charts I and II, and may stay there for the next five years. The move to a great power or nuclear deterrent posture – if this does happen at all – is likely to be built on worst-case scenarios. Such scenarios, whether entirely convincing or not, may become more acceptable to Indian authorities as the procurement of weapons capabilities to meet such expanded threat projections become more readily feasible. In other words, what can be done may have a tendency to become what needs to be done.

Thus, for example, the decision on whether to become a nuclear weapons power may simply be a function of India's *ability* to deploy sufficient IRBMs and ICBMS so as to possess a credible retaliatory strike capability. Similarly, the expansion of Indian naval capabilities may be a function of *sufficient* economic and technological resource capabilities whereby India could demonstrate its sea power in an

Table 3.2   Implicit doctrines in India's military policy

A. *Sufficient Conventional Defence 1963–1971*
(The *Minimalist* Posture)

Pakistan: Maintain slight edge in ground forces against West Pakistan, qualitative parity but quantitative superiority in the air, and superiority at sea but at low resource levels. Maintain superior but minimum land, air and sea forces against East Pakistan.
China: Maintain sufficient ground forces along Himalayan borders to adequately fight the last war of 1962.

B. *Limited Conventional Deterrence, 1972–1988*

Pakistan: Move towards conventional military superiority over Pakistan. Develop SRBM capability.
China: Maintain sufficient ground forces along Himalayan borders. Develop intermediate missile delivery systems (IRBMs).
Indian Ocean: Commence naval expansion for defence of coastline and of the maritime economic zone.

C. *Latent Nuclear Deterrence, 1989–1995*

Pakistan: Maintain conventional military superiority. Deploy short-range nuclear delivery systems (SRBMs and bombers) while maintaining nuclear weapons capabilities on the threshold of production and deployment.
China: Maintain sufficient ground forces along Himalayan borders. Deploy intermediate-range delivery systems (IRBMs) while maintaining nuclear weapons capabilities on the threshold of production and deployment.
Indian Ocean: Expand naval capabilities in the extended Bay of Bengal and Arabian Sea regions.

D. *Regional Nuclear Deterrence 1996–2000*
(The *Maximalist* Posture)

Pakistan: Maintain conventional and nuclear deterrent capabilities based on conventional superiority and short range nuclear delivery systems (SRBMs and bombers).
China: Maintain sufficient border ground forces and adopt minimum nuclear deterrent capability based on intermediate and long-range delivery systems (IRBMs and ICBMs).
Indian Ocean: Expand naval capabilities to demonstrate 'sea power' among the littoral states from the Horn of Africa to the Straits of Malacca.

---

extended arc of the Indian Ocean. Until recently, the 'doves' in India have been able to restrain the more ambitious military objectives of the 'hawks'. What is apparent, however, is a steady move toward the strategic scenarios projected by the 'hawks', especially in naval and nuclear weapons and missile capabilities. These moves are raising concerns in the United States, in some of the Southeast Asian countries and in Australia.

III THE CONVENTIONAL MILITARY POSTURE: BALANCE VERSUS PREPONDERANCE

There are fundamental differences between India and Pakistan on how to measure the military balance in South Asia. To apply some of the American terminologies used during the early SALT I negotiations with the Soviet Union, Pakistan has sought to establish an 'essential equivalence' with India in the distribution of forces on land, air and at sea (the American expectation during the SALT I negotiations), while India has sought to achieve 'equal security' taking into account the Chinese threat, its long land boundaries that it has in common with several states in the region, and its long coastline and several island territories in the Bay of Bengal such as the Andaman and Nicobar Islands (the Soviet expectation).

However, there are some crucial differences in the opposing Indian and Pakistan expectations compared to the American and Soviet objectives during the SALT I negotiations. First, India's population and land area is almost eight times the size of Pakistan's, as compared to the essentially equivalent populations sizes of the United States and the Soviet Union. Second, the difference in the size of forces that appear between 'essential equivalence' and 'equal security' are less relevant in measuring the nuclear military balance as compared to the conventional military balance. To maintain India's conventional military strength at the level of Pakistan would make India vulnerable to threats from China and to great power naval interventions. Third, the problem of the conventional threat appears more crucial for India because its main adversaries (Pakistan and China) are on its borders and therefore within ready striking distance. In contrast, the main population and industrial centres of the United States and the Soviet Union are separated by the Pacific and Atlantic oceans.

From the Indian defence standpoint, measurement of the conventional military balance in South Asia must also take into account three other significant considerations: (a) the quality of the weapons procured by either side; (b) the terrain on which wars must be fought; and (c) the expected time duration of likely wars on the subcontinent. India claims disadvantages in all three categories. Soviet and, to a lesser extent, British, French, Swedish and German weapons do not quite compare with the best American weapon systems obtained by Pakistan. This qualitative Indian disadvantage was only partly offset by the Pakistani need to rely on Chinese weapons as well. Again, the conduct of wars in the defence of Kashmir (the Indian state claimed by Pakistan) and Arunachal Pradesh (claimed by China) were perceived to be more difficult from the Indian side than that of its adversaries. Finally, India's quantitative military superiority over Pakistan was generally considered to be quite irrelevant in the case of the short duration wars of the subcontinent. If the element of surprise is also added to the three disadvantages described above, Pakistan and China may be capable of seizing Kashmir and Arunachal Pradesh at critical moments.

From the Pakistani defence standpoint, Indian demands for clear military superiority in proportion to its size and perceived extended security requirements are unacceptable. If an 'essential equivalence' of military forces did not prevail between India and Pakistan, then Pakistan would really have no defence at all. Either Pakistan must possess a rough military balance with India or Pakistan would be at the mercy of India. There would be little point in maintaining only one-eighth or even half the military force capabilities of India. Pakistan may just as well eliminate almost all of its forces and adopt the policies of Bangladesh and India's other neighbour: viz., limited military capabilities for the maintenance of internal security alone.

However, Indian military preponderance in South Asia is precisely the goal of Indian defence policy and is considered to be the desirable state of affairs to maintain peace and stability in the region. India has constantly rejected 'balance of power' politics in South Asia, both during and after the Nehru era, although the reasons were fundament- ally different in each period. Under Prime Minister Nehru, European- style balance of power politics was considered dangerous and immoral. He preferred the policies of nonalignment and *panchsheel* as offering the best prospect for peace and security among nations. He believed that military capabilities became irrelevant if such policies were pursued successfully. On the other hand, under Prime Ministers Indira Gandhi and Rajiv Gandhi, Indian military preponderance was the preferred posture to avoid wars on the subcontinent.

The policies of the two Gandhis essentially followed the analysis of Professor A. F. K. Organski of the University of Michigan, who had argued that under conditions of military preponderance, the weaker state dare not attack, while the stronger state need not attack. Even when wars do take place, often they occur because the weaker state is attempting to catch up in the military balance with the stronger state – a situation which Organski has called the 'rear-end collision' theory. The fact that there has been no Indo–Pakistani war since December 1971 – including during the revival of the Kashmir crisis in 1990 – may perhaps be attributed to India's military preponderance. Similarly, we could argue that the lack of a military balance between India and China has prevented the Himalayan border dispute from erupting into another war between the two states.

These differing outlooks on the distribution of forces between India and Pakistan are not likely to be easily resolved. In practice, Pakistan may have no choice. After the creation of Bangladesh out of the old Pakistan in 1971, India now appears determined to maintain its military superiority on the subcontinent. New Pakistani military acquisitions have a tendency to produce Indian procurements that greatly exceed the Pakistani gain, at least quantitatively if not qualitatively. For example, the Pakistani purchase of forty F-16s from the United States in the 1980s, triggered the purchase of more than twice as many French Mirage-2000s and Soviet MiG-29s by India. This was quite unlike the earlier Indian policy of 'matching capabilities' that was pursued in the 1950s and 1960s. This Indian inclination to overreach Pakistan in the arms race is also paralleled by a tendency to compare Indian capabilities with those of China, especially in the nuclear field and in maritime conventional capabilities. Although no effort has yet been made to engage in a major arms race with China, there are signs that India may eventually seek to move towards a *maximalist* defence posture.

IV THE ORDER OF BATTLE

An assessment of Indian military power needs to be measured against the power capabilities of present and potential military rivals. Such an assessment was relatively simple in the past since it was gauged in terms of India's two traditional rivals, Pakistan and China. Indian force levels and weapons procurement strategies were generally intended to maintain a defensive 'slight edge' against Pakistan in the case of full-scale wars, and the ability to carry out a 'holding operation' against China in the kind of limited land war that was fought in 1962 along the Himalayan borders.

Thus, on the eve of the 1971 war with Pakistan over the Bangladesh issue, the Indian Army consisted of about 830,000 men and officers, and included one armoured division, with a second almost completed.[12] There were thirteen infantry divisions for deployment against Pakistan, and ten mountain divisions deployed against China along the Himalayan frontiers. These were complemented by three armoured brigades, six independent infantry brigades, and two parachute brigades. As against this, the Pakistan Army consisted of 365,000 men and officers, which included two armoured divisions, twelve infantry divisions, one independent armoured brigade and another air defence brigade. On the ground, Pakistan had continued to match the Indian land forces both in men and equipment.

There was a greater quantitative imbalance in the air and at sea. In December 1971, the strength of the Indian Air Force was estimated at 80,000 men and 625 combat aircraft which included the Indian-made or assembled HF-24 *Maruts*, *Ajeets*, and Mig-21s, and the Soviet-supplied SU-7BS. IAF squadrons also possessed the British *Hunter* and French *Mystère* fighters purchased in the 1950s. As against this, the Pakistani Air Force consisted of 17,000 men and 285 combat aircraft which included the older American B-57B *Canberras*, F-86 *Sabres*, and F-104 *Starfighters* obtained in the 1950s, Chinese Mig-l9s, and French *Mirage*-IIIEs. Neither side had significantly advanced aircraft at the time. The Indian-made *Maruts*, and especially the Soviet-supplied SU-7Bs, proved disastrous in operations, with many of the SU-7Bs crashing before they were engaged in combat.

In 1971, the Indian Navy consisted of 30,000 men and included one refurbished aircraft carrier, two cruisers and three destroyers, all obtained from Britain and all of the immediate post Second World War vintage. The Indian navy also possessed nine destroyer escorts (including five Soviet *Petya*-class vessel), four Soviet *Foxtrot*-class submarines, about five Soviet *Osa*-class missile boats, together with several other lesser vessels such as patrol boats, minesweepers, seaward defence boats and landing craft. In comparison, the Pakistan navy consisted of 10,000 men and operated four smaller Italian *Daphne*-class submarines, three destroyer escorts, two fast frigates and other lesser vessels, most of which were obtained from China. Although the Indian navy was small, the Pakistan navy was comparatively quite insignificant, enabling India to crush the latter during the first few days of the war. It then proceeded to bombard the coastal ports of Karachi in West Pakistan and Chittagong in East Pakistan with virtually no Pakistani naval resistance.

Almost twenty years later, the situation has been substantially changed in the South Asian region.[13] By 1990, the Indian Army consisted of approximately 1.2 million military personnel organised into five Regional Commands and ten Corps Headquarters.[14] This included nineteen infantry divisions, eleven mountain divisions, two armoured divisions and one mechanised division. These major formations were supplemented by 8 armoured, seven infantry, one mountain, and three independent artillery brigades. The Indian Army possessed 3,150 main battle tanks (MBT). Organized into five Air Commands, the Indian Air Force comprised 115,000 men and carried 836 combat aircraft and twelve armoured helicopters distributed among fifty squadrons. There were another 186 planes as part of twelve transport squadrons, and 140 helicopters as part of six helicopter squadrons. Likewise, the Indian Navy had expanded to 47,000 military personnel organized under three Naval Commands headquartered at the ports of Bombay, Fort Cochin and Vishakapatnam. The Navy included two carriers, five destroyers, twenty-one frigates, seventeen submarines including one that is nuclear-powered, and another 34 patrol and coastal combat vessels.

Compared to the growth of the Indian armed forces, the Pakistani military consisted of 480,000 men in the army organized into seven Corps Headquarters that included fourteen infantry divisions, two armoured divisions, five independent armoured brigades, four independent infantry brigades, eight artillery brigades, and three anti-aircraft artillery brigades. The Pakistan army had 1,750 main battle tanks. There were 25,000 men in the air force equipped with 451 combat aircraft organized into twelve fighter squadrons. There were another two transport squadrons comprising fifteen planes. The navy had 15,000 men and included seven destroyers, ten frigates, six submarines, and another twenty-nine patrol and coastal combat vessels.

Proponents of the Indian military buildup will argue that this kind of comparison with Pakistan is not only misleading but even somewhat irrelevant because India's security problems are much wider than expressed by the Indo–Pakistani military balance. The fact that India before 1971 sought only a 'slight edge' against Pakistan, and a minimum capability that would allow it to conduct a limited border 'holding operation' against China (i.e., the *minimalist* defence posture), merely demonstrated the Indian government's past restraint in responding to the serious threats that it faced. Moreover, despite the quantitative military advantage carried by India, there still exists today a rough qualitative military balance with Pakistan especially with regard to the frontline weapon systems of the army and air force.

Therefore, taking the combined power capabilities of India's two traditional rivals, Pakistan and China, as well as the length of India's land and sea frontiers, the present distribution of military forces in South Asia is not necessarily in India's favour. As in the past, a military balance on the subcontinent based on the concept of 'essential equivalence' of military forces has remained, but only at a much higher level of capabilities on all sides. Indeed, from the standpoint of the *maximalist* perspective, India has not achieved its projected objective of 'equal security' with its traditional military rivals considering all the past wars that India has fought and the new and continuing security problems that it faces.

The Indo–Pakistani balance of military forces on the ground measured in terms of military personnel is 1.2 million to 480,000 (ratio of 2.5:1), and measured in terms of main battle tanks is 3,150 to 1,750 (ratio of 1.8:1). Since eleven Indian divisions are deployed against China and some sections of Indian infantry divisions are intended for deployment in the troubled northeast sector where there are several separatist movements, the actual order of battle against the Pakistan army is only marginally in favour of India. On the other hand, the qualitative military balance on the ground may actually be shifting in Pakistan's favour as it proceeds to acquire American TOW anti-tank missiles and M-1 *Abrams* tanks as compared to the quality and effectiveness of recent Indian procurements such as the Indian-made T-72 tanks of Soviet design.

Perhaps a comparison between India's military exercise in 1987 (Operation 'Brasstacks') and Pakistan's exercise in 1989 (Operation 'Zarb-e-Momin' or 'the Strike of the Faithful') may be suggestive of the likely order of battle on the ground. The Pakistani exercise was of an even larger scale than India's earlier exercise, utilizing more than half of its 480,000 regular land forces.[14] Indeed, if Pakistani reservists, numbering as many as its regular forces and concentrated mainly in Pakistani Punjab, are taken into account, then the numerical advantage may even lie with Pakistan. Add to this the threat of the Pakistani army Chief-of-Staff, General Aslam Beg, to pursue a strategy of 'offensive defence' in future wars with India, and the tilt may seem even more pronounced.[15] Since the bulk of Indian army divisions are stationed in central and southern India, Pakistan may carry the advantage in any preemptive conventional strike across the border.

Meanwhile, the eleven Indian mountain divisions intended for defence of the Himalayan frontiers with China have remained relatively unchanged since this deployment was first conceived following the war with China in 1962. China has approximately the same number of forces deployed or intended for deployment along its frontiers with India. Note, however, that in the early 1990s, both India and China had begun to reduce their military deployments along their Himalayan borders, signifying a considerable thaw in Sino-Indian relations.[16]

The numerical superiority of India in the air is not in question. India carries an advantage in combat aircraft of 836 to 451 (ratio of 1.8:1), and has 115,000 uniformed personnel to Pakistan's 25,000 (ratio of 4.6:1). Unlike the Indian army, air force deployments would appear to be primarily directed against Pakistan, since Indian military deployments against China appear intended to 're-fight' the last war of 1962 in which the Indian Air Force was not engaged in a combat role. However, numerical balances – or imbalances – do not always reflect the qualitative nature of the aircraft on either side, which on the subcontinent has fluctuated between the two sides. India, for instance, has claimed that the introduction of the forty American F-16 *Fighting Falcons* to the Pakistan Air Force (with the promise of another sixty in 1990) constituted a qualitative leap forward in the Indo–Pakistani military balance compared to the Indian procurement of French and Soviet aircraft.[17]

The Indian response to the Pakistani acquisitions of forty F-16s from 1982 onwards has been to acquire forty Mirage-2000s from France and another forty Mig-29s from the Soviet Union on the grounds that this numerical leap forward did not sufficiently offset the qualitative combat effectiveness of the Pakistani acquisitions. (Note that the Indian negotiations for the *Mirage*-2000s had begun before the American decision to supply F-16s to Pakistan, although the decision to acquire them almost immediately in 1982 was essentially a knee-jerk reaction to the American decision to sell F-16s to Pakistan in 1982.) Pakistani acquisitions of 100 hand-held *Stinger* missiles is believed to have further eroded the combat effectiveness of the Indian air force.[18] It was the introduction of this missile among the Afghan *mujahideen* that effectively turned the tide of the war against the Soviet occupying forces in Afghanistan. By the early 1990s, Pakistan had successfully negotiated the delivery of another sixty F-16 aircraft from the United States while India continued to negotiate for more Mig-29s from the Soviet Union in response to this move.

From the Indian standpoint, the Indo–Pakistani military balance on the ground and in the air must also be viewed in the context of the terrain on which wars are fought and the short duration of the wars (three weeks in 1965, and two weeks in 1971). India claims to have the disadvantage in defending Jammu & Kashmir on the Indian side from any Pakistani attempt to wrest that state away by force. In 1965 and 1971, such attempts were thwarted only by opening new battle fronts and pushing forward across the Indo–Pakistani frontiers in divided Punjab and Rajasthan-Sind. With Indian Punjab in turmoil since 1984, and Sikh loyalties no longer certain, even this type of defence appears less certain. Unless India and Pakistan were to fight a war of attrition in the future, India's numerical superiority in men, tanks and combat aircraft would be quite meaningless in another Indo–Pakistani war.

Despite all the international concerns expressed about India's naval expansion, India has only forty-five combat vessels and thirty-four patrol vessels compared to Pakistan's twenty-three and twenty-nine (ratios of 2:1 and 1.2:1). This 'superiority' would appear meaningless when measured against the disparate lengths of the two country's respective coastlines and India's additional island territories in the Bay of Bengal and the Arabian Sea. India has argued that its expansion at sea is merely to compensate for past neglect and to produce a better internal military 'balance' among its armed services.

India's naval expansion is generally unrelated to the traditional Sino-Pakistani threat.[19] Unlike the Indian army and Indian air force, the Indian navy cannot point to a specific and more immediate threat to national security where naval forces could play a decisive or substantial role. The threat from Pakistan was always perceived to come by land and air. Pakistan's more recent naval expansion is largely a belated response to the growth of Indian naval power. The threat from China is perceived to be primarily land-based and (to a lesser extent) from conventional air power and intermediate-range nuclear-tipped missiles. The Chinese navy does not operate west of the Straits of Malacca in the Bay of Bengal and southern Indian Ocean region.

The steady growth of the Indian navy since the mid 1960s has been based on a wider strategic perspective that included a mix of four distant and proximate objectives: (a) to establish 'sea power' befitting a nation of its size and central peninsular location; (b) to defend India's growing sea-borne trade; (c) to improve India's coastal defence capability within its 12-mile territorial waters; and (d) to protect its potential mineral resources within its 200–mile economic zone.[20]

Although a measurement of the Indian navy's capabilities against those of Pakistan may be irrelevant from the Indian standpoint, nevertheless Indian naval growth poses a serious threat to Pakistan's major port of Karachi and the rest of its short coastline. As during the 1971 Indo–Pakistani war, the Indian navy could readily blockade the Pakistani coast, or bombard Karachi with some limited resistance posed by the Pakistan Air Force. Given these circumstances, it is not unusual to see that the Pakistan navy has begun to expand in response to the threat from the Indian navy, setting the stage for a major Indo–Pakistani naval arms race in the 1990s.[21]

Of greater consequence for the Indian Ocean littoral has been the Indian navy's search for a blue water capability. The leasing of a nuclear-powered submarine from the Soviet Union in 1988, the INS *Chakra*, is indicative of this wider naval objective.[22] There were also some reports that this acquisition may be the forerunner of a program to produce nuclear-powered submarines in India.[23] Together with the purchase of five Kashin-II destroyers from the Soviet Union over the last decade, India has begun to affect the naval balance among the littoral states of the Arabian Sea and Bay of Bengal, and to worry countries as far away as Australia.[24] These trends could conceivably lead to the forging of a naval alliance by the three major Islamic states of Iran, Pakistan and Indonesia in order to counter the growth of Indian naval power. Or, it may provoke the entry of the Chinese navy into the Indian Ocean at the behest of some of the littoral states.[25]

V THE NUCLEAR AND BALLISTIC MISSILE ARMS RACE

Apart from issues arising from the conventional arms race and the regional military balance in South Asia, of increasing concern is the latent nuclear arms program and the development of missile capabilities in India and Pakistan. Both countries have acquired the technological capability to produce nuclear weapons. India tested an atomic device in 1974 but refrained thereafter from proceeding with a nuclear weapons program. On the other hand, Pakistan has been threatening to carry out a nuclear test over the last decade – at least implicitly – but has thus far refrained from carrying out that threat. With the launching of *Agni* in May 1989, an intermediate range ballistic missile, and with the second test launching of *Prithvi* in September 1989, a shorter range surface-to-surface missile, India has demonstrated that it is virtually a nuclear weapons power with delivery systems short of actual deployment.[26] Apart from the existing five nuclear weapons powers, only Israel with its *Jericho*-II missiles possess such IRBM capability. The *Agni* test has produced domestic pressures to embark on further testing with accompanying external pressures from the United States to conform to the American-sponsored Missile Technology Control Regime.[27]

The strategic repercussions of these developments are as yet unclear. Pakistan has already started to seek similar capabilities in nuclear weapons and missile systems. However, more significant will be the effects of these Indian military programs on the Sino-Indian military balance. Whereas at one time the Chinese threat was considered likely to be limited to another Himalayan border war, the growing Indian capability in nuclear weapons and missile systems will make Chinese capabilities in these areas more relevant and significant in measuring the military balance between the two countries. Indeed, the distant Chinese nuclear threat to India that prevailed in the past will have been brought nearer with India's growing nuclear and missile capabilities.

The nuclear environment in South Asia has gone through several phases that follow approximately the periods indicated earlier in India's strategic doctrines and war-fighting capabilities. The Chinese atomic test of 1964, just two years after the 1962 Sino–Indian war, first raised the question of whether India should become a nuclear weapons power. From that time on, India watched the political and military relationships between China and Pakistan, and those between China and the two superpowers. Given the combined hostility of both superpowers against China before 1971, India considered it unnecessary to embark on a nuclear weapons program. Any possible Chinese nuclear threat to India was perceived to have been effectively curbed by the counter-threat of the two superpowers against whom China at the time possessed no retaliatory strike capability. However, by continuing to develop its nuclear energy capabilities, India was able to maintain its nuclear weapons option (i.e., the ability to develop nuclear weapons from its peaceful nuclear energy programs) should this favourable strategic nuclear environment change in the future. In the late 1960s and early 1970s, the time needed by India for a diversion to nuclear weapons was generally assessed at between eighteen months and two years.

The Indian atomic test of 1974, about two years after the December 1971 Indo–Pakistani war, ushered in the second phase. The decision to proceed with the development and testing of an atomic bomb was probably taken soon after the 1971 Indo–Pakistani war. During that war, the American nuclear-powered carrier *Enterprise* sailed into the Bay of Bengal in a show of gunboat diplomacy against India while there were fears that China might intervene on the Pakistani side. Sino-American rapprochement in 1972 further implied that the hostility of both superpowers against China had been reduced to just that of the Soviet Union. Thus, in any future military confrontation with China, either directly or indirectly on behalf of Pakistan, Chinese nuclear threats would appear more credible.

Similar reckoning had also taken place in Pakistan, which saw the severance of East Pakistan through Indian military intervention in the civil war. Moreover, Pakistan perceived at this time that one method of negating the new Indian dominance (the 'new realities of the subcontinent', as India called the situation), would be the acquisition of nuclear weapons. A nuclear Pakistan would be able to deter both nuclear and conventional attacks by India in the future. The Indian atomic test of 1974 further sparked and accelerated Pakistan's drive for nuclear weapons. From about 1980–81 onwards, several Indian and foreign reports indicated that Pakistan had acquired a nuclear weapons capability through the uranium enrichment process at Kahuta.[28] By the late 1980s, nuclear conversion time from civilian to military purposes was about six weeks for India and perhaps somewhat longer for Pakistan, assuming that Pakistan had not already built and stockpiled nuclear warheads.

The situation that prevailed during the 1980s, and is likely to continue through the 1990s , may be termed a case of 'Mutual Nuclear Brinkmanship' (MNB) between India and Pakistan.[29] The strategy of 'brinksmanship' on the subcontinent carries three basic characteristics. First, both sides remain on the threshold of nuclear weapons production and deployment through their civilian nuclear energy programs. In effect, Pakistan is following India's policy of 'maintaining the option'. Second, both sides periodically allege that the other has begun the covert stockpiling of untested nuclear weapons. Such allegations, however, have never been fully substantiated but it would be enough if one or both believe the other to have already 'gone nuclear' even if they have not. That would immediately produce a counter response by the other. Third, both sides periodically threaten to 'go nuclear' while attempting not to carry out that threat. Under these contradicting pressures, one side may be tempted to forestall and finesse the other side's nuclear decision so as to be the first to 'go nuclear' (mainly India's inclination), or may seek ways to provoke the other side into 'going nuclear' first so as to justify a nuclear weapons program of its own (mainly Pakistan's inclination).

This unusual nuclear posture may lead eventually – if this has not already happened – to the more unstable situation of 'Mutual Bombs-in-the-Basement' (MBB). Thus, the hitherto 'latent' nuclear arms race between India and Pakistan from 1972 to 1989 may lead to a 'covert' nuclear arms race in the early 1990s. An MBB policy by India and Pakistan may prove to be risky because the degree of uncertainty and paranoia may be unusually high. Since neither side officially claims to have nuclear weapons, formal checks and verification become impossible. The relationship would be a competition in concealment and one of constant denials. Moreover, no nuclear arms control talks would be possible since nuclear weapons are officially not in existence on either side. Unable to check, verify or even discuss the issue of such a covert nuclear arms race, both India and Pakistan may be compelled to assume the worst possible scenario thereby leading either to an intense nuclear arms race, or even to nuclear preemptive attacks. Thus, the slide from 'mutual nuclear brinkmanship' to 'mutual bombs-in-the-basement' will further move quickly to an overt and unabashed Indo–Pakistani nuclear arms race in South Asia. Should this happen in the 1990s, then conditions of stability and instability in India's two-way nuclear arms race with both China and Pakistan will need to be formulated so as to avoid nuclear wars through misconceptions of each other's nuclear strategies.

There is, perhaps, no significant reason to assume that the same stable relationships as found at the global level among the United States, the Soviet Union and China should not occur at the regional level if India and Pakistan were to join the nuclear club. Indeed, the China-India-Pakistan nuclear relationship would resemble the United States-Soviet Union-China nuclear relationship during the Cold War. A state of mutual assured destruction would exist between China and India resembling that between the United States and the Soviet Union, while a similar deterrent relationship would exist between India and Pakistan, resembling that between the Soviet Union and China.

In the past, there were fears in the United States that communist China's entry into the nuclear club would be more dangerous than the earlier entrants (all white European or European-descended states) because Chinese leaders were more likely to be irrational or irresponsible. Indeed, fears of the 'illegitimate' communist regime in China produced an American policy that for more than thirty years sought to prevent China's entry into the United Nations until President Nixon's visit to Beijing in 1972. Yet, in retrospect, few American analysts today would claim that China was more dangerous and irresponsible with its nuclear weapons than the other four nuclear powers.

So too, perhaps, fears of a nuclear India and Pakistan may be unfounded. Despite the emotional nature of Indo–Pakistani issues that are derived largely from religious antagonism, the two countries' actual behaviour does not indicate irrationality or irresponsibility. In the Indo–Pakistani wars of 1947–48, 1965 and 1971, there was overall caution, restraint and even gentlemanliness in their military behaviour. Civilian targets were scrupulously avoided and prisoners-of-war were well-treated. The formal agreement in December 1988 not to attack each other's nuclear installations signed by Prime Ministers Benazir Bhutto of Pakistan and Rajiv Gandhi of India is further evidence that the nuclearisation of South Asia does not necessarily mean greater levels of instability.

Despite the probable parallels between the global and regional relationships, extrapolating the likely regional nuclear relationships based on the global nuclear experience may not always be satisfactory in practice. In particular, four differences may be noted as between the global and regional relationships that may affect South Asian stability: (a) the rate of nuclear change and transformation; (b) the problem of geographical proximity; (c) the problem of emotional intensity; and (d) the experience of more frequent wars on the subcontinent.

First, whereas the basic relationships between the United States, the Soviet Union and China evolved over a period of almost twenty-five years, the nuclear relationship between China, India and Pakistan is likely to be dramatic and uneven. To be sure, Soviet nuclear capabilities have swiftly followed those acquired by the United States (e.g., the atomic bomb, the hydrogen bomb, ICBMs, MIRVs, cruise missiles, ASATs), while the Chinese rate of nuclear development has lagged well behind the two superpowers. However, despite this uneven rate of nuclear growth, including some dramatic spurts over the last three decades, there was sufficient time for the United States, the Soviet Union and China to adapt and develop nuclear strategy in response to each other's growing capabilities and technological break-throughs.

The rate of nuclear change and development in South Asia may be more sudden and erratic, providing little time for strategies among the three countries to evolve and adapt to each other. Both India and Pakistan may choose to become nuclear weapons states overnight and simultaneously. At present, China does not appear to have seriously considered the consequences of a two-way nuclear arms race with the Soviet Union and India, and there is no indication in Indian and Pakistani official circles (nor could there be one because both countries have denied nuclear intentions) as to how they would conduct a nuclear arms race against each other.

On the other hand, a mitigating factor that may provide some stability in South Asia is the ability of China, India and Pakistan to learn quickly from the experience of relationships between the United States, the Soviet Union and China. Possible regional instability caused by dramatic change may be cushioned by the rational and sobering lessons derived from the global nuclear relationships, as well as by the prolonged gestation period that has existed in South Asia between technological nuclear capability and the decision to acquire nuclear weapons.

Second, unlike the great distances between the major industrial and population centres of the United States, the Soviet Union and China, the industrial and population centres of India and Pakistan (if not China and India) are very close to each other. For both India and Pakistan, the location of nuclear weapons and their targets will be so close to each other as to generate greater paranoia and sense of nuclear discomfort. Consequently a 'preemptive' mentality may prevail in South Asia despite the existence of stable retaliatory strike capabilities. Even in the case of India and China, the location of Chinese nuclear weapons close to the Indian border may create similar psychological nuclear discomfort so as to make Indian leaders nervous and more inclined to pull the nuclear trigger first during times of crises.

However, there is a counterpoint to this argument too. Geographical proximity may also produce mutual deterrence since the attacker may suffer collateral damage from the blast effects and radioactive fall-out. Almost every major city or industrial and nuclear site in Pakistan is close to the Indian border, with similar numbers of targets so placed in northwest India. A Pakistani nuclear attack on Indian cities, whether located near or far from the border, would have the additional disadvantage that it would involve the deaths of large numbers of Indian Muslims.

Third, the relationships between the United States, the Soviet Union and – to a certain extent – China were mainly determined by ideological differences as well as the more classic type of great power rivalry. The Cold War was a confrontation between western capitalistic ideology and democratic systems against communist ideology and totalitarian systems, where both the United States and the Soviet Union sought to advance their global influence and power. Similarly, the confrontation between the Soviet Union and China was also mainly ideological, being based on differences about communist beliefs and doctrines, although this may have been also a cover for the rivalry between Russian and Chinese nationalism. But there is no historic basis for such antagonistic nationalism between Russians and Chinese as between the Germans and French, or the French and British; nor does there appear to be deep animosity among Russian and Chinese peoples at the level of the masses.

In contrast, the relationship between India and Pakistan is mainly determined by religious antagonism that encompasses leaders and masses, a far more emotional state of affairs than rivalry based on ideology or even differences in language and race. This emotional intensity exists despite the fact that the peoples of the Indian subcontinent carry common historical, racial, linguistic and cultural ties. The spontaneous and uncontrollable conflict between Hindus and Muslims on the subcontinent when religious passions are aroused is much more intense than when such conflict is based on linguistic or racial differences.

Elsewhere in the world, the problem of emotional intensity may be seen in the case of conflict between Israeli Jews and Arab Muslims, Lebanese Christians and Muslims, or Azerbaijani Muslims and Armenian Christians in the Soviet Union. It is usually much more difficult to appeal to reason when there is religious antagonism and stress. There are, of course, exceptions in South Asia, as in the case of the Punjabi slaughter of Bengalis during the civil war in East Pakistan in 1971, a case of Muslim against Muslim based on linguistic and cultural differences. In general, all of this suggests that an Indo–Pakistani nuclear confrontation in South Asia may prove emotionally more stressful than nuclear confrontations between the United States and the Soviet Union, or the Soviet Union and China, at the global level. By the same token, however, Sino–Indian confrontations based on ideology or power rivalry may prove to be less intense than Indo–Pakistani confrontations within the South Asian regional nuclear triangle, providing a somewhat mitigating factor.

Fourth, India and Pakistan have been more prone to wars, at least since the Second World War, than the present five nuclear powers. India and Pakistan have fought wars in 1947–48, 1965 and 1971, while India and China have fought a war in 1962. No doubt, wars have also been fought by the existing nuclear powers since 1945. Both the United

States and the Soviet Union fought wars in Vietnam (1964–74) and Afghanistan (1979–89) against each other's proxies. Under the United Nations flag, the United States also fought a war against China between 1950 and 1953. China has fought a border war with Vietnam in 1979, Britain fought a war against Argentina over the Falkland Islands in 1982, and France has fought wars in Vietnam and Algeria in the early and late 1950s.

However, we may argue that there are some qualitative differences between the origins and causes of such wars compared to the wars of the subcontinent. These differences relate to the earlier arguments of geographical proximity, ideological versus religious intensity, and additionally, colonial control as in the case of France in Vietnam and Algeria. Wars between India and Pakistan, as between Israel and the Arab states, continue to relate back to the original causes of their conflict, especially the establishment of a new state based on religion. These conflict issues have as yet defied solutions.

VI CONCLUSIONS AND PROSPECTS

The essential thesis of this chapter is that Indian military capabilities have been expanding so that India may eventually be able to adopt an Asian or even global great power posture by the year 2000. While the rise of such capabilities is not necessarily reflected in annual resource allocations to defence measured as a percentage of the GNP, (which has remained steady at about 3.5 per cent), the total quantity of resources being allocated is accelerating because the Indian GNP as a whole has been increasing at a much faster rate than during earlier decades. Moreover, the substantial qualitative improvements in military capabilities tend to make India more visible and threatening. The acquisition of T-72 tanks, MiG-29s, Mirage-2000s, nuclear-powered submarines, aircraft carriers, *Kashin*-II destroyers, IRBMs, and eventually, perhaps, nuclear weapons, project India as a burgeoning great power. While critics may complain that such growth is unreasonable and unwarranted, India perceives the growth as modest, normal and natural. Compared to China, Pakistan, South Korea and Taiwan, India spends less of its GNP on defence and less military expenditures *per capita*.

Whether the growth has been modest, normal and natural, Indian military capabilities have been moving steadily from a *minimalist* conventional defence posture, directed primarily against Pakistan and secondarily against China, to a *maximalist* nuclear deterrent posture that would extend India's military reach throughout Asia and the Middle East. Much of this will be built on a major nuclear weapons capability and long-range delivery systems, and through the expansion of Indian naval power. However, as Charts I and II earlier indicated, the *maximalist* posture has not been reached. Thus, although there will continue to be various pressures that push India towards policies of global nuclear deterrence and sea power, there will be other constraints that will pull India back towards the old policy of sufficient border defence against Pakistan and China.

Pressures on the *minimalist* strategic posture towards the maximum will arise from some of the traditional conflict issues that have begun to resurface towards the end of the last decade. These include the re-enactment of the Tibetan rebellion and Chinese crackdown in 1988, the continued failure to formally settle the Sino–Indian boundary dispute, the resurgence of the Kashmir crisis in 1990, and the continued arms race between India and Pakistan that has moved towards the threshold of a nuclear arms race as well. With respect to China, the unabated arms buildup in that country may compel India to develop a military counter-balance, especially as the old Cold War rivalry of the superpowers recedes in Asia. Such an Indian policy would involve a nuclear arms race with China that would draw in Pakistan as well. With respect to Pakistan, India's conventional deterrent posture based on superiority is being imitated by Pakistan in an attempt to frustrate the Indian objective. That may prompt an even greater Indian military response to render Pakistani efforts futile. And that, in turn, may prompt Pakistan to go nuclear so as to neutralise and paralyse India's conventional military superiority. An Indo–Pakistani nuclear arms race would aggravate the Chinese nuclear threat, making it even more critical.

There is now also a greater desire in India to claim its 'rightful place under the sun' as a major Asian power of equal status with China. The rapid growth in India's technological capabilities will accelerate the 'mad military momentum' whereby weapons that are possible become essential. The competition among the Indian armed services for greater shares of the defence resource allocations is also likely to produce the familiar 'balloon effect' whereby greater allocations to one service will call for compensatory allocations to the other services so as to maintain a military balance among the services.

Constraints on the *maximalist* strategic posture towards the minimum will arise again from some of the same traditional conflict issues.

The Sino-Indian boundary dispute may be considered settled on a *de facto* basis since both sides have essentially held that territory which they want: India holds the North East Frontier Agency (renamed Arunachal Pradesh) south of the McMahon Line, which it considers strategically crucial to defend the northeast Indian states, and China holds the Aksai China plateau off Kashmir, which it considers strategically crucial for access to its nuclear weapons sites in the Sinkiang province. Meanwhile, the increasing likelihood of reduced Soviet support for India in the aftermath of the Cold War – one of the major roots of past Chinese hostility towards India – may well push India and China back towards the old 1955 spirit of Bandung.

From another standpoint, Indo–Pakistani issues may be considered less volatile for a variety of reasons. Pakistan's claim to Kashmir has weakened with the creation of Bangladesh in 1971, when Mohammed Ali Jinnah's 'two nation theory' of Hindus and Muslims on the subcontinent was shattered. An almost equal number of Muslims live in each of the three states of India, Pakistan and Bangladesh, thus weakening Pakistan's claim to represent Muslim interests on the subcontinent. Despite the violent dissatisfaction that was expressed in the Kashmir valley in 1990, the Kashmir issue between India and Pakistan is more likely to settle itself along the lines of the *status quo*. This slow resolution of Kashmir through the passage of time is being aided through the meetings of the South Asian Association for Regional Cooperation (SAARC). Despite the occasional pressures within this organization arising from India's military intervention in Sri Lanka and its economic sanctions against Nepal in 1989, SAARC has encouraged an emphasis on 'low politics' that concern economic cooperation rather than 'high politics' that concern national security issues. The SAARC process may perhaps emulate the uniting of Europe in the future.

Meanwhile, neither India nor Pakistan has gone the nuclear route, suggesting that both recognize the irretrievable and irreversible consequences of embarking on a nuclear weapons arms race. If threats by both sides to 'go nuclear' during the 1980s did not materialise, then it is quite possible that similar threats during the 1990s may not materialise either. Constraints on 'going nuclear' also arise from the growing world-wide recognition of the disutility of nuclear force and a shift from an emphasis on nuclear weapons as the symbol of great power status to that of economic power. In the future, prestige will be determined by GNP *per capita*, the trade balance, and the world-wide qualitative competition in goods and services. Japan,

South Korea, and Taiwan are setting the Asian and global agenda by defining issues based on economic power, thus rendering obsolete China's nuclear power and the potential nuclear power of India and Pakistan. Under these circumstances, even India's acquisition of sea power may appear to belong to the politics of the nineteenth century rather than to those of the twenty first. Should India recognise these trends, then the *maximalist* objective may yet become superfluous.

NOTES

1.   In an interview in January 1990, senior political officers at the Embassy of India in Washington, D.C., denied that there was a significant relative increase in Indian allocations to defence beyond the usual annual increases. One official expressed surprise to hear from me that there had been one. Interviews.
2.   Figures derived from *The Military Balance, 1989–90*, International Institute for Strategic Studies, London, 1989.
3.   The average Indian GNP growth rate figures were obtained from *Statistical Outline of India, 1988–89*, Tata Services Limited, Bombay, 1988, p. 5.
4.   See *The Military Balance: 1988–89* and *1989–90, op. cit.*
5.   Note that there is not necessarily a close correlation between GNP growth rates and annual increases in the defence allocation in previous years. This may be due to time lags or delayed official responses, or urgent military demands given arms procurement by India's military rivals. In the past there were increases in defence allocations of 4.3 per cent from 1978 to 1979, 18.3 per cent from 1979 to 1980, 16.2 per cent from 1980 to 1981, 2.8 per cent from 1981 to 1982, and 5.5 per cent from 1982 to 1983. There were annual GNP growth rates of −4.8 per cent in 1979 to 1980, 7.5 per cent in 1980 to 1981, 5.2 per cent in 1981 to 1982, and 1.8 per cent in 1982 to 1983. Percentage defence increases over the previous year were calculated from annual Indian defence budget figures provided by issues of *The Military Balance* from 1980–81 to 1984–85. GNP growth rates were derived from *India 1981: A Reference Annual*, Ministry of Information and Broadcasting, New Delhi, p. 34; and from *The Times of India Directory and Yearbook*, 1984, Times of India Press, Bombay , no date, p. 288.
6.   For an analysis of the Tamil crisis in Sri Lanka, see Dilip Mukerjee, 'Grim Lanka Scenario', *Times of India*, 16 January, 1990.
7.   For some contemporary analyses of the Kashmir problem, see two reports by Askari H. Zaidi, 'Politics: Behind the Increasing Militancy in Kashmir', and 'Personality: A Conversation with Abdul Ghani Lone,' *Times of India*, 1 January, 1990. Abdul Ghani Lone is the 'founder chairman' of the Kashmiri People's Conference. He and his daughter,

Ms. Shabnab Lone, are representing several arrested Kashmiri militants in various cases filed by the Government of India under the Public Safety Act and the Anti-Terrorist Act. See also reports by Balraj Puri, 'Roots of Terrorism in Kashmir Valley,' and K. Shankar Bajpai, 'Kashmir and Indo–Pakistani Relations', *Times of India*, 11 January , 1990; and Raju G. C. Thomas, 'Tug-of-War over Kashmir', *Christian Science Monitor,* 30 January, 1990.

8. For an assessment of Indo–Pakistani relations in 1989, see *Dawn Overseas Weekly* (Karachi), 20 July and 2 August , 1989. See also Jasjit Singh, 'Indo–Pakistani Relations: Simla Holds the Key', *Times of India*, 19 January, 1990; and K.R. Malkani, 'Towards Warmer Indo–Pakistani Ties', *Times of India*, 23 January, 1990.

9. See Raju G. C. Thomas, 'The Melancholy Chapter of Tibet', *Christian Science Monitor*, 22 October, 1987.

10. For recent analyses of the Sino-Indian dispute, See Sumit Ganguly, 'Sino-Indian Border Talks, 1981–89', *Asian Survey*, vol. 29, no. 12, December 1989, pp. 1123–35. See also Allen S. Whiting, *The Chinese Calculus of Deterrence: India and Indochina*, University of Michigan Press, Ann Arbor, Michigan, 1975. For an earlier controversial assessment of the dispute, see Neville Maxwell, *India's China War*, Jaico Publishing House, Bombay, 1971.

11. See Raju G. C. Thomas, *Indian Security Policy*, Princeton University Press, Princeton, N.J., pp. 19–50.

12. From *The Military Balance, 1971–72, op. cit.*

13. The figures that follow are from *The Military Balance: 1989–90.*

14. See Jasjit Singh, 'Pakistan Mounts Big Military Exercise', *Times of India*, 6 December, 1989.

15. See *News India*, New York, 22 December, 1989.

16. See reports in the *Times of India*, February 1 and 2, 1990.

17. *Times of India*, 9 February, 1988.

18. See Mohan Guruswamy, 'Stingers: A New Threat in South Asia', *Times of India*, 25 February, 1988.

19. For a recent study of the growth and development of this service, see Robert H. Bruce (Ed.), *The Modern Indian Navy and the Indian Ocean*, Centre for Indian Ocean Regional Studies, Perth, Australia, Curtin University of Technology, 1989.

20. See Raju G. C. Thomas, 'The Sources of Indian Naval Expansion', and Ashley J. Tellis, 'Securing the Barrack: The Logic, Structure and Objectives of India's Naval Expansion', in Robert H. Bruce, *Ibid.*, pp. 95–108, and pp. 5–50.

21. See reports in the *Times of India*, 24 February, 1988; and 21 March, 1988.

22. For an analysis, see K. Subrahmanyam, 'Nuclear Submarines Vital for Defence', in *India Abroad*, New York, 18 March, 1988

23. See remarks made by Vice Admiral (Retd.) K. K. Nayyar in *Navy News and Undersea Technoloqy*, Washington D.C., vol. 6, no. 13, 3 April, 1989, pp. 1–2.

24. See report by Michael Danby entitled, 'India Rules the Waves', in *The West Australian*, 12 July, 1988. The synopsis of the article reads:

'Australia's Defence Minister, Kim Beazley has described it as 'intriguing' . . . but there is nagging worry among some nations of the Indian Ocean basin, including Australia, that it could herald something more dangerous'.

25. See two articles by Harvey Stockwin, 'Chinese Ambitions in South China Sea', *Times of India*, 2 March, 1988; and 'Prolonging Tension in South China Sea', *Times of India*, 3 March, 1990 . See also earlier report entitled, 'China's Bid to Strengthen Its Navy', *Times of India*, 9, February, 1988 .

26. For a report on the *Agni* IRBM launch, see report in *The New York Times*, 23 May, 1989; and for the second *Prithvi* SRBM launch, see *The Hindu*, Madras, 28 September, 1989.

27. For a rationalization proposing a major Indian missile program, see K. Subrahmanyam, 'Missile Control Regime: Case for a Stepped-Up Indian Effort', *Times of India*, 31 January, 1989.

28. Pakistani as well as Indian nuclear weapons developments are discussed in Leonard Spector, *The Undeclared Bomb*, Ballinger Publishers, Cambridge, Mass., 1988, pp. 69–153.

29. Parts of this section from here on are derived from my paper entitled, 'The Nuclear Question in South Asia' delivered at the International Studies Association Convention, in Washington D.C., April 10–14, 1990. See also Raju G. C. Thomas, 'Should India Sign the NPT?' in Robert Pendley and Joseph Pilat, *Beyond 1995: The Future of the NPT*, The Plenum Press for Los Alamos National Laboratory, New York, 1990, pp. 133–50.

4 Directions in India's Defence and Security Policies
Manoj K. Joshi

The decade of the 1980s has ended with the recognition that India is a major actor in the vast South Asian region. This was the inevitable consequence of the Indian ventures in Sri Lanka and Maldives. But equally, it arose from the visible capabilities acquired by the Indian defence forces in the area of maritime reach, air mobility, as well as acquisition of the less tangible 'will' to act when required.

For the South Asian region, the 1980s has been a tumultous decade. Beginning with the Soviet intervention in Afghanistan, it led to the point where not only did the Soviet Union withdraw, but actually began the process of reform that seems to be a major world development. The Afghan issue brought Pakistan, an old Indian adversary, to the forefront of world affairs since its territory was used by the US to fight a not-so-covert war against the USSR.

In 1983 the decades-old ethnic problem in Sri Lanka erupted into a bloody massacre against the Tamil minority. This touched off a militant movement that was supported covertly by India. In these circumstances, Indian policy was largely reactive.

The response to the US aid package to Pakistan assumed near-hysterical proportions in the Indian media. But official policy under Indira Gandhi switched tracks as soon the government realised that there was nothing India could do to prevent the emergence of a new US–Pakistan relationship. Mrs Gandhi herself decided to woo Washington, not in a precipitate fashion, but in a serious, systematic way that was reciprocated by the US administration.

Indian worries about a possible regional imbalance in arms holdings were met by an almost automatic Soviet underwriting of Indian conventional weapons requirements.

Mrs Gandhi also attempted to exploit the nonaligned movement (NAM). The 1983 summit of the NAM was a major event in New

Delhi. However, the Indian stand on Afghanistan had alienated a significant section of Third World opinion and the NAM glitter could not hide its irrelevance. Moreover, by 1984 Mrs Gandhi was deeply embroiled in the Punjab disturbances. Externally, India was involved in the Sri Lanka venture. The stepped-up violence of Sikh militants brought latent tensions with Pakistan to a boiling point again.

The accession to power of Rajiv Gandhi following the assassination of his mother served to provide a level of continuity to Indian policies. Moreover, his penchant for travelling abroad and meeting foreign leaders bespoke of a high interest in the foreign policy area. Following his mother, he kept the Soviet Union firmly with him, even though Mr Gorbachev was outlining his own substantial agenda.

The message Mr Gorbachev brought in his first visit to New Delhi in 1986 was simple: we are undertaking major changes in our society and, as part of this, we plan to resolve our problem with China. We think there is a government in Beijing with whom we can do business and we advise you to do the same.

It is not clear whether the import of the Soviet message sank in immediately or whether it took some time, till after the Afghan withdrawal, to do so. However, that winter India became involved in a potentially dangerous situation with regard to China when the incident relating to Sumdorong Chu touched off a border buildup by both sides. While there was considerable excitement across the world, with some alarmist reports predicting border clashes in the summer of 1987, the situation was controlled by diplomatic action.

There was one positive consequence of the border imbroglio. India and China decided that they had to do something more than just talk on their border dispute. The firm Indian response to extremely strong language from the Chinese side provided the 'proper' psychological backround for Rajiv Gandhi to visit Beijing at the end of 1988.

The warming climate of Sino–Indian relations also took place against the backdrop of Chinese difficulties in Tibet. Riots in Lhasa followed by the imposition of martial law in 1987 and 1988 made the Chinese nervous of Indian intentions. However, the Government of India made it clear that its stand on Tibet was unchanged – Tibet was an autonomous region of China. Further, the Indian side reassured the Chinese that it would not allow its territory to be used for anti-Chinese activity by exiled Tibetans.

The Indian stand on the issue of Tibet was reconfirmed by the reiteration of New Delhi's position in the joint press communique following Rajiv Gandhi's visit in 1988. From the Chinese point of view, the best proof of India's determination to improve relations came following the Tiananmen massacre. The Government refused to take a condemnatory approach to the incident. Such an approach seems to have paid positive dividends in terms of the PRC's response to India's problems with Nepal and Pakistan.

I INDIA–US–USSR RELATIONS

Through the 1980s, even as India was opening up to the West in terms of arms acquisitions and exploring the US as a potential supplier, the relationship with the Soviet Union remained the more important. In part reacting to India's new Westwards orientation, the Soviets agreed to look at a range of Indian requests which included their most modern armaments.[1]

The most significant purchase, or lease to be precise, was the *Charlie* II type nuclear propelled submarine, rechristened *Chakra*. Though contracted for earlier, this became a symbol of continuing Indo–Soviet ties in the arms transfer area in late 1987 and early 1988, a period wrought with some anxiety over the direction of Indo–Soviet relations.[2]

Caught in the throes of internal reform, the Soviets appeared to have become quite disinterested in developments in the region in the latter half of the 1980s. While stressing the wider design of Asia-Pacific cooperation envisioned by Mikhail Gorbachev, there was little by way of initiatives on the Indian front. The Soviets were content to remain silent on the Indian intervention in Sri Lanka and Maldives and the Indians contented themselves with the nice sounding Delhi Declaration.

However, as budgetary constraints caught up with New Delhi, it became clear that the Soviet Union could not be entirely left out of India's calculations. For their part, the Soviets made it clear that they would also like to play a 'responsible' role in the region as part of their overall settlement with the West. When for a while it seemed that the US might supply AWACs to Pakistan, Moscow assured India that it would redress the balance with its own technology.

The 'bottom line' of Gorbachev's thinking was, however, that the Soviet Union did not think it had exclusive rights and interests in India and therefore would not object to closer Indo–US relations. Whether this conceptual change concealed a realistic assessment on the part of

Moscow of its inability to do anything about the situation remains to be seen. In their response to the Kashmir issue in early 1990, the Soviets quietly backed India but also made it clear that they were supportive of Washington's peace initiative.

Some of these trends became sharper by the time of Mr Gorbachev's second visit in 1988. The thrust of the visit appeared to be to promote economic relations. This involved shifting the emphasis of relations from trade based on the exchange of commodities to industrial cooperation through joint ventures and the joint development of advanced technologies.[3] Unlike the previous visit, on this occasion there was no press conference in which the Indian correspondents grilled Mr Gorbachev on the issue of China. However, the reference to the Indo–Soviet Treaty of 1971 in the joint communique appeared to underline the continuing security nature of Soviet concerns in India.[4]

The most portentous development to take place in the 1980s was the steady improvement in Indo–US relations. Mrs Gandhi's cautious wooing of Washington became more ardent under the Rajiv Government. The Government articulated a vision of a high-tech India and actively promoted an economic liberalisation regime that was widely welcomed in the US.[5]

Since the invasion of Afghanistan, when US attention once again reverted to the region, US leaders had been looking at the Indo–Soviet relationship as being hinged on arms transfer ties. To break this perception, there were several suggestions that the US promote ties with India in the same area, especially since New Delhi, which had contracted to acquire submarines from the FRG and the *Mirage* 2000s from France, seemed inclined to shop in the West for some systems. Little came from these suggestions.

Anyone who had seen the figures would have appreciated that there was an area of opportunity in Defence Research. The Defence Research and Development Organisation (DRDO) budget, which stood at Rs. 125 crores (one crore equals 10 million) in 1982–83, had by 1985–86 grown to Rs. 321 crores. Besides the Integrated Guided Missile Development Programme and a number of smaller projects, the DRDO was developing the Main Battle Tank (MBT) project and had initiated the Light Combat Aircraft (LCA) project.

Negotiations had been continuing between India and the US since 1983 for an agreement on the transfer of high-technology. After protracted discussions, an agreement was concluded relating to areas of sensitive technology. It was signed by the then US Ambassador, Harry Barnes, and M. K. Rasgotra, the Indian Foreign Secretary.

Later a memorandum of understanding was signed between Indian Commerce Minister P. Shivshankar and US Commerce Secretary Malcolm Baldridge for cooperation in the area of science.[6]

The thrust of the negotiations was to build up a relationship on the basis of scientific and technical cooperation which would meet the US needs of preventing leakage of technology to the East Bloc as well as the Indian desire to remain as self-reliant as possible. If the US could not break the Indo–Soviet arms linkage directly, it could achieve this end on a longer time-span by encouraging an indigenous Indian weapons design and development effort. The US therefore 'targeted' for cooperation the LCA project. The first stage was a series of visits by officials from India to the US and *vice versa*. This resulted in the agreement in 1986 for the purchase of eleven GE 404 engines to be used as an interim power plant for the LCA. In 1987, the Pentagon actually came out with a 'Blue Book' which was distributed to the aerospace industry. It outlined the areas cleared for deals with India.[7] Shortly after it was announced in the Indian parliament that a mutually agreed framework for cooperation had been developed. However, budgetary and other constraints have since imposed delays on the LCA programme.

The restriction imposed on the export of a combined acceleration vibration test system (CAVCTS) following the launch of the *Agni* (Fire) IRBM technology demonstrator in May 1989 points to the clear limits of the Indo–US understanding.[8] However, it appeared that some kind of balance had been achieved in the Indo–US relationship. The US was clear in expressing its 'world order' concerns relating to missile and nuclear proliferation, but did not take a shrill view with regard to India.[9]

The US response to *Chakra* and *Agni* was moderate. In exchange, the Indian stance on the US–Pakistani arms transfer relationship also lost its harsh edge. The second arms aid package to Pakistan, agreed in 1986 and worth $4.02 billion, did not see the kind of responses that the earlier package had engendered. By 1987–88, New Delhi also began to shift from its earlier policy of blaming the US for not taking steps against the Pakistani nuclear programme. The annual certification exercise of the US President with regard to the Pakistani nuclear programme did not excite too much comment.[10]

It is difficult to put a finger on the precise mechanics of the transformation of the relationship. Suffice to say it was not reflected in any enunciated policy change in New Delhi. The nuances could be picked up but not the detailed contours.

One example was the stepping up of US Navy port calls to India. These were related partially to Gulf deployments. But there were other missions involved, as illustrated by the US request for permission in late 1987 to bring an aircraft carrier to Bombay and the request for a visit by the USS Missouri, which may or may not be nuclear armed. On the floor of Parliament the government tabled statistics to illustrate that more Soviet than US ships had visited Indian ports, but these included Soviet navy ships that put in with supplies for the Indian navy.[11]

There was an accompanying development. In 1986 the Indian stand on foreign fleets was made clear by the foreign minister, B. R. Bhagat, when he said in the context of the visit of the USS Enterprise to Karachi:

> We have been consistently against Big Power presence in our neighbourhood and our stand on the implementation of the UN Declaration on the Indian Ocean as a Zone of Peace has been consistent and steadfast.[12]

Yet two years later when the unfortunate incident relating to the shooting down of an Iranian Airbus by the *Aegis* Class ship took place, the Indian reaction was 'somewhat belated' and, in the context, unbalanced. The Indian statement now was that India had 'consistently maintained that great power naval presences in the Gulf are aggravating tension in the region and has accordingly urged the utmost restraint by all concerned'.[13]

The harmony that had developed between India and the US was confirmed by the cooperation between the two countries at the time of the Indian military intervention to thwart the coup bid in the Maldives in November 1988. The US was kept fully informed of the action. In fact US ships were nearer to Maldives at the time of Mr Gayoom's SOS than were Indian ships, but they did not have the manpower for intervention. They provided the Indian forces with meteorological and navigational data and the end result was warmly applauded by Washington.[14]

The 'bottom line' was that India had come to accept US security interests in the north Indian Ocean in exchange for the benign US attitude and, indeed, encouragement to play a more significant role in regional affairs. This was made amply clear by Rajiv Gandhi himself when in response to a question from Indian correspondents while returning from the US in 1987, he said: 'I believe they [the US] will act in a proper manner [with regard to the the Pakistani nuclear programme]. They are worried. I believe they are also seeing a more positive role for India than they have seen in the past for the region specially'.[15]

The confirmation of this trend came out of the crisis that developed in the period after December 1989. The civil disturbances in the Kashmir Valley became a revolt against India and assistance from the Pakistani side was stepped up. On at least two occasions, according to media reports, the US averted an India–Pakistani clash.

In the spring of 1990, as the situation in Kashmir continued to remain grim, the US was active in cautioning restraint on both sides. Though it was never made public, there was considerable pressure from the US on Pakistan to reduce its support to Kashmiri militants. At a public level, the United States disclaimed any desire to mediate and supported the bilateral Simla Agreement that followed the Bangladesh War of 1971 and its major provision that the two sides solve their dispute through direct negotiations.

In May 1990, the situation had become sufficiently serious for the US President to send a special envoy in the person of Deputy National Security Adviser, Robert M. Gates, to both countries. While at a public level the Gates mission was essentially a fire-fighting operation to persuade the two sides to pull back forces, it was also an exploratory mission to see if the US could serve as an 'honest broker' in facilitating a permanent settlement in Kashmir.

At the end of May 1990, there was considerable speculation that the Bush-Gorbachev summit might see a joint US-Soviet initiative on the subcontinent. However, despite American efforts, the Soviets backed out of a joint appeal on Kashmir. In fact, Mr Gorbachev's spokesman, Arkady Meslennikov, made it clear that while the Soviets too supported dialogue through the Simla Agreement, they were reluctant to back Washington's initiative since it did not adequately address the issue of Pakistani complicity in the disturbances.[16]

II   REGIONAL ISSUES

Indian relations with Pakistan in the Rajiv Gandhi period were coloured by the rising tempo of violence in Punjab which the Indian government believed was orchestrated from across the border. However, under consistent pressure from the US, there were moves at various times to get out of the spiral of mutual recriminations. The first step was the decision taken during Prime Minister Rajiv Gandhi's visit to Islamabad in 1985 to work out an agreement on the non-attack of each other's nuclear facilities.

Following this, two rounds of talks were held in January and June 1986 to resolve the Siachen Glacier issue. These talks were presented as part of a series of official level consultations on other issues of concern to both sides. However after two rounds, there was a hiatus of two years.

In the intervening period came the crisis stemming from the 'Brasstacks' exercise, which brought India and Pakistan close to war.[17] The Brasstacks issue had another significant outcome. On January 29-30, 1987, just as the crisis over the Pakistani movements opposite Punjab and the Indian decision to man its forward defences was peaking, Dr Abdul Qadeer Khan, the head of the Pakistani nuclear programme, in an interview with Indian journalist, Kuldip Nayar, which was published in *The Observer* declared: 'America knows it. What the CIA has been saying about our possession of bomb is correct and so is the speculation of some foreign newspapers'.[18]

The Indian reaction to the interview was at two levels. On one level it confirmed their fears expressed loudly and not so loudly in the previous period. But on another level it was taken as a signal from Pakistan, one that deliberately expressed the ambiguity of the situation. In the circumstances it was up to India to accept or reject Pakistan's bluff, if indeed it was one. Whatever the consequences, it would seem that this development in conjunction with the Brasstacks episode may have persuaded the Government of India to have another look at its own 'ambiguous programme'.[19]

The death of General Zia in 1988 and the election of Benazir Bhutto as Prime Minister produced a thaw in relations between India and Pakistan. Rajiv Gandhi visited Islamabad in late December 1988 to participate in the South Asian Association for Regional Cooperation (SAARC) meeting and one of the agreements signed was for the non-attack of nuclear facilities.[20]

Another outcome of the change of government in Pakistan was the agreement to withdraw to pre-1972 positions in the Siachen Glacier area to facilitate negotiations on the border dispute. The implementation of this agreement has been subsequently stalled due to mutual suspicion.[21]

By late 1989 and early 1990, the Indo–Pakistan relationship had again hit rock bottom. The revolt in Kashmir, accompanied by a stepping up of Pakistani assistance to Kashmiri militants, had created an extremely dangerous situation. The Indian perception was that there were so many centres of power in Pakistan that there was a kind of competitive promotion of anti-Indian hostility. Nevertheless, there remained a perception that important power centres in Pakistan, including those close to the Prime Minister Bhutto, were not averse to having good relations with India.[22]

The years from 1987 to 1989 were ones of crisis for the Rajiv Government. Those close observers of the situation in New Delhi could see the extent to which the Rajiv gloss had been lost. However despite the government's preoccupation with a host of domestic crises (such as a debilitating clash between Rajiv Gandhi and President Zail Singh, the Punjab situation and the crisis-management for the emerging Bofors scandal) foreign and defence policy issues could not remain entirely 'on the backburner'.

The issue that came up next related to the ethnic conflict in Sri Lanka. The Sri Lankan army offensive against the Tamil militants reached Vaddamarachi in the Jaffna peninsula in May 1987. The outcry in India was enormous. The Indian Government first attempted to force the situation by sending an expedition of fishing boats loaded with food for Jaffna city. This was stopped by the Sri Lankan Navy. Following this, IAF transports escorted by *Mirage* 2000s carried out an air drop over the peninsula.

This action served to break the logjam in the Indo-Sri Lanka communications. By the end of July, New Delhi and Colombo had signed an agreement under which Sri Lanka was to accept India's security concerns regarding the presence of foreign elements in Sri Lanka and in relation to the port of Trincomalee, in exchange for which India would disarm the militants. For their part, the militants were promised a united North and Eastern Province, a political package, and a guarantee of their safety.

The signing of the agreement was accompanied by an immediate Indian military commitment to the island. One under-strength Indian division and an independent brigade, less their heavy firepower, were despatched to Palili Kankesanturai and Trincomalee in July–August 1987. The instructions to the forces were that their role was to disarm the Tamil Tigers and to reassure the militants with regard to their security. New Delhi's assessment of the Tigers' political goals was grossly inaccurate, as was its appreciation of their military strength. That realisation came after a slogging battle to capture Jaffna in October 1987, one year's intense jungle operations by four divisions of the Indian Army and 1100 officers and men dead.

By the end of 1989, with some 80 per cent of its goals achieved, New Delhi decided that the time had come to thin out forces in the island. At this point the Sri Lankans and the Tigers did a *volte face* and decided to talk to each other, leaving Indian policy in limbo. It was clear that Indian forces would have to leave. Indeed, by the end of March 1990, all Indian forces had returned home.[23]

India's venture in Sri Lanka has brought home to the region New Delhi's power projection capabilities. However, it has also brought out the limits of such a policy. Though the Indian commitment took place at the express invitation of the Sri Lankan government and was backed by powerful western countries, it did not have the overwhelming support of people in India. Indifference rather than widespread opposition was the broad Indian reaction and further economic and human cost could have converted the intervention into a liability.

Juxtaposed with the Sri Lankan venture has been the positive end result of India's Nepal policy. Piqued by consistent anti-Indian attitudes held by a coterie surrounding the King of Nepal, New Delhi utilised the renewal of trade and transit treaties to pull the rug from under Nepal in 1989. New Delhi's complaint was that despite considerable economic aid and extraordinary provisions, such as access to virtually any job in India for Nepalese citizens, the Nepalese Government persisted in squeezing Indian interests. The last straw was a large importation of arms from China which went against the spirit if not letter of Indo-Nepalese agreements.

New Delhi's squeeze was criticised around the world. Nepal was seen as a tiny landlocked country fighting a bullying giant. Significantly China, Nepal's neighbour, provided little comfort even if other regional countries like Bangladesh seemed willing to do more.

In the end, the train of events led to the rise of a pro-democracy movement in Nepal led by leftists and the traditionally pro-Indian Nepalese Congress. The movement finally brought down the Panchayat Raj Government and is currently in power under a constitutional monarchy framework. Considerable goodwill exists between the Nepalese Congress Party and India and the trade and transit issues have been settled.

III DEFENCE PLANNING

During the 'Gandhian decades' of 1947–62, expenditure on defence was accorded the lowest priority and there was little effort to focus on the need for planned expenditure for the services. However, as the border with China began to hot up in the late 1960s, a crash effort was launched to modernise the forces.[24]

Following the border war with China, the Emergency Committee of the Cabinet (ECC) formulated the first clearcut goals for the expansion of the Indian armed forces. The first Five Year Defence Plan was approved in early 1964. The plan allowed for a total outlay of Rs. 5,000 crores. Under it the army was to be expanded to a force of 825,000 and the air force to forty-five squadrons. The plan also outlined the need for replacing old aircraft and improving air defence radar and communications facilities. For the navy, the plan envisaged a phased programme for the replacement of ships as well an overall buildup. The exact stages of the navy plan are not known, but officers currently observe that even now the navy has not reached the figures laid down in that plan.[25]

K. Subrahmanyam, the noted strategic analyst, has observed that the first plan was essentially a compilation of the annual plan budgets. The same happened with the second plan and by the time of the third plan the situation arose where the requirements of the services exceeded what could be allocated. Though a Directorate of Planning was set up to reconcile the service requirements with the budget, it could achieve little and according to Subrahmanyam, the Directorate slowly vanished from sight.[26]

Subrahmanyam also notes that the first plan was based on a threat assessment of the Chinese deployment in Tibet and the Pakistani deployment on the western border. This was updated in 1966 and 1969. He also points out that until 1962, the defence services expected policy to be handed down from the political executive. Available intelligence was not processed into threat assessments, and until 1963 policy makers were not even aware of critical issues such as the impact of the PLA air force's condition following the Soviet withdrawal from China or which airfields in Tibet were available for attacks against India.[27]

Skipping over the intervening period to the present, we find that the defence planning process has yet to get off the ground. Responding to a question in Parliament in 1988, then Defence Minister K. C. Pant admitted that the Seventh Defence Five Year Plan (1985–90) had not yet been given formal approval. He went on to add:

Formal approval of the Seventh Defence Five Year Plan involves consideration of complex issues, reassessment of the threat scenario, allocating resources including foreign exchange to the services, Defence Research and Development and for Defence Production Units. These considerations have taken more time than assessed earlier.[28]

The Government subsequently approved the defence plan. But even this formal approval was ambiguous since it was given 'minus its financial implications', which meant that officials would have to obtain sanction for each item and that its fate would depend on the availability of resources. However, Mr Pant's answer made it clear that it was not as though Government was not spending money on defence, nor that it was lax or lazy, but that its hands were so tied with regard to resources that it was unable to provide any advance commitments to the defence services.

So far nothing has been heard of the eighth defence plan, though its preparation should have begun by 1990.

Whatever has happened in the area of defence planning has been an *ad hoc* exercise which may be seen through the matrix of the annual budgets (see Table 4.1).

Table 4.1   Indian defence budget, 1985–91 (rupees in crores – note, 1 crore = 10 million)

Year	Budget estimate (BE)	Revised estimate (RE)	Per cent change
1985–86	7,686	7,862	18.0
1986–87	8,728	10,477	24.9
1987–88	12,512	12,000	14.5
1988–89	13,000	13,200	10.0
1989–90	13,000	14,500	9.8
1990–91	15,750	15,750	8.6

Source: Defence Services Estimates

What the figures do bring out is the variation between the budget estimate and revised estimate figures. This is partly the result of poor planning. However there is also an element of fudging to show lower allocations on Budget Day when these things are noticed, the Government knowing full well that some of the expenditure will have to come through a supplementary allocation. Exchange rate fluctuations and failure to allocate adequate foreign exchange in the budget have also played a part. In this period, the rupee has continued to decline drastically against hard currencies. Its value against the rouble has also halved in the period under review.

From 1984 onwards, Indian forces were involved in a small but expensive war with Pakistan in the Siachen area. Even accepting the figure for defence spending put forward by the Government, what has not been allowed for both in the Siachen and Sri Lanka ventures is the enormous attrition forced on equipment by the widespread use of airmobility. Since these were not part of 'planned' expenditures, the implication is that the readiness levels of the Indian forces has been seriously affected.

Budget constraints began appearing from 1987–88, when the budget estimate of Rs. 12,512 crores went down to a revised figure of Rs. 12,000; and then in 1989–90 the Government actually presented a budget estimate that showed a 0.2 per cent cut. The cut was presented as a 'signal' to Pakistan. Whether that country accepted this preposterous signal cannot be ascertained. It was clear at the outset that this figure made little sense and following the 1989 general election, the government hurriedly brought out a supplementary demand for grants to Parliament that raised the figure to Rs.13,500 crores, which became Rs.14,500 crores by the time of the 1990 budget. The defence budget for 1990–91 shows an 8.6 per cent hike, amounting to Rs. 15,750 crores. However, despite this growth, India's defence spending now seems to have touched a plateau.

This plateauing of defence expenditure is due largely to pressures from other areas for resources. In the Indian system, the annual budgets comprised of the plan and non-plan heads. All developmental expenditure is part of the five year plan and annual figures are supposed broadly to conform to the plan document's allocations.

Defence, interest payments and subsidies come in the non-plan head. With a rising bill for interest payments and subsidies as well as a growing budget deficit, little flexibility has been left in the resource position (see Table 4.2). There is little the government can do about interest payments and subsidies. Further, it faces constant pressure for resources to be allocated to development needs. For this reason, the government has found it convenient to take an *ad hoc* approach to the funding of defence.

The consequences of this situation can also be seen through the annual defence services estimates. The burden of the pay and allowances and pensions is a palpable one (see Table 4.3). While 40 per cent of the Army's budget is allocated to pay and allowances, there are estimates that 75 per cent of the money in fact goes towards establishment costs.

Table 4.2   Expenditure of the Union Government (rupees in crores)

Year	Plan	Interest	Defence	Subsidies	Total	Deficit
1980–81	8,994	2,604	3,604	2,028	13,062	2,477
1987–88	24,277	11,236	11,948	6,729	40,791	5,816
1988–89	26,906	14,150	13,200	7,790	48,877	7,940
1989–90	28,476	17,710	14,500	9,166	59,220	11,750
1990–91	28,401	21,850	15,750	9,550	60,946	10,772

Source: Government of India Budget papers

Table 4.3   Army pay allowances and pensions (rupees in crores)

Year	Total army demand	Pay and allowances (% of demand)	Pensions
1985–86	4552	1601 (35)	
1986–87	6053	2032 (34)	
1987–88	6526	2408 (37)	1034
1988–89	6617	2629 (42)	1509
1989–90	7449	2994 (40)	1509
1990–91(BE)	7910	3173 (40)	1415

Source: Government of India Budget papers and Defence Services Estimates

Table 4.4   Capital outlay for defence services (rupees in crores)

Year	Army	Navy	Air Force	Ordnance factories
1985–86*	264	412	88	133
1986–87*	334	583	103	181
1987–88	776	828	1172	238
1988–89	1055	1026	1266	310
1989–90	1201	1114	1431	342
1990–91(BE)	1420	1274	1620	307

* The substantial figure for aircraft and aeroengines and heavy vehicles over Rs. 200,000 in value were shifted to this head in 1987–88.

Source: Defence Services Estimates

The figures for the capital outlay for the services do not show any unusually sharp increases. It is clear from Table 4.4 that the modernisation programme of the three services is in full swing. However the rupee values shown here do not reveal the full picture. Some of the amounts are against foreign exchange requirements and their utilisation would depend on the availability of foreign currency. Interestingly, the proportion of money being spent on capital outlay for the army is steadily increasing. In the case of the navy, the capital outlay in 1990–91 exceeds the navy demand and in the case of the air force, it is 78 per cent of the air force demand.

The impact of the restraints placed on expenditure by the Rajiv Gandhi Government in the last three years has now become a matter of public debate. Prime Minister, V.P. Singh, roundly criticised his predecessor for allowing defence preparedness to slip. There is little doubt that the restraints were applied across the board in all areas except pay and allowances. There were maintainance slippages in all formations and reductions in training sorties and exercises. Navy sailings were also reduced. Permission to sail the aircraft carrier *Viraat* had to be given by the Naval Headquarters itself. The distribution of cuts were of necessity uneven since the services were in an operational mode in Siachen and Sri Lanka, where restrictions could not be applied.

IV THE NEW GOVERNMENT AND DEFENCE POLICY

When the National Front Government came to power and was faced with a potentially serious military threat across the border because of the Kashmir disturbances, it realised the impact of the cuts on the defence forces. The new Prime Minister made it a point to inform the meeting of the Consultative Committee of Members of Parliament that the cuts had a negative impact on the readiness status of the services. In the campaign for the State Assembly elections in February 1990, Mr Singh attacked the former Congress (I) ruling party for defence policies which 'had threatened the country's security'. He said that, given the cost escalation of equipment and recent Pakistani acquisitions, the Indian defence budget should have gone up, but instead it went down.[29]

However, looking back at the figures in Table 4.1 it can be seen that despite attempts to curtail the budget as reflected in the Budget Estimates (BE), the budget did grow at roughly 15 per cent *per annum* between 1985 and 1990, a figure that ensured that by and large it outpaced inflation.

The approach of the new Government has also been made clear. After a hike of 8.6 per cent in 1989–90, Prime Minister Singh promised a new and integrated approach to the three services as well as an enhancement of the 1990–91 allocation.[30]

There have been several more developments in connection with the defence policy. The Government has announced a high-powered consultative panel on defence expenditure, to be headed by Arun Singh, Minister of State for Defence under Rajiv Gandhi. It also announced a scheme for the establishment of a National Security Council.[31]

The clouds of war that gathered over South Asia also brought forward the National Front Government's more hawkish posture on defence and security issues. Whether this was a rhetorical response to the serious situation on the border or a policy posture is not clear. However it needs to be noted that the minority Government depended on the support of the Hindu chauvinist Bharatiya Janata Party (BJP). V. P. Singh also criticised the Congress Government for allowing Pakistan to alter the ratio between Indian and Pakistani forces in its favour. In addition, he put forward propositions that seemed to presage doctrinal changes for the Indian defence services.[32]

It has been noted that the two principal Indo–Pakistani wars were brief two to three week affairs. Mr Singh argued during his intervention in the Defence debate in Parliament that 'A longer conflict is in our interests. With greater depth and capabilities, I think, if it is forced on us, we are not going to stop till we achieve our objective.'[33]

V   TRENDS IN FORCE STRUCTURE

At one level, the budgetary problems being faced by the defence services stem from the upward spiral of arms prices in the past two decades and the declining value of the rupee. The late 1970s and early 1980s saw the second modernisation programme of the defence forces. As this process continues, what has been driven home has been the price that is required to be paid.

While modernising, the services have not yet paid sufficient attention to the corollary to the process – the reduction of the manpower component – a problem which really pertains to the army. During the seventh plan (1985–90), the army proposed an expansion of the manpower level by 85,000 personnel. The army's case was that with the improvement in communications on the part of the Chinese in the North-East, areas previously undefended would have to be secured.

However, this figure was scaled down to 45,000 and, while the exact size of the Indian Army is not known, it is clear that instead of showing a downward trend, manpower levels show a persisting upward swing. The new developments in southern India involving fresh fighting in Sri Lanka point us to the other as yet 'uncatered' for areas, requiring higher manpower levels.

Fiscal pressures have led to some restructuring and reduction of manpower in the technical arms. However, there is a complaint that some of the reductions have been introduced in anticipation of modernisation to follow. Obviously, manpower cutbacks cannot be introduced without a comprehensive approach to the problem. But there has been movement in one related issue though no new policy has yet been announced. This concerns the proposal to revert the colour service of army personnel to seven years so as to prevent the accumulation of a pension bill which is the emerging nightmare of the Defence Finance officials.

The call for a 'machine rich' army also imposes its own compulsion to reduce manpower. However, senior army officials do not promise any immediate reductions. Some restructuring is also beginning and the old infantry divisions are being made more mobile or RAPID (Reorganised Army Plains Infantry Divisions). This implies changes in the war-fighting doctrine.[34]

Given the enormous costs associated with equipping modern air forces, the Government is unlikely to permit any enhancement of the IAF's combat squadrons. The IAF does not possess any deep strike aircraft like the *Tornado* or the F-111. Moreover, bureaucratic battles are still being fought for a dedicated advanced jet trainer, for which several aircraft like the *Hawk*, *Alpha Jet* and the F-5 are competing.

The most important item on the IAF's agenda in the coming decade will be the need to re-equip its work-horse Mig-21 squadrons. Currently, six squadrons, two each equipped with Mig 29s, Mirage 2000s and Mig 23MFs, occupy the top niche of the IAF order of battle. There are twelve squadrons flying the Mig-21 bis and another seven flying the older Mig-21 variants. The Mig squadrons are to be replaced by the indigenous LCA in the 1990s. The cost and capability of the LCA is likely to compel a lower level of acquisitions. This could be lower still if the LCA fails to meet schedules and imports are needed.

A similar scenario seems likely for the navy. Currently the Indian navy does not have any ship on order from any foreign shipyard.

By the year 2000 all the *Petya* corvettes of the 1967–72 vintage will have retired. The first three *Leanders* will be over twenty years old and the first of the *Kashins* decommissioned. The Indian navy anticipates that the first of the Type 15 destroyers and 16A frigates will have been commissioned by 1994 and that four or five of them will be ready by 2000. Some four Type 25 corvettes as replacements of the ten decommissioned *Petyas* may also be ready by then.

At the same time, the first of the fleet tankers, *Deepak*, will be thirty-three years old and the second twenty-five. The two current aircraft carriers, *Viraat* and *Vikrant*, will be more than forty years old. All the *Foxtrot* class of submarines will also be on the retirement list by then. In fact, by present schedules of construction and plans, the current 125-ship Indian Navy will be down to a 100-ship force by the year 2000. By the same token the *Chakra* will be an ancient boat. As of this juncture the navy's plans to acquire more SSNs are uncertain. Media reports that India is to get another nuclear propelled submarine appear to be incorrect. One major reason cited against additional acquisitions is the enormous cost. It is not even clear whether the Soviets would still be willing to supply an additional vessel.[35]

VI RESEARCH AND DEVELOPMENT: PROVIDING FOR THE THIRD MODERNISATION CYCLE.

To partially offset the enormous burden imposed by the rapid obsolesence of weapons systems and their sky-rocketing costs, India has been investing heavily in research and development (see Table 4.5). However, this is not the only reason. There has always been an autarkic streak in post-colonial India and even now it impacts on decision-making. 'Indigenous' and 'indigenisation' are words that are conferred with an almost mystic meaning in India.

However, there is a problematic side to the 'indigenous' mystique. Indian R&D and industry is permitted to try its hand on every product with a mindlessness that is amazing. This often results in a constant endeavour to reinvent the wheel. Only now, faced with the problem of making the 'indigenous' LCA and the MBT, has the Indian R&D setup been able to alter its purist approach. The Defence Research and Development Organisation (DRDO) no longer hesitates to admit that it will obtain non-critical sub-systems from manufacturers anywhere in the world. Of course, given the backwardness of the Indian industrial base, the 'non critical' items include the GE F404 aeroengine and MTU tank engine, though the official position is that these are interim power plants.

Table 4.5 Research and development expenditure of defence services

Year	Rupees	Capital (crores)	Total outlay	Percent of total expenditure
1982–83	113.74	11.74	125.48	2.3
1984–85	187.96	35.49	223.45	3.3
1985–86	258.45	62.60	321.05	4.0
1986–87	361.11	76.63	437.74	4.2
1987–88	481.45	79.10	560.55	4.6
1988–89	466.56	115.94	582.50	4.4
1989–90	507.25	127.60	634.85	4.4
1990-91(BE)	607.31	169.60	776.91	4.9

Source: Defence Services Estimates

At present the DRDO is involved in three major projects, the MBT, the LCA and the Integrated Guided Missile Development Programme (IGMDP). Most observers consider this to be more than enough. However, the DRDO also has a host of other projects in the area of electronic warfare, arms and armaments, and so on. In conjunction with the navy it has developed an electronic warfare suite and a sonar and in conjunction with the IAF it has been working on an airborne early warning scheme using an HS-748 platform.

Other projects, such as the Advanced Technology Vessel (ATV) for designing an indigenous nuclear propelled submarine, are funded through several different budgets. Similarly, naval design and development comes through its own budget and the ordnance factories and public sector units provide some funding for R&D as well.

The DRDO has reached a critical stage in its endeavours. It has to come up with productionised versions of the *Arjun* MBT and the *Trishul* and *Prithvi* missiles by the early 1990s and to provide a prototype for the LCA by 1995.

The army at least has ensured that the slippage of the DRDO's MBT project will not affect it too much. The T-72 is already in licensed production and can meet the MBT requirements of the army through upgrades up to the year 2010 and beyond.

The biggest dilemma is faced by the IAF and the Indian navy. In the case of the IAF, the lack of the LCA will impose some tough decisions with regard to replacement fighters for retiring Mig-21s and Mig-23s. The navy has to depend on the continued and sustained budgetary support of the state-owned dockyards for getting replacements for its retiring fleet. While the frigate and corvette construction programs are progressing well, the aircraft carrier to be constructed at Cochin is still some distance from keel-laying. Moreover, there appear to be no plans to manufacture additional submarines. According to estimates, the major DRDO products like the guided missiles, the MBT and LCA will require investments of some Rs. 1200 crores *per annum*, half of which could occur in foreign exchange in the next five years. There seems to be little indication in the budget that such investments are being made.

VII DECISIONS AND DECISION-MAKING

In India, the process of decision making in defence and security policy is quite difficult to pinpoint, there being very few institutional arrangements to tackle such problems.

The principal and highest body, the Cabinet Committee on Political Affairs, (CCPA) must approve of projects above a certain value. It also reviews defence planning and military movements in peacetime. Thus the military exercise 'Brasstacks' was authorised in size, location and scope following a presentation to the CCPA. Similarly the CCPA authorised the scheme for the defence of Tawang that led to the imbroglio over Sumdorong Chu.[36] There has, however, been a uniform complaint that the CCPA does not have the time to apply its mind on specialist and involved issues of national security. Authorisation is based on a perfunctory look at the issues involved. More often than not, approvals are given without discussion and in many cases ministers neglect to even read their agenda papers.

The CCPA is, of course, a political body and politicians in India have never pretended to be too knowledgeable on defence and security affairs. The 'real' decisions, as per British tradition, are taken by bureaucrats. To coordinate the work of the Ministries, an informal Secretaries Committee, chaired by the Cabinet Secretary, meets as and when required.

In 1982 and 1983, a 'core-group' was created at the insistence of Mrs Indira Gandhi's Security Adviser and former Chief of Research and Analysis Wing (RAW), Ram Nath Kao. This group, comprising the principal secretaries of the government, the Director, Intelligence Bureau, Director, RAW and the Chairman, Chief of Staffs Committee, took up the task of handling security and defence issues. It is this group that handled the major domestic and foreign policy issues such as the Punjab crisis and the Sri Lankan situation.

As in other countries, the principal decision-making and coordination functions have drifted into the hands of the Prime Minister's Office (PMO), at the expense of the Cabinet. This has been a special feature of the governments of Indira Gandhi and Rajiv Gandhi. The key directions on virtually any policy of the government in the past five years were provided by the PMO. The 'core group' or Secretaries' committee and other 'quasi-institutional' bodies existed basically to implement and manage policy, as worked out by the PMO, in consultation with the departments, presumably with the sanction of the Prime Minister.

At the Ministry of Defence level, the primary coordinating function is carried out by the weekly Monday morning meeting between the Chiefs of Services, Secretaries and Ministers.

However, besides the CCPA, there is no real institutional establishment for decision-making. The theory of Parliamentary Government whereby elected representatives make policy and the bureaucrats serve as advisers has over the years become less and less relevant, since neither the politicians nor top bureaucrats are able to apply their minds to any problem in-depth.

An important indicator of the effectiveness of any decision-making process is the intelligence gathering and processing arrangement. Naturally, nothing much appears on these subjects before the public eye, but by all accounts the Indian weakness in this area is substantial. While tactical intelligence on Pakistan is passable, it is poor in relation to China. Beyond those countries, it is a clean slate.

All the problems facing Indian intelligence such as poor conceptualisation, inadequate leadership and low *esprit de corps*, were manifest in the Sri Lankan operation, which in one sense had to be undertaken precisely because of poor intelligence work. More than anything, one of the lessons of Sri Lanka was that India cannot afford to continue to allow its military intelligence to remain in a strait jacket. Unfortunately the political masters have been happiest using or misusing the intelligence agencies against their political opponents in a manner that would be considered not just scandalous but treasonable in most democratic countries.

In preparing the defence plan the various services put up their proposals to the Defence Finance Department, where they are examined critically. A total allocation is then worked out in consultation with the services and sent to the Finance Minstry, which makes its allocation not by looking at threat assessments but by considering the amount of the money left over in the non-plan head after the interest payments and subsidies have been accounted for!

Since 1986, there has been an attempt to undertake integrated planning under a Defence Planning Staff (DPS) headed by an officer of the rank of Lt. General. The DPS has put forward several plans, including integrated fifteen-year defence plans, but since no one is willing to commit resources beyond a year at a time they have been shelved. Most bureaucrats defend the current system, arguing that despite the lack of planning the services have been receiving their budgets, and generous ones too. However, they miss the point. The constraints being faced now as well as the need to shift to equipping the forces with Indian-made weapons and weapon systems imposes requirements that call for careful investment planning, optimum utilisation of resources, tighter equipment and re-equipment schedules and inventory control. All this requires a substantial degree of advance planning and commitment of resources.

In its 1989 election manifesto the National Front unexpectedly declared that it would set up a National Security Council (NSC) on assuming office. The Front accused the Gandhi Government of endangering national security. It promised a new security doctrine and linked the absence of such a doctrine with *ad hoc* decision-making and imports of arms leading to kickbacks, which in turn affected national security.[37]

The National Front promised to evolve a security doctrine for India and set up a National Security Council to develop consensus on foreign and defence policies.[38]

Within two months of coming to power, the government began discussions on the proposal for the NSC. It used the medium of the Consultative Committee of Members of Parliament attached to the Defence Ministry, an advisory body, to sound out ideas for the NSC.

In debating the formation of a NSC, MPs were in the main concerned to ensure that the new body did not violate the principle of the supremacy of Parliament and the Cabinet system of government. It was, however, the Cabinet Secretariat rather than the Defence

Ministry that was responsible for the processing of the proposal. All the relevant Ministries were asked for their position papers, but the Cabinet Secretariat prepared the final paper.

The basic proposal is a 'minimalist' one; the NSC will be nothing but a truncated CCPA. That is, it will consist of the Chairman, the Prime Minister and the Finance, Home, Defence and External Affairs Ministers. This body would be helped by a 'Strategic Policy Group' (SPG) which would really be the Committee of Secretaries of the above Ministries or the 'Core Group'.

The only innovative tier, but the most crucial, is the NSC Secretariat, headed by a Secretary rank officer who would head a specialist team of 'senior officials' and be guided by the SPG. In essence, the Secretariat would consist of officials junior to those in the SPG, which would retain the exclusive right to provide inputs to the NSC. It was proposed in the last meeting of the Consultative Committee that the Joint Intelligence Committee (JIC) serve as the Secretariat 'for the present'. The JIC is under the Cabinet Secretariat and is supposed to provide assessments based on intelligence supplied by RAW, the Intelligence Bureau (Counterintelligence) and the Departmental agencies such as Military Intelligence and the Ministry of External Affairs. The proposal has been severely criticised in India and the Cabinet Secretariat has been accused of executing a coup of sorts to ensure that the NSC would be new wine in old bottles. The NSC idea remained infructuous.[39]

Leaving aside the bureaucratic manoeuvers, a background paper provided to the MPs notes that 'no country can achieve effective defence against its adversaries and protect its security interests except through long-term strategies . . . development of a national security scenario calls for [an] inter-disciplinary group to work in a dedicated manner'.

VIII CONCLUSION

On close inspection, the Indian scene appears to be a roller-coaster ride through a storm. Far from working to a set policy plan, Indian security and defence policies have consisted of a series of firefighting operations. In the 1980s the governments of Indira Gandhi and Rajiv Gandhi appeared to have considerable coherence in their first two years. However, those governments then became bogged down in a variety of intractable internal problems. The domestic difficulties of recent Indian governments appear to put those of Indira Gandhi and Rajiv Gandhi in the shade.

With the onset of the Kashmir rebellion, the dividing line between India's always serious internal revolts and external security concerns seems to be disappearing. Pakistan, which has 'facilitated' the insurgency in Punjab and Kashmir seems to be putting India in a very grave position. Nevertheless, those troubles seem to be nothing but an old fire not adequately extinguished.

In all this, India bungles along towards the twenty-first century with only the certainty that there will be progress, development, crisis and turmoil. Without any plan of its own, it will react to those of others. Given its size, it will compel others to modify their plans by the unstudied responses that will undoubtedly be the primary feature of Indian policy.

In the area of security and defence policies, the success of the *Agni* programme and the momentum of the military modernisation spiral ought to compel a degree of strategic thinking. It appears at this juncture that India's best-handled area – relations with China – will pay dividends. The possibility of a Sino–Indian detente is a real one in the 1990s. Relations with Pakistan are not likely to alter until the tide of Islamic fundamentalism begins to recede. It can be only hoped that the counter-tide of Hindu fundamentalism will not in the meantime overwhelm India.

Peace with China and an improvement in relations with Pakistan would probably encourage India to turn towards the Indian Ocean area. Indian economic interests in the Southeast Asian region are slowly emerging and despite the recent setback, India will perforce again engage itself in Sri Lanka. Beyond that there is still a question mark, more likely to be determined by the end of the US-Soviet rivalry than the aims and objects of the Indian Ocean littoral powers.

Indian history does not boast of Alexanders and Napoleons. In fact the Alexanders and Napoleons were the ones who wanted to come to India. The vast and rich variety of the subcontinent and the problems of governing it seem to have acted as a self-limiting factor. In recent times, the military interventions and withdrawal from Bangladesh, Sri Lanka and Maldives, could fancifully be attributed to some racial memory. But they are more likely the outcome of an essentially cautious and democratic policy.

NOTES

* Many of the points made in this paper have been based in 'off-the-record' conversations with senior officials. Since they are woven into the argument, I have not footnoted them separately.

1. 'A Steady Evolution', *Frontline*, (Madras), 15–28 November, 1986, pp. 20–23.

2. Rita Manchanda, 'Nuclear Subs for India', *The Indian Post*, 18 January, 1988; see also, 'India Getting Soviet Nuclear Submarine', *The Hindu*, 27 December, 1987.

3. 'Qualitative Shift in Indo–Soviet Ties', *The Hindu*, 21 November, 1988.

4. 'Rs 5,300 Crore Soviet Credit', *The Hindu*, 21 November, 1988.

5. Manoj Joshi, 'Will India Buy US Arms', *Frontline*, 24 August–6 September, 1985 pp. 51–5.

6. The Rasgotra-Barnes agreement seems to be a confidential one with little official reference to it. The MOU on Science and Technology signed by the two officials at the time of the visit of the US Commerce Secretary, Malcolm Baldridge was the outcome of the earlier document. See G.K Reddy, 'Hurdle to US high-tech transfer overcome', *The Hindu*, 18 May, 1985; See also R. Ramachandran for a critique: 'MOU: the missing understanding', *Frontline*, 24 August–6 September, 1985, pp. 46–50.

7. G.K Reddy, 'Superpowers vying with each other to woo Rajiv', *The Hindu*, 1 May, 1985; and 'US team highlights Soviet Threats', *The Hindu*, 4 May, 1985, describing the visit of Fred Iklé, US Under-Secretary of State for Defence Affairs.

8. 'Indo–US accord on light combat aircraft', *The Hindu*, 7 November, 1987; 'Setback to Indo–US Defence relations', *The Hindu*, 20 July, 1989; Starred question No. 294 Lok Sabha, 7 August, 1989.

9. USIS Press release, 'US Response to Agni', 23 May, 1989.

10. 'India Building bridges with the US', *The Hindu*, 18 January, 1988.

11. Manoj Joshi, 'Port Calls and Politics', *The Hindu*, 2 March, 1988.

12. *Ibid.*

13. K.K. Katyal, 'India concerned at naval presence in the Gulf', *The Hindu*, 5 July, 1988.

14. 'Swift Effective Action', *The Hindu*, 5 November, 1988.

15. K.K. Katyal, 'New Fields of Cooperation', *The Hindu*, 23 October, 1987. Following his visit to the U.S., the then Defence Minister, K.C. Pant, also emphasised this point, see 'U.S. accepts India's regional role', *The Hindu*, 11 July, 1989.

16. See Manoj Joshi, 'U.S. concerns over Kashmir', *The Hindu*, 2 June, 1990; 'U.S. For Political Dialogue on J-K', *Times of India*, 26 May, 1990; and 'Reciprocate India's Step, U.S. tells Pak', *Hindustan Times*, 3 June, 1990.

17. *The Hindu*, 7 March, 1987, p. 1 and p. 9. See also Manoj Joshi, 'From Maps to the Field', *The Hindu Sunday Magazine*, 29 March, 1987, p. 17 and p. 19.

18.   The details of the story and the subsequent controversy may be found in
       Sreedhar, Ed. *Dr. A.Q. Khan on Pakistan Bomb*, ABC Publishing
       House, New Delhi, 1987, pp. 151–60.
19.   G.K. Reddy, 'Decision this year on nuclear option', *The Hindu*, 8
       March, 1987.
20.   *The Hindu*, 31 December, 1988. However it is believed that the two sides
       have yet to exchange data about the facilities they regard as being
       covered by the agreement.
21.   'Its a long road to peace in Siachen', *The Hindu*, 20 June, 1989; 'Siachen
       Zone to be demilitarised', *Ibid.*, 26 June, 1989.
22.   'Tough response tells on bellicose Pak', *The Hindu*, 25 January, 1990;
       'Centre assessing situation in Kashmir', *Ibid*, 26 January, 1990.
23.   'PM hints at getting back bulk of IPKF', *The Hindu*, 25 April, 1989.
24.   A.L. Venkateswaran, *'Defence Organisation in India'*, Publications
       Division, New Delhi, 1967, pp 361–2.
25.   *Ibid.*
26.   K. Subrahmanyam, *Perspectives in Defence Planning*, Abhinav, New
       Delhi, 1972, p. 201
27.   *Ibid*, p. 133 and p. 126.
28.   Rajya Sabha unstarred question no. 211, July 28, 1988. See also Manoj
       Joshi 'Indecision cramps defence planning process', *The Hindu*, 25 June,
       1988.
29.   'V.P. flays Congress (I) defence policy', *Indian Express*, 16 February,
       1990.
30.   'Raids on camps in Pak not ruled out', *The Telegraph*, 29 April, 1990;
       'Extra Fund for Defence Likely', *The Statesman*, 29 April, 1990.
31.   'New post for Arun Singh', *The Hindu*, 16 May, 1990; 'Congress (I)
       opposes proposed NSC', *The Hindu*, 17 May, 1990.
32.   The views of the new Government are clearly visible in the remarks of
       Prime Minister, V.P. Singh while intervening in the debate over the
       Defence Ministry Demand for Grants. See also 'V.P. asks people to be
       prepared for war, '*Times of India*', 11 April, 1990.
33.   See uncorrected text of the Parliamentary debate on Defence on April
       10, 1990, p. 12046.
34.   Lt. Gen. Mathew Thomas, 'The RAPID: An Appraisal of India's new-
       look infantry division for warfare in the plains, *Indian Defence Review*,
       January, 1989, pp. 92–101.
35.   Some of this information has been obtained through senior serving
       officials who cannot be named. One of the officials in fact noted that at
       the present rate, the Navy will become 23 per cent smaller in the year
       2000 and by the year 2010, it may become 50 per cent smaller.
36.   'How to Break the Logjam in the Tawang sector', *The Hindu*, 22 July,
       1987.
37.   National Front: *Lok Sabha Elections 1989 Manifesto*, New Delhi, V.P.
       Singh, n.d p. 35.
38.   *Ibid.*
39.   Manoj Joshi, 'NSC: Form not Substance', *The Hindu*, 23 May, 1990; See
       also editorials by the *Times of India* entitled 'Poor Homework', 18 May,
       1990, and the report 'Congress (I) opposes proposed NSC', *The Hindu*,

17 May, 1990. On 24 August the Government announced the setting up of the NSC. See *The Hindustan Times*, 25 August, 1990.

5 Chinese Perspectives on India as a Great Power*

Gary Klintworth

China and India are both important Asian great powers, often regarded as threshold superpowers. They both announced increases in defence expenditure for 1990 at a time when most countries were under pressure to make cuts. They are closer to Australia than either Japan or the United States. Their total population is almost two billion. They have the largest military forces in the Asia–Pacific region and a common interest in seeing an end to European military influence in Asia. They have developing economies and are close neighbours. They share the world's longest stretch of disputed border and are not yet agreed on how to divide the region between them. But their historical relationship over the past two thousand years has been one of friendly though not close cultural exchanges, without hostility, rivalry or war.

India was one of the first countries to establish diplomatic relations with the People's Republic of China (in April 1950). The two countries had an amicable relationship in the 1950s based on their jointly developed Five Principles of Peaceful Coexistence and a common background as newly independent anti-colonial Asian states. This initially auspicious state of affairs was upset by the border war in 1962, the effects of the Sino–Soviet dispute, the Chinese annexation of Tibet, misconceptions, domestic politics, Chinese support for insurgency in India, and an emerging rivalry between the two countries in South Asia.

Relations began to improve in the mid-1970s, a period that coincided with the era of post-Mao pragmatism in China's domestic and foreign affairs. Diplomatic relations were restored to ambassadorial level in 1976 and annual talks on the border began in 1981. However, from mid-1986 to mid-1987 the two countries were again huffing and puffing – possibly bluffing – over disputed territory in the Bhutan–India–China triborder area. A well prepared Indian army was confident it could prevent a recurrence of India's humiliating defeat in the 1962 border war (of thirty-two days) while China's PLA reinforced its presence in Tibet and threatened India with 'an unpleasant event'.[1]

Since then both sides have pulled back from what looked like the brink of another border war and relations have subsequently improved.

There have been no reports of border incidents or military tension on the border since December 1988 when Indian Prime Minister Rajiv Gandhi met Deng Xiaoping in Beijing, the first high-level Sino–Indian summit in twenty-eight years. Deng told Gandhi that India and China should forget the past and look to the future.[2] Gandhi and Chinese Premier Li Peng signed accords to establish direct commercial flights between New Delhi and Beijing, to increase cultural, scientific and technological exchanges and to hold annual ministerial level talks.

Gandhi reaffirmed that his government recognised Tibet as an autonomous region of China and that it would prohibit Tibetans from conducting political activities inside India.[3] Tibet is an important part of the Sino–Indian equation. China feels vulnerable in Tibet which is one of the most rebellious parts of the country and the back door to the strategically important and equally troublesome Xinjiang Autonomous Region. China's hold over Tibet and Xinjiang is based in part on Chinese control of Aksai Chin, in the western sector of the Sino–Indian border and claimed by India. Beijing is suspicious of India's continued willingness to host the Dalai Lama and his Tibetan government in exile[4] so the Gandhi statement was well-received in Beijing (although not amongst India's influential Tibetan lobby).

In October 1989 Vice Premier and former Foreign Minister Wu Xueqian visited New Delhi and reaffirmed the generality of China's wish to improve relations with India on the basis of the Five Principles of Peaceful Coexistence. He said China 'sincerely hoped to see a fair and reasonable settlement of the issue . . . [and] as long as the two sides conducted friendly consultations in a spirit of mutual understanding and mutual accommodation, a mutually acceptable solution could be found'.[5]

As Chinese President Yang Shangkun noted in a message to Indian President Ramaswamy Venkataraman on India's Republic Day on 26 January 1990, Sino–Indian relations 'have been continuously improving because of the combined efforts of the two sides'.[6] In a message to Indian Prime Minister Vishwanath Pratap Singh on the same occasion, Chinese Premier Li Peng emphasised that friendship between China and India was in the basic interest of both countries; he would continue to make concerted efforts towards that end[7] and, speaking in Islamabad, he said that 'the border dispute between the two countries could be solved through peaceful negotiations and consultations'.[8] Meanwhile, India's relative silence after the June 1989 crackdown in Beijing by the PLA was well regarded by the Chinese leadership as it contrasted with the critical response of much of the Western world at a time when China was, and still is, looking around for new friendships post-Tiananmen.[9]

The Sino–Indian relationship is nonetheless an uneasy one. India still regards nuclear China as a major threat to its security. It sees China's South Asian policies as anti-Indian, divisive, opportunistic and interfering.[10] China for its part perceives India to be an ambitious, overconfident yet militarily powerful neighbour with whom it may eventually have to have a day of reckoning. The PLA's General Staff Department lists India as one of China's most likely opponents in possible small war contingencies on China's southern borders in the 1990s (the others being Vietnam and Taiwan).

One of the problems is territorial sovereignty, something about which both sides feel strongly. India and China dispute border territory totalling almost 125,000 sq kms (or four times the size of Taiwan). China has previously offered to swap its claim for Arunachal Pradesh (about 90,000 sq kms) in the eastern sector (the precise delineation of which is in itself a matter of dispute) for Indian acceptance of its possession of Aksai Chin (about 33,000 sq kms) in the west with some adjustments to the disputed middle sector (about 2000 sq kms). India's preference has been for a more detailed sector by sector approach, subject to the exigencies of India's domestic politics – no Indian leader can concede Indian territory to China without risking accusations of a sellout and jeopardising his or her political base.[11] But without Indian concessions, China has said it will not accept 'the illegal McMahon line and the so-called Arunachal Pradesh'.[12] Despite annual border talks and the suggestion of mutual accommodation, the position of both sides has hardened with China asking concessions on the western side of Arunachal Pradesh. No progress has been made or seems likely in the near future.

As well as their territorial differences, China and India have failed to develop close cultural, economic and political ties. They are physically divided by the Himalayan mountain chain. Bilateral trade in 1988 was $US247 million out of China's total trade in that year of $103 billion. India and China are moreover competitors for aid, certain export markets and sources of capital. While China accepts that Kashmir is a bilateral issue between Pakistan and India, it refuses to recognise

India's 1975 annexation of the small Himalayan state of Sikkim. China has adopted contrary positions to India on Vietnam–Cambodia and Afghanistan. And China is a major arms exporter to countries in Southwest Asia, including CSS-2 medium range (3000kms) ballistic missiles to Saudi Arabia in a deal that may have included Pakistani technical inputs[13] and adversely affects India's regional security environment.

An underlying cause of unease in Sino–Indian relations is that both are newly rising great Asian powers, conscious of an illustrious past and sensitive about their place in the world. The withdrawal of the European powers and the rise of China and India in the last few decades has brought the land between them into sharper focus. India is clearly the dominant power in South Asia, from the Suez to the Andaman and Nicobar Islands adjacent to the Malay peninsula. China has been emerging as an influential East Asian power, from Singapore up to the Koreas. Both China and India have shown a willingness to act as regional policemen in their spheres of influence – India in East Bengal in 1971, in Sri Lanka in July 1987 and in November 1988 in the Maldives. China displayed a growing disposition to intervene to establish what it believes the regional order ought to be when it attacked Vietnam in 1979, used force in the South China Sea in 1974 and 1988, and materially supported the Khmer Rouge in Cambodia.

China and India are intuitively rivals for hegemony in South Asia, Burma, Indochina and Southeast Asia. Mainland Southeast Asia in particular is an area of growing interest for India and China. Their cultural influences have seeped into the region over many centuries with Cambodia caught roughly in the middle. China has built up a close relationship with Thailand, has strong opinions about Cambodia and has made inroads into Burma and Bangladesh, both of which might, from New Delhi's perspective, be seen as Indian territory. In fact, China might be seen to be cultivating a security belt on its southern flank running through Thailand, Burma and Bangladesh. China has a close defence cooperation program with Thailand. In February 1990 the PLA airforce Commander Wang Hai paid an official visit to Bangladesh and Thailand.[14] A few days later Chinese Defence Minister Qin Jiwei followed up with a visit to Dacca and Islamabad aimed at developing closer military cooperation between China and Bangladesh and Pakistan.[15] For its part, India has a small foothold in Vietnam and Cambodia, diplomatic and cultural contacts with Phnom Penh and political and intelligence exchanges with Hanoi.[16]

As well as their territorial dispute and incipient great power rivalry, the Pakistani factor has long been a sensitive issue for China and India. Pakistan, India's most immediate security concern, is one of China's few reliable friends and allies. China constructed a strategically important two lane all weather highway to Pakistan across the Karakoram mountains in the 1970s. China is a major supplier of military equipment to Pakistan and the two countries collaborate closely on modern aircraft and tank design. China is fundamentally the prime source of nuclear technology for Pakistan.[17] China's National Nuclear Industry Corporation has provided Pakistan with a mini-reactor and in 1989 agreed to build a 300,000 kw nuclear power station in Pakistan.[18]

Pakistan might be expected therefore, as India anticipates, to act in concert with China so as to divide Indian military forces by presenting New Delhi with the possibility of tension on two fronts. In 1965 China gave India an ultimatum whilst it was engaged in its second war with Pakistan. In 1971 when India was engaged in its third war with Pakistan, China was only checked by a Soviet warning to keep its 'hands off'.[19]

The possibility of a two-front dilemma for India was illustrated in the tension in Kashmir in early 1990: India is reported to have been forced to pull back nine army divisions from the Sino–Indian border for redeployment to Kashmir.[20] What would happen if the Sino–Indian border simultaneously flared up?

China's response, however, has been to urge caution on both Pakistan and India and call for a settlement based on peaceful negotiations. Mrs Bhutto's adviser on foreign affairs and national security, Iqbal Akhund, in Beijing to brief the Chinese government on the crisis in Kashmir, was told that the Chinese government was 'very concerned' but 'hoped the situation would calm down very quickly'. Premier Li Peng's message to Prime Minister Bhutto was that India and Pakistan should resolve what was an historical problem through 'talks instead of violence in order to avoid further escalation'.[21]

China has been used as a counter-weight to Indian domination by other small South Asian states. Land-locked Nepal for instance has moved closer to China in recent years: Lhasa and Kathmandu are linked by a Chinese-built road and in 1988 Nepal began to buy arms from China (including anti-aircraft guns) as 'a sovereign independent country'.[22] contrary to a 1965 agreement whereby Nepal promised to buy arms only from India, or, if India could not meet its needs, from Britain or America.[23] India in consequence began to squeeze Nepal.

China's response, as with Kashmir, was cautious. Its criticism of India has been indirect and while it sympathises with Nepal, it has called for friendly negotiations between Nepal and India in the spirit of their membership of the South Asian Association of Regional Co-operation.[24] In fact it advised the Nepalese government that China could not be a substitute for India in economic matters.[25] Similarly with Sri Lanka – its civil war is a sensitive foreign policy issue for New Delhi. China, friend and supplier of aid to the Sri Lankan government, has been careful to keep New Delhi informed of the scale and delivery date of Chinese military aid sought by Colombo.[26]

Privately China may be critical of India's interventionism in South Asia but it has tried to avoid public condemnation. Recent Chinese media commentary stressed the good beginning Prime Minister Singh made in improving India's relations with its South Asian neighbours while expressing Beijing's hope that the current trend towards peace and stability and economic progress in South Asia would continue.[27]

China's somewhat more relaxed attitude toward Indian activities in South Asia matches the improvement in Sino–Soviet relations. The normalisation of China's relations with the Soviet Union, interrupted by the Soviet intervention in Afghanistan in 1978 and Vietnam's invasion of Cambodia in 1979, got underway again in the early 1980s. China had hitherto seen India in the context of what it perceived to be a hostile Soviet-inspired encirclement strategy. From the early 1980s, however, it saw India as just another great power disconnected from China's primary strategic concerns.

China's primary security interests are focused on the superpowers and Japan. Developments in the Korean peninsula, China's inner maritime zone (particularly in the South China Sea), Taiwan, Hong Kong, Indochina and Southeast Asia also rate more highly than India and the subcontinent.

China is not threatened by any other great power for the first time in perhaps two centuries. The Soviet Union has withdrawn from Afghanistan, from Cam Ranh Bay in Vietnam and from Mongolia. Vietnam has ceased to be regarded as an agent of Soviet socialist imperialism. Sino–Soviet relations have been normalised and cross-border trade and economic cooperation has developed rapidly. China's key northern border is no longer of immediate security concern to Beijing. At the same time, China has an important economic relationship with Japan and – despite Tiananmen – an important strategic relationship with the United States. China no longer feels encircled; on the contrary it is confident in its surroundings. China is clearly having its share of serious domestic social, economic and political crises. And it may not be admired for its recent record on human rights in Lhasa or Beijing. But it is still, in the community of nations, one of the biggest and most important countries in the world with growing offshore interests. It is a member of the UN Security Council and is the world's third largest nuclear power. The superpowers defer to its claims to regional hegemony at least in Indochina, Hong Kong and the Taiwan Straits.

China's favourable strategic circumstances and its expanding maritime activities are matters of direct security interest to India. The Sino–Soviet dispute in the 1960s and the Indo–Soviet Treaty of Peace Friendship and Cooperation of August 1971 cushioned the impact of China's nuclear weapons for non-nuclear India. Sino–Soviet rapprochement in the 1980s therefore might be seen to release Chinese military forces and missiles for deployment against India. It might also mean that the Soviet Union is unlikely to want to side with India against China as Mikhail Gorbachev intimated when he was in Delhi in November 1988. While Sino–Soviet rapprochement means China may be less paranoid about being encircled by hostile forces it also strengthens rather than lessens China's ambition to assume its rightful place as a great Asian power. Sino–Indian rivalry picked up in Indochina with the withdrawal of the United States in 1975.[28] Sino–Indian rivalry, one might surmise, may be less constrained with the decline of Soviet military activities in the Asia–Pacific region and the Soviet withdrawal from Cam Ranh Bay in Vietnam.

India has thought about the implications of China's favourable strategic circumstances. It believes that China, secure from external threat in the north and the east, may feel free to try and recover lost territory in the south and assert its influence over adjacent regions.

There is logic to this assessment and indeed it is one that Chinese strategists in Beijing have considered. It has influenced the PLA's military doctrine to the extent that China has graduated from the concept of people's war in defence of the homeland to people's war under modern conditions and, in certain circumstances, preemptive offensive operations. The PLA has shown growing interest in developing a capability to project military force beyond China's physical borders. China has trained rapid reaction 'fist' battalions, marines, the air transport of troops and supplies and long distance tridimensional naval operations. It has developed staging facilities and airfields on islands in the South China Sea to support naval activities as far south as the Malacca Strait. In 1985 China deployed naval ships into the Indian Ocean for the first time since the voyages of the Ming dynasty Admiral, Zheng He, in the fifteenth century. It has sought air-to-air refuelling technology and considered the cost of British Harrier jump jets and the construction of an aircraft carrier at Dalian shipyard. Recent increased defence funding for the PLA is to be spent on improved at-sea support for the navy, and helicopters and long range transport aircraft for the army and the airforce.

In other words, China is on a parallel track to India in developing its navy and rapid deployment forces.

China's SSN programme and its growing naval presence in the South China Sea have fuelled Indian concern about a Chinese challenge to India in the Bay of Bengal via the Malacca Straits. This has given impetus to New Delhi's plans to develop its carrier task forces, long range airlift and maritime patrol capabilities, SSNs and a forward naval perimeter in and around the Andaman and Nicobar Islands on the western side of the Malay peninsula to meet what might be seen in New Delhi as a Chinese thrust in the South China Sea on the other side of the peninsula.

There is what might be described as a competitive duality in the Sino–Indian relationship. China exploded a nuclear bomb in 1964. India followed suit in 1974. China has short range ballistic missiles that can cover India; in May 1989, India test fired the *Agni*, an intermediate range (2500 kms) ballistic missile that can reach much of southwest China. India had the support of one superpower while China sought a tacit strategic understanding with the other. India's East Sea Fleet Commander took two destroyers and a submarine to Vietnam in May 1982. In December 1985 China matched this development by sending the PRCN's East Sea Fleet Commander with a destroyer and supply ship to Karachi, Colombo and Chittagong. India has acquired the first of several nuclear powered submarines that it plans to obtain to offset China's small fleet of SSNs and SSBNs. China meanwhile is reported to have offered a nuclear powered submarine to Pakistan.[29] New Delhi in turn has, in a move that with a stretch of imagination might be seen as tit for tat, agreed to help Vietnam with an 'atomic energy program for peaceful purposes'.[30]

China and India have each cultivated a security relationship with the enemy of the other – China with Pakistan and India, less overtly, with Vietnam. India invited Vietnamese Defence Minister Senior General Van Tien Dung to New Delhi in March 1985 to discuss Chinese military tactics with Indian military leaders[31] while India's Chief of Army Staff, General Sundarji, went to Vietnam in March 1987 to study Vietnamese tactics against Chinese forces in mountainous areas.[32] Vietnam is likely, however, post-Cambodia, to reach an accommodation with Beijing rather than provoke its large neighbour for the sake of an uncertain relationship with India, a distant ally and a non-superpower.

China's military doctrine, given the favourable strategic circumstances of its northern borders, envisages the concept of 'using a bullock's knife to slaughter a chicken' to deal with smaller states on its southern borders. But as the Vietnamese have shown, albeit at great cost, the Chinese knife is not so sharp. China's defence expenditure has been heavily constrained since 1979 and modernisation of the PLA's new group armies has been a slow process. Much of the PLA's equipment is dated or is still being upgraded.

China's frontline F-7 fighter aircraft is derived from the Mig-21, a design that first flew in 1956. The programme to re-equip the F-7 with modern American avionics has been cancelled. China's newest fighter, the F-8 has yet to enter series production. The reality for the PLA is, notwithstanding Tiananmen and its increased political prominence, that China has many more urgent priorities than increasing defence expenditure at a time of low external threat.[33]

However China will, for the foreseeable future, remain circumscribed by problems of size, poverty and regionalism, as well as the dilemmas of economic modernisation and political reform. China might have the capability and be prepared to try and punish a small country like Vietnam over some real or imagined slight, or possession of a few square kilometres of disputed border territory or off-shore islands. Vietnam is small, physically accessible and militarily weak. The cost of China's 1979 lesson to Vietnam, however, was in the vicinity of $US2–3 billion, a sum that generated doubts within the Chinese leadership over whether or not the operation was necessary or even worthwhile. Chen Yun for example is reported to remain opposed to China's involvement in avoidable border wars that drain resources at a time when China is trying to restrain defence expenditure and increase spending to fix bottlenecks in the civilian economy like education, transportation and energy. China's modernisation presupposes a no-war environment.

The modernisation imperative weighed heavily against China's initial impulse to try and teach India a lesson as it threatened to do in 1987.[34] It remains a key factor affecting the state of Sino–Indian relations in the 1990s. Other important considerations are China's more relaxed security outlook and its sense of obligation as a responsible member of the United Nations and a net consumer of global capital and technology. China in 1990 is much less intolerant of adverse foreign policy developments than it was in 1962 or even 1979 when Vietnam bore the brunt of its anger. The leadership in Beijing can also draw on competitive position papers from well informed advisers in the PLA, the Foreign Ministry and learned academic and strategic institutes. Chinese diplomacy in other words is not framed in stark either/or choices but is sensitive to 'the ambiguous complexities of international relations' in South Asia and elsewhere.[35] China realises it will have to learn to live with India, the strongest power in South Asia.

The most important factor tempering China's Indian policy has been a realistic assessment of India's military capabilities by the PLA. India is no small border state. It is a major Asian military power. Since 1962, India has trained its army and airforce in joint operations. It has a modern airforce of *Jaguars, Mirage* 2000s and MiG-29s and a well-equipped army that includes at least eleven specially trained mountain divisions equipped with long range artillery. India has also devoted considerable effort to avoid being caught unprepared for war with China as it claims it was in 1962. In particular it has upgraded airfields, roads, rail links, communications and other infrastructure in the eastern sector of the Sino–Indian border. According to press reports at the time of increased tension on the Sino–Indian border in 1986 and 1987, the Indian Army was confident it could repel any Chinese incursion across the McMahon line.[36] China, on the other hand, is handicapped by the exposed high altitude terrain of Tibet and very limited all-weather road access from Lhasa to the Sino–Indian border. Lhasa, which would be an important rear base area in the event of conflict with India is a tense city under martial law and, like the rest of Tibet, it tolerates a Chinese presence only at the point of a gun. The nearest rail links to Lhasa are at Golmud in Qinghai over 900 kms distant or Chengdu in Sichuan almost 1500 kms away. Furthermore, most of China's best ground force units, aircraft and other equipment are concentrated in the strategically more important east and northeast sectors of the country. China does not have the numbers of personnel or the supplies of POL, food and equipment to launch a decisive attack against Indian forces in Arunachal Pradesh or to support major hostilities on the border for more than a few weeks. To inflict a 'punishment' on India, China would have to choose ground for a thrust where it was least expected, for example, in the corridor between Sikkim and Bhutan or in Ladakh rather than in the more obviously disputed Sumdorong Chu area of Arunachal Pradesh. Either way China would have to decide, as it did in 1987, whether a small war with India was winnable and worthwhile. If the Foreign Ministry in Beijing felt inclined to go to war with India in 1987 over the principle of China's territorial integrity, the PLA's detailed cost-benefit analysis concluded that India was simply too strong and that China could not really afford the risk of war. The Indian Army's General Staff, it seems may have made a similar appreciation and reached the same conclusion.[37]

OUTLOOK

The Chinese Communist Party is preoccupied with internal economic adjustment and political instability in the wake of the June 1989 crisis and the lead up to the Deng succession. The border dispute with India could generate renewed tension but neither side appears to have any compelling interest in disturbing the existing stalemate for the time being. Each state holds the portion of disputed territory most valuable to it. Aksai China, held by China, is not materially important to India. India's Arunachal Pradesh in the west is a sparsely populated mountainous area of no significant strategic value to China. A simple swap of claims based on the line of actual control giving each what it values most would seem a logical solution. Both sides have reportedly been close to such a solution in the past.[38] While rational considerations may be discounted in a situation where each side perceives its regional prestige to be at stake or where domestic political factors become important, a costly drawn out war in remote mountain border regions remains an avoidable and unnecessary distraction to China's more pressing internal economic and political priorities. Prudent Chinese defence planners have no doubt prepared contingency plans for conflict in the Himalayas but China is in no position to initiate hostilities. A similar attitude seems to be prevailing on the other side of the Himalayas. For the time being, therefore, the border is likely to remain quiescent. In the longer term, however, competitiveness between China and India for regional political influence seems likely to increase. If this is carried over into missile-nuclear or naval rivalry, adverse consequences for regional security and stability could easily follow as pressure develops for neighbouring countries to follow suit or choose sides.

NOTES

* The suggestions of J. Mohan Malik and A. D. Gordon are gratefully acknowledged.

1. *Beijing Review*, no. 20, 18 May, 1987, p. 7.
2. *India Today*, 15 January, 1989.
3. Shen Chun-chuan, 'Peking's Relations with India and Pakistan', *Issues and Studies*, vol. 25, no. 9, September, 1989, p. 119 and p. 125.
4. For a discussion, see Colin Mackerras, 'Tibet and the Chinese', *Current Affairs Bulletin*, vol. 64, no. 12, May 1988, pp. 22–8.
5. *Beijing Review*, 30 October–5 November 1989, p. 5.
6. Radio Beijing, in *Foreign Broadcasting Information Service-China* (FBIS), 29 January, 1990, p. 13.
7. *Ibid.*
8. *Beijing Review*, 27 November–3 December 1989, p. 6.
9. *Times of India*, 13 December, 1989; *Beijing Review*, 17–23 July, 1989, p. 7.
10. *The Telegraph*, Calcutta, 5 February, 1987.
11. See Sumit Ganguly, 'The Sino–Indian Border Talks, 1981–1989', *Asian Survey*, vol. XXIX, no. 12, December, 1989, p. 1123.
12. *Xinhua,* Beijing, 21 February, 1987, *FBIS China*, 24 February, 1987, Fl.
13. J. Mohan Malik, 'Chinese National Security and Nuclear Arms Control', unpublished PhD Thesis, Department of International Relations, ANU, Canberra, 1990, p. 47.
14. *Xinhua*, Beijing, in *FBIS China*, 7 February, 1990, p. 4. According to the South China Morning Post, 10 February, 1990, Wang Hai's visit was related to the sale of fighter aircraft to Bangladesh and Thailand.
15. Xinhua, Islamabad, in *FBIS China*, 22 February, 1990, p. 10; and Xinhua, Dhaka, in *FBIS China*, 28 February, 1990, p. 8.
16. For a discussion see Mohammed Ayoob, 'Southeast Asia in Indian Foreign Policy: Some Preliminary Observations', *Contemporary Southeast Asia*, vol. 9, no. 1, June, 1987, p. 1.
17. Malik, *op. cit.*, ch.IV, 'China and Nuclear Non-Proliferation', 43ff; also R. R. Subramanian, *Strategic Analysis*, November, vol. IX (8), 1985, p. 761.
18. Reported in a short article carried in FBIS China, 16 February, 1990, p. 36.
19. Comments by Dr M. A. Bhatty, Seminar 'Pakistan's Relations with India and China', Department of International Relations, RSPacS, ANU, Canberra, 5 April, 1990. Dr Bhatty was Pakistan's ambassador to China from 1982–86 and Director General of Pakistan's Ministry of Foreign Affairs 1971–75.
20. *Asiaweek*, 23 February, 1990.
21. Xinhua, Beijing, FBIS China, 15 February, 1990, p. 6.
22. *Xinhua,* Kathmandu, 4 November, 1988, *FBIS-China,* 7 November, 1988, p. 19.
23. *Far Eastern Economic Review*, 25 May, 1989.
24. *Beijing Review*, 24–30 July, 1989, pp. 11–12.

25. *Times of India*, 15 June, 1989.
26. *Far Eastern Economic Review*, 9 August, 1990.
27. Beijing Radio in Hindi to India, transcribed in FBIS China, 8 February, 1990, p. 6.
28. John W. Garver, 'Chinese–Indian Rivalry in Indochina', *Asian Survey*, Vol XXVII, no. 11, November, 1987, p. 1205.
29. *Far Eastern Economic Review*, 18 January, 1990.
30. *Xinhua*, Beijing, 16 August 1988, in *FBIS China*, 17 August, 1988, p. 20.
31. Garver, *op. cit.*, 1213.
32. *Far Eastern Economic Review*, 14 May, 1987.
33. For a discussion, see Gary Klintworth, *China's Modernisation and the Strategic Implications for the Asia–Pacific Region*, AGPS, Canberra, 1989, 31ff.
34. *Far Eastern Economic Review*, 4 June, 1987.
35. Surjit Mansingh and Steven I. Levine, 'China and India: Moving Beyond Confrontation', *Problems of Communism*, March–June 1989, p. 30 and p. 39.
36. See for example *The Hindu*, New Delhi, 27 December, 1986.
37. U.S. Bajpai, *India's Security*, Lancers, New Delhi, 1983, pp. 24–5 and p. 90; or K. Subrahmanyam, *The Times of India*, 9 May, 1987.
38. In 1983 and again in 1985 according to A.P. Venketeshwaran, 'Just Neighbours, Or Friends', *Indian Express Magazine*, New Delhi, 5 July, 1987, quoted by Mansingh and Levine, *op. cit.*, p. 38.

6 Southeast Asian Perceptions of India's Strategic Development: An Indonesian View

Lt. Gen. (Rtd) A. Hasnan Habib

During the past two decades the international system has undergone great changes. New powers have emerged. Bipolarity has given way to multipolarity. Multipolarity is more evident in Asia than in any other region, including Europe. And as Soviet–American strategic competition is diminishing, the increasing economic, political and strategic weight of Japan, China and India is coming more and more into focus.

Over the years, India, a country of vast resources and great aspirations, has shown a very significant growth in its industrial and military might. As such, it has become recognised as a preeminent power in South Asia and gained increasing influence in the Indian Ocean region. More recently, it has been referred to, especially in Australia, as a possible military threat, even a potential enemy.[1] Its acquisition of a nuclear submarine from the Soviet Union, as part of its naval buildup program, has raised questions as to its motives and intentions in the region.

This chapter does not dwell on each Southeast Asian country's perception of India's strategic development. To the best of the author's knowledge, India's military buildup has never been on the agenda of the ASEAN Senior Officials' Meetings. Neither has it been a topic of discussion at the annual ASEAN Foreign Ministers' Meetings, let alone among the officials of the Southeast Asian countries. Apart from the non-existence of a Southeast Asian forum for exchanging views on strategic issues, the countries of the region are all preoccupied with their own problems.

This chapter presents an Indonesian perspective; it does not necessarily reflect the official Indonesian view. Also, it is designed to stimulate further discussion rather than serve as a definitive statement

107

India's activities in Southeast Asia or about the response of ASEAN nations.

I GENERAL PERCEPTIONS OF INDIA IN SOUTHEAST ASIA

As noted earlier, India's strategic development has not attracted much attention in Southeast Asia, beyond personal statements made by some officials or political observers or reports in the media. This is in stark contrast with the reaction a few years ago to the planned expansion of the Japanese navy's role to safeguard the international sealanes in the South China Sea up to a distance of 1,000 miles from Tokyo.

The Southeast Asian countries recognise India's unique position in South Asia, its great past, its big power potential, and its leadership role in the nonaligned movement. But they have also been critical of its stance on some international and regional issues of great concern to them. India's propensity for high-handedness in settling its differences with its smaller neighbours and its occasional big power attitude have not particularly endeared it in the region, especially not among the South Asian countries. A journalist who studied India's relations with Pakistan, Sri Lanka, Bhutan, and Nepal concluded that 'India has good relations with none of its neighbours. It has no friends in the region.'[2] On the whole, however, India is regarded in Southeast Asia as just another developing country with a host of problems. Most of these countries have generally a good relationship with India, though not necessarily a close and warm one.

This is not to suggest that the Southeast Asian countries have been completely indifferent to India's strategic buildup and its foreign policy. The region's non-communist countries which, in the past had been subjected to communist insurgencies and subversion, have watched with interest, albeit without undue alarm, New Delhi's growing close relations with Moscow, especially after India signed the Treaty of Peace, Friendship and Cooperation with this communist superpower in 1971. This treaty enjoined each party immediately to consult each other in case of a military threat to either one and not to join any alliance hostile to either of them. Following its signing it was an interesting subject for discussion at seminars and even among officials in the ASEAN countries. New Delhi's support of the pro-Soviet Kabul regime in Afghanistan, its recognition of the Vietnamese-installed Heng Samrin government in Pnom Penh and its failure to make a public condemnation of the Soviet invasion of Afghanistan could not but hurt India's credibility and reputation as a nonaligned and self-reliant country.

Nonetheless, there was a general belief and hope that India could not have become, or would ever become, Moscow's instrument for its global policy, in particular for its Asia policy. At least the Southeast Asian countries were willing to give India the benefit of the doubt.

As far as ASEAN countries were concerned, apart from a few personal statements made by private individuals or officials which did not reflect official views, India's willingness to use military force for power projection (Sri Lanka in 1987, the Maldives in 1988, and the naval exercises in and around the Andaman and Nicobars Islands) had not been a cause for alarm. The Coordinating Minister for Political and Security Affairs and former Commander for the Restoration of Order and Security (KOPKAMTIB) of the Republic of Indonesia, Admiral (Rtd.) Sudomo, told the press that Indonesia was not concerned about what observers regarded as 'provocative Indian naval exercises' in the Andamans and Nicobars from time to time. He added, that 'the ASEAN concept of national and regional resilience has taken deep roots'.[3]

II INDIA'S SELF-PERCEPTION AND AMBITIONS

India has the potential to be a great power. Its size, population, strategic location, the past creativity of its people and its abundant natural resources endowment have led its elite to believe that it is destined to play a major role in the world. This perception has been carefully nourished ever since winning independence in 1947. As one Indian scholar puts it:

It is precisely India's perception of itself as a potential great power – however distant that may seem – that led to the policy of nonalignment in the first place. Underlying the policy of nonalignment, however, was a perception of a future great power role for India. Here Nehru was not only the exponent of nonalignment, but also the one who gave expression to such a role for India in the future. Indeed, he articulated his vision of such a role long before independence though he often masked it in moral language.[4]

As Nehru himself said in clarifying these aspirations:

A free India with her vast resources can be of great service to the world and humanity. India will always make a difference to the world; fate has marked us for big things. Leaving the three big countries, the United States, the Soviet Union and China aside for the moment, look at the world. There are many advanced highly cultured countries. But if you peep into the future and if nothing goes wrong, wars and the like – the obvious fourth country in the world is India.[5]

The cultural influences that flowed from India into Southeast Asia have been attributed by Indian and some European scholars to its effort at cultural expansion and colonization. Members of the Greater India Society, for instance, which was founded in 1926 saw the countries of Southeast Asia as 'ancient Indian colonies'. Even Siam was claimed as an Indian colony. Radhakumud Mookerji's *Indian Shipping: A History of Seaborne Trade and Maritime Activity of the Indians from the Earliest Times*, published in 1912, conjured up a vision of 'huge fleets of Indian adventurers, crossing the sea to Farther India and Indonesia, founding kingdoms, establishing colonies, expanding the trade of their mother-country, and in due course bringing over talented artists from Bengal, Kalinga and Gujerat to erect matchless monuments'. In a Foreword to Phanindra Nath Bose's book *The Indian Colony of Siam*, Lahore, 1927, Dr P. C. Bagchi wrote 'The history of the Indian colonization of Indo–China and the Malay Peninsula forms a glorious chapter to the history of India'.[6]

The Indian colonization theory has been rejected by many scholars. The generally accepted theory now is that Southeast Asia was not at the receiving end playing a passive role. It was more a case of ambitious local rulers who, eager to copy the grander style of the Indian courts, employed Brahmans to consecrate them as god-kings in accordance with the ideas and ritual of the Indian classics.[7]

But history has also shown that however great a power India was in the past, it was no match for a great foreign naval power such as Britain, a factor which led to the subjugation of the former by the latter for hundreds of years. The role of naval technology seemed to have inspired the Indians, especially the elite, to work for an independent India which is now more powerful than in the past. These elites seek to establish an India that is self-reliant and influential, not only on the Indian sub-continent, but also in the Indian Ocean region and ultimately in the world, a country that can never again be conquered by any foreign power. In short, a big power which not only has a major role to play in global politics, but at the same time also has the power to deter any potential external aggression or foil coercive diplomacy from any outside power.

To this end, all elements of national power must be harnessed and developed into an effective national power.[8] India's endeavours to realize this objective during the past two decades and a half have made it a preeminent country in South Asia or, perhaps, even a predominant one.

As the most powerful country in the subcontinent, India expects its smaller neighbours to submit to its 'rightful role' in subcontinental affairs. It will not tolerate external intervention in a conflict situation in any South Asian country, especially if the intervention has any implicit or explicit anti-Indian implication. No South Asian government must therefore ask for external military assistance to deal with a serious internal conflict situation. Instead, it must ask help from India or from neighbouring countries. The exclusion of India from such a contingency will be considered to be an anti-Indian move on the part of the government concerned.[9]

But much to India's irritation, its ambition to be the predominant regional power has always been challenged by Pakistan, which could not accept India's 'natural right' to play the role of the guarantor of peace and security in South Asia. In India's view, Indo–Pakistani relations had been determined primarily by Pakistan's search for power-parity with India and its efforts to prevent the natural balance of power in the subcontinent from developing. And in the process it was even prepared to 'borrow power' from abroad, justifying it in terms of its own search for security.[10]

III INDIA'S THREAT PERCEPTION

Influence of past experiences

The nation-building experiences of third world countries have not been similar. Some countries have experienced insurgencies during the process of national integration. Both from the point of view of the nature and the intensity of insurgency and the extent of external involvement in it, the experience of some has been more traumatic than others. Still other countries have faced more serious external threats. Each country's experience, therefore, influences its threat perception.

Many, if not all, of the Southeast Asian countries have experienced serious domestic insurgencies, which some of them continue to face. This has led to a perception of threats arising from internal insurgencies with or without external encouragement or support. In dealing with these threats Indonesia and the other ASEAN countries have been developing the strategies of *national resilience* at the national level and *regional resilience* at the regional level, with *self-reliance* and *self-confidence* as the core principles. National development which emphasises the socio-economic sector and regional cooperation is most crucial in the implementation of these strategies. The Kuala Lumpur Declaration of 1971 on Southeast Asia as a 'Zone of Peace, Freedom and Neutrality' (ZOPFAN) and *regional resilience* are correlated and mutually reinforcing.

Unlike the ASEAN countries' experience, India tends to highlight the dangers arising out of external threats, with the possibility of great power involvement. As an Asian country with a long historical pluralistic heritage and with the potential of vast human and natural resources, India is aiming at speedy national development in a rapidly changing world. In identifying the sources of adverse external pressures, India, like others, refers to the factors that are relevant to its experience. Of the five international wars in which India has been involved since independence, great power intervention was perceived as a real threat in two.[11] This has greatly influenced India's threat perception.

Whereas *national resilience* and *regional resilience* are the hallmarks of the ASEAN response to adverse situations emphasising domestic sources of threat, India's strategy in responding to its external sources of threat is *military self-relianc*e. Both strategies, however, have evolved out of the basic philosophy of nonalignment and self-reliance. But unlike Indonesia and the other ASEAN countries, which are striving for increasingly close cooperation among themselves and are trying to widen the geographical area of cooperation eventually to include the whole of Southeast Asia, India's approach to the South Asian region has tended to emphasise the potential for tensions within the region. This has had a destabilising effect in the region.

India's thrust for regional supremacy is also motivated by its perception that a threat to any of the northern buffer states is considered a threat to India. At the time of the Chinese invasion of Tibet in 1950, Nehru said, 'The fact remains that we cannot tolerate any foreign invasion from any foreign country in any part of the Indian subcontinent. Any possible invasion of Nepal would invariably involve the security of India.' This statement of policy applies to the whole of the northern frontier and is enforced by formal treaties with Bhutan, Sikkim and Nepal, which defined these countries' respective roles in the Indian-managed regional security system.[12] This policy is essentially a British colonial heritage which the Indians saw as their right to retain in terms of continental security and foreign policy postures.[13]

India's land environment

India, the largest democracy in the world, is surrounded by Pakistan – an Islamic country and until very recently governed by a military regime; Bangladesh – another Islamic country and one of the poorest in the world, plagued by frequent severe natural disasters such as draught, cyclones and tidal waves, and refugee problems; two small monarchies – Bhutan and Nepal; one giant Communist state – China, which is still troubled with the aftermath of the Tiananmen square massacre and with problems in Tibet; one small and turbulent democracy – Sri Lanka, facing serious insurgency from the Tamil and Sinhala militants; and Burma, for many years unstable because of continuing secessionist movements aggravated by popular revolt against the autocratic military regime.

Thus, India finds itself surrounded on all sides by current and potential instability. The fact that India has chosen a secular, democratic and a federal system of government, which is in contrast to surrounding military authoritarianism and religious fundamentalism, has contributed to the atmosphere of distrust and disharmony between India and the countries around it.

Pakistan has always figured very high in India's security considerations. Indo–Pakistani enmity has been the outgrowth of the Congress–Muslim League rivalry long before independence, which resulted in the partition of the subcontinent into secular India and Islamic Pakistan. Independence was preceded by an undeclared war between the two rivals which caused much suffering, bitterness and hundreds of thousands of casualties.[14]

India, by reason of its much greater size and by virtue of a much more rapid take-off into nationhood, has always been dominant. This fact has made Pakistan very conscious of its taking second place, which was not conducive to a friendly relationship between the two countries. Pakistan's adversary relationship with India was also seen by the latter as the result of the absurd nature of the geographically divided Pakistani state and to the exclusive and socially narrow character and composition of its ruling elite.[15] Traditionally India was threatened from the northwestern frontiers. Invasions by the Greeks, the Kushans, the Huns and the Mongols came through that sector. But since independence, due to the drastic change of its geopolitical environment, India no longer directly confronts threats from Central Asia or Iran. Pakistan and Afghanistan are supposed to act as a buffer.[16] Instead, Pakistan has become the number one threat. Throughout most of the 1980s Indo–Pakistani relations improved, especially following Benazir Bhutto's rise to power and Pakistan's return to democracy. Nevertheless, in the 1990s India's security environment will still be directly dependent, to a significant extent, upon the nature of the relationship with Pakistan.[17]

The People's Republic of China impinges upon India's security environment because it occupies the entire northern fringe of the Indian subcontinent, with Nepal and Bhutan sandwiched in between. China has a direct accessibility to Pakistan through Pakistan Occupied Kashmir (POK), and Bangladesh is just across an 80km strip of Indian territory. China can easily cause trouble for India by playing upon the fears of smaller neighbours such as Nepal and Bhutan.

China also emerged as a major military challenge to India in the late 1950s. The Sino–Indian border war of 1962 caused damage to India's strategy of 'self-reliance'. The Government, under intense parliamentary and public pressure, urgently called for British, Commonwealth, and American assistance. British guns and American bombers were rushed in, but China suddenly and unilaterally ended the war by announcing that it was withdrawing its forces back to the lines of actual control before the conflict.[18]

The disastrous twelve weeks Sino–Indian war, followed by China's first nuclear explosion two years later, had a significant effect on Indian defence policy. Military strength had come to be viewed as an indispensable and vital component of national power and its use a vital necessity to defend and promote India's national interests. Indeed, successive events in South Asia since 1984 (the occupation of the no-man's-land of Kashmir's 20,000ft high Siachen Glacier, 1984; the penetration into unoccupied and disputed territory along the China–India border, summer 1985; an extensive Indian military exercise close to the frontier with Pakistan, winter 1986-87; India's intervention in Sri Lanka and occupation of the northern and eastern parts of the island, 1987; intervention in the Maldives, 1988)[19] suggest India's predilection to use military force as the main element of power projection.

Although they never broke off their diplomatic ties, Sino–Indian relations remained frozen till 1976, when the two countries exchanged ambassadors. Since then there has been significant progress in improving bilateral relations. However, problems like Afghanistan, Kampuchea and Tibet, the unresolved border issue and China's alleged nuclear aid to Pakistan, are the stumbling blocks in the process of normalizing bilateral relations.

Strategic linkages with external powers

Pakistan is the only south Asian power which India perceives as a potential threat to its security. The two countries are entangled in a race for superiority in military technology, such as nuclear and missile technology, and an arms buildup. Over the years India has made significant advances in its industrial, technological and military might. Pakistan would not be a formidable adversary for India on its own. Because of India's vast population and, consequently, much larger GNP, it has been able to develop a modern advanced sector in the midst of its prevailing poverty.

What is of more concern to India is Pakistan's inclination to compensate for its inferiority by establishing strategic linkages with extra-regional powers in its search for security and parity *vis-à-vis* India. The signing of the Mutual Security Pact between Pakistan and the United States in 1954 had started the flow of arms to Pakistan. This was followed by Pakistan's joining SEATO and CENTO linking it with Southeast Asian (Thailand and the Philippines) and Middle East countries (Iran and Turkey), all allied to the West. Pakistan has also established closer affinities with Iran, Turkey and other Muslim countries in the Middle East and the Gulf Area.

The fall of the Shah's regime in Iran and the Soviet invasion of Afghanistan made Pakistan strategically the most important country in the region for the United States. Pakistan's security was seen as essential to prevent the Soviets gaining a foothold from which they could influence events in the Gulf area. The result was a massive arming of Pakistan, which included sophisticated systems like F-16 aircraft and ultra-sensitive radar stations for several airfields, to name a few.

Pakistan has also forged a strategic link with China, India's other potential adversary. Ever since the Sino–Indian border dispute began in 1959, the PRC has gradually moved towards total support for Pakistan. On all major issues of conflict between Pakistan and India, (i.e. Kashmir, the Indo–Pakistani War of 1965, the Bangladesh crisis of 1971), China fully supported Pakistan. Although lately both China and India have taken steps to resolve the border issue and normalise relations, the Sino–Pakistani relationship must be still a major factor in India's strategic considerations.

India for its part has also established a strategic link with an external power, and a superpower at that, by signing the Treaty of Peace, Friendship and Cooperation with the Soviet Union during the Bangladesh crisis of 1971. Besides the provisions on military cooperation, the treaty also introduced as a new stage of economic cooperation between the two countries. India's justification of its signing the treaty was that in a situation in which two of the big powers (the USA and China) took the side of Pakistan, the Indo–Soviet treaty provided a countervailing influence to prevent India from being subjected to the joint pressures of Washington and Peking.[20]

The maritime environment

Geopolitically, India occupies a unique position in the Indian Ocean. India juts into the northern Indian Ocean and virtually cuts it into two halves, the Arabian Sea and the Bay of Bengal. This situation encourages India to develop its maritime strategy from three distinct angles. One is oriented to the south towards the Indian Ocean to take into account India's interests in the region, such as safeguarding its security against possible encroachments emanating from the presence of big powers, its interests further south in Antarctica and in the deep sea-bed resources of the region. The other two are geared to meet events from the Arabian Sea and the Bay of Bengal, which are governed not only by local power equations but also by the links between the local and the major extra-regional powers.

During the past two decades or so the Indian Ocean region has undergone a gradual transformation from a relatively peaceful 'British lake' into an area of turbulence, tension and crises of all descriptions. Soon after the vacuum created by the British withdrawal from east of Suez was filled by the great powers, the latters' competing strategic, political and economic interests led to a rapid buildup of military arsenals in the region, both conventional and nuclear.

The Indian Ocean region comprises the largest chunk of the developing world. There are no great powers among its thirty six littoral and eleven hinterland states. Except South Africa and Australia all are developing countries and excepting these two countries and Thailand, the rest are all nonaligned nations.[21] The region is very diverse in almost every aspect: religious, cultural background, tradition, economic structure, resources, area, population, level of development, strategic significance. Therefore, there is a wide disparity in power potential of these states. These divergencies contribute to the lack of the spirit of unity, and evoke intraregional rivalries making room for external involvement.

The resources which this region contains are vital for the world, especially the industrialized world, thus offering excellent prospects for economic exploitation by the big powers. It is, therefore, in the interest of the Western world that the sea lanes and oil supply lines in the Indian Ocean remain open and safe. Mindful of the far-reaching implications of these facts and of the increased military and strategic activities of both superpowers and other major powers, the littoral and hinterland states took the 'Indian Ocean Peace Zone' initiative at the Nonaligned Summit at Lusaka in 1970. They were in broad agreement that the region should be protected from the East–West conflict. This initiative was supported by United Nations General Assembly Resolution of 1971. Unfortunately, the peace zone proposal was rejected by the Western powers.

India's maritime interests have been increasing due to its gradually expanding trade and commerce. These interests will become even more vital in future as a result of factors like the exploitation of living resources in its 200-mile EEZ, mineral resources in its continental shelf, development of its island resources and the exploitation of minerals in the deep sea-bed. India will have to develop its maritime strategy to defend these growing interests, taking account of the rejection of the peace zone concept by the industrialized major powers, their naval presence in the Indian Ocean and the linkages they might develop with regional powers not friendly to India.

India is developing an autonomous modern blue-water navy with a balanced sea-denial and sea-control capability as an integral part of its strategic buildup. It has also developed a coastguard to perform 'part-time' operations like patrolling its EEZ, protecting the oil installations in the continental shelf and checking illegal immigration, etc.

But India is still a long way from becoming a major maritime power. It will be years before it can sufficiently build up its maritime infrastructure in order to have the capability of launching a sustained offensive outside its neighbourhood – even if it should wish to do so.

For the foreseeable future, no navy of the Indian Ocean littoral countries has any significant intervention potential, including the Indian Navy.

IV THE PROSPECT OF INDIA'S STRATEGIC BUILDUP

The fundamental changes that have been taking place on the global level since late 1985 have brought about changes in international agendas. As superpower dialogue and negotiation are replacing confrontation, thereby changing the paradigms of the Cold War, as industrialized nations are trying to maintain their economic and technological predominance while at the same time preparing themselves for the post-industrial era and as the Third World countries are struggling not to be left too far behind, economics will increasingly be the prime mover of actions and the prime cause of conflicts. Prestige and power will be increasingly measured in terms of economic power and technological strength. To be sure, politics will continue to be important, especially when national security is involved. However, in today's world, non-military factors such as economic, industrial and technological backwardness, environmental deterioration, rapid population growth and social inequities, pose significant threats to the security of nations. These changes will not fail to have their impact on South and Southwest Asia and the Indian Ocean region.

Given the basic tenets of India's defence and foreign policies since independence, (i.e. nonalignment and peaceful coexistence to contribute to world peace and the welfare of mankind), one may expect India to seize the opportunity to erase its image as a destabilising factor in the region.

Nonetheless, pragmatism and *realpolitik*, to which it also subscribes, will not allow its leaders to take things for granted. India will continue to develop strategic power commensurate with its size, economic and technological strength and geographic position. It will continue to search for power to enable it to deal with any sudden changes in the global and regional situation, given the many uncertainties which will continue into the next century. India appears to have made a doctrine of K. Sundarji's advice, one of the architects of its military buildup after the Sino–Indian border war in 1962, who said: 'To be weak is not virtuous, being prepared is not being provocative'.[22]

V CONCLUSION

India's military and political predominance in South Asia and its growing naval capability in the Indian Ocean region is an established fact. But India is still a long way from becoming a major maritime power in the Indian Ocean region.

Its military buildup is motivated first and foremost by its self-perceived manifest destiny to play a dominant role in the South Asian subcontinent and the Indian Ocean region. At the same time it is striving to become a global power commensurate with its great power potential. However, in this drive to realize its ambitions and aspirations, it will not constitute a threat to its region and adjacent regions if it upholds the tenets of its foreign and defence policies since independence, which are nonalignment and peaceful coexistence.

Ever since independence India has been challenged in its ambition by Pakistan, the country's largest potential adversary on the sub-continent. The People's Republic of China is the only other potential adversary in the region. The close Sino–Pakistan ties will continue to require India's special attention.

India's immediate environment is characterised by current and potential instability, providing the opportunity for extra-regional involvement and the establishment of linkages which are detrimental to India's aspirations. This is a factor that has an important bearing on India's strategic thinking.

Like the ASEAN countries, India wishes to see the Southeast Asian region become a Zone of Peace, Freedom and Neutrality, and to establish the Indian Ocean as a Zone of Peace. The Peace Zone concept is supported by the majority of the world community. The absence of Western agreement to this concept has been an important factor in India's resolve to become a major maritime power.

In pursuing its ambition it is essential for India to understand that no developing country can alone ensure its national security and the security of the region in which it finds itself. It must establish and develop cooperation with neighbouring countries. This goes for India too, perhaps even more so. India has to build bridges of under-standing, confidence and trust with its neighbours, so as to promote close regional cooperation in developing South Asia into a secure, peaceful and prosperous community of nations. To this end the South Asian Association for Regional Cooperation (SAARC) could best serve the purpose.

Finally, the common search for peace, stability, tranquillity and prosperity for the peoples in both South Asia and Southeast Asia, in combination with recent fundamental geopolitical changes, provides a good opportunity for ASEAN and SAARC to establish inter-regional cooperation.

NOTES

1. *The Canberra Times*, 19 February, 1990.
2. John Seeger, *Straits Times*, 24 June, 1989.
3. Muhammad Jusuf, 'India and Strategic Developments in the Indian Ocean', *Telstra*, 02–1989, p. 50.
4. Ashequa Irshad, *Indian Military Power and Policy*, as quoted from Baldev Raj Nayar's 'A World Role: The Dialectics of Purpose and Power', *BIISS Journal*, vol. 10, no. 4, 1989, p. 389.
5. *Ibid.*
6. D.G.E. Hall, *A History of Southeast Asia*, Second Edition, London – Macmillan & Co Ltd, New York – St Martins Press, 1964, p. 16.
7. *Ibid*, p. 19.
8. Ray S. Cline argued that national power 'is determined in part by the military forces and the military establishment of a country but even more by the size and location of territory, the nature of frontiers, the population, the raw-material resources, the economic structure, the technological development, the financial strength, the ethnic mix, the social cohesiveness, the stability of political processes and decision-making, and, finally the intangible quantity usually described as national spirit.' See Ray S. Cline, *World Power Assessment, A Calculus of Strategic Drift*, Georgetown University, The Center for Strategic and International Studies, Washington, DC, 1975, p. 11.
9. Bhabani Sen Gupta, 'The Indian Doctrine', *India Today*, 31 August, 1983.
10. Mohammed Ayoob, *Developments in the Subcontinent – The Post-Bangladesh Phase* in K. Subrahmanyam (Ed.), 'Self-Reliance and National Resilience', Abhinav Publications, New Delhi, 1975, p. 12.
11. The five wars involving India's territorial integrity and national security are: (1) With Pakistan over Kashmir in 1947; (2) The border war with China in 1962; (3) With Pakistan at the Rann of Kutch in April 1965; (4) With Pakistan in August 1965 (Operation Gibraltar and Operation Grand Slam launched by Pakistan against India); (5) The 1971 war with Pakistan resulting in the birth of Bangla Desh. See K.C. Pant, 'Philosophy of Indian Defence', *Strategic Analysis*, vol. XII no. 5, August, 1989, p. 479.

12. Pradyot Pradhan, 'Indian Security Environment in the 1990s – External Dimension', *Strategic Analysis*, vol. XII, no. VI, September, 1989, p. 653.
13. Ashequa Irshad, *op. cit.*, p. 391.
14. *The New Encyclopaedia Britannica*, vol. 9, 15th Edition, 1978, p. 423.
15. Mohammed Ayoob, *op. cit.*
16. K. R. Singh, 'India and the Indian Ocean Region in the Coming Decade'. Paper presented at the Indo–Malaysian Seminar, New Delhi, 7–9 March, 1988.
17. Parminder S. Bhogal, 'India's Security Environment in the 1990s: The South Asian Factor', *Strategic Analysis*, vol. XII, no. VII, October, 1989, p. 771.
18. *The New Encyclopedia Britannica*, *op. cit.*, p. 425.
19. *Time*, 3 April , 1989.
20. Nilufar Choudhury, 'The Indian Ocean: A Zone of Peace or A Zone of Conflict?', *BIISS Journal*, vol. 6, no. 2, 1985, p. 247.
21. Ashequa Irshad, *op. cit.*, p. 410.
22. *Ibid.*

7 The Future of India and Southwest Asia

Amin Saikal

Since obtaining its independence in 1947, India has conducted a very complex foreign policy. Two guiding objectives have underpinned this complexity, even though different personalities – and even different parties – have been responsible for shaping foreign policy. The first of these objectives has been to enable India to act as the central regional power; and the second, as a corollary to this, has been to make other regional actors acquiesce to such an Indian role and to induce the major powers to tolerate it. These objectives have set India's broad foreign policy parameters and played a major role in determining the character of India's relations with important actors in the wider world arena, most notably the USSR and the USA. They have also influenced the strategic and security perceptions and priorities of successive Indian governments to the extent that most of their foreign policy actions and the outside reactions to them have either directly flowed from them or been closely inter-woven with them.

While this is not to suggest that Indian foreign policy makers have remained utterly unresponsive to changes in global conditions, they have thus far demonstrably gone to considerable lengths to harness such changes to support their guiding objectives. The same may well prove to be the case with the dramatic changes which have recently shifted the international environment in the direction of greater cooperation between the superpowers. It is in this context that this chapter focuses on India's relations with Southwest Asia, which is often classified as a region in its own right but for our purpose can be viewed as a sub-region in relation to India's overall region of security and interests. This sub-region consists of Pakistan, Afghanistan and Iran as well as, to some extent, the Persian Gulf.

The aim of the chapter is three-fold: to evaluate both India's constant desire for regional centrality, and the consequent obsession that it has displayed in seeking to prompt Pakistan to accept such a centrality; to assess the implications of this for India's Southwest Asian relations in general; and to cast an eye on the future of India's regional position.

I INDIA'S GOAL OF REGIONAL CENTRALITY

Despite New Delhi's repeated official denials that it has sought to achieve a position of regional centrality, this is one goal which has consistently underlined India's foreign policy behaviour. 'Regional centrality' in this sense signifies a capability on India's part, at best, to prempt and, at worst, to deter any political, economic or military threats originating from within states in its vicinity. This objective has had its foundations in what Indian leaders inherited from their colonised past, as well as in the imperative to protect the integrity of a state highly fractionalised on sectarian, linguistic and ethnic bases, in the face of both longstanding and more recently perceived threats.

There is no doubt that at the time of the partition of the Indian subcontinent into the two independent states of India and Pakistan, many of those within the Indian National Congress who formed India's leadership were not well positioned for the task that confronted them, primarily for two reasons. First, while being Indian by birth and social background, they had grown to be Anglicised by training and politicisation. This had heavily influenced their understanding of not only politics in the mould of British democratic ideas and practices, but also India's position in the world – a position which under the British had been inflated in regional affairs beyond that which could have been justified by the resources that India could have mustered on its own. This had two broad implications.

On the one hand, the leadership had grown to value Western democratic principles as good for them and India; and viewed themselves as the natural inheritors of British rule and India's British-backed status in its region. On the other, as a consequence, they had not managed to have their feet firmly on the ground with regard to actual Indian circumstances. In the absence of British rule, these circumstances made it difficult for them either to pursue their democratic ideals or to uphold the regional role that India had played under the British. In fact, upon independence, which came much sooner than many of them had expected, they instantly found themselves torn between what they had inherited from the British and what the existing Indian national conditions demanded of them. These conditions were marked by extensive political-social divisions and mass poverty which made it difficult for them to achieve their post-independence objectives. The result was the accentuation among many of them of a crisis of identity, security and political vision. This crisis was pithily summed up by Jawaharlal Nehru when he remarked:

I am a stranger and alien in the West. I cannot be of it. But in my own country also, sometimes, I have an exile's feeling. I often wonder if I represent anyone at all, and I am inclined to think that I do not, though many have kindly and friendly feelings toward me. I have become a queer mixture of the East and the West, out of place everywhere, at home nowhere.[1]

The second factor which added to this crisis and changed the situation of regional acquiescence that the British had promoted for India was the creation of the independent Muslim state of Pakistan. This development, which many Indian leaders had opposed as anathema to their whole nationalist stance, shocked the Nehru leadership to its foundations. It confronted it with a major foreign policy problem with wide domestic implications, given the serious dislocations that it caused for the Indian population and the precedents that it set for secessionist movements in India. What Nehru feared most was that the successful breakaway of Pakistan could result in the 'balkanisation' of India.[2]

Meanwhile, the way Pakistan desperately set out to establish and protect its own identity as a sovereign Islamic state did not help the situation. Its rapid move to enlist support from the Islamic world and, more importantly, from the United States through bilateral and multilateral military and security agreements (which soon led to Pakistan's joining the Western-sponsored Baghdad Pact and its successor, the Central Treaty Organisation (CENTO) and Southeast Asian Treaty Organisation (SEATO)), left the Nehru leadership high and dry. It not only provided it with little opportunity to come to terms with the idea of Pakistan as a separate and equal state born out of India, but also jolted it out of its Anglicised state. The involvement of Britain and the United States in the Baghdad Pact and CENTO and the US's orchestration of SEATO could not but deeply hurt Nehru. Although the two Western powers' policy attitudes towards Pakistan were primarily motivated by their opposition to Soviet Communism rather than to India, they nonetheless made one thing clear to Nehru: that all his commitments to Western democratic ideals and to the goal of building a secular democratic system based on the institutions which the British had built in India were no guarantee against the Western powers acting contrary to what New Delhi perceived as its vital interests.

This seemed to have several implications. First, while unable to prevent the creation of Pakistan, New Delhi found it imperative, on the one hand, to do whatever possible to contain the effects of the partition on its domestic and foreign policy, and limit Pakistan's capacity to act as an equal to India in the region; and, on the other, to draw on the 'Pakistan' factor (just as the latter did from the outset in respect of the 'Indian' factor) to make a claim of major regional threat to India. This eroded any possible immediate chance for an amicable and peaceful settlement of the issues arising from the partition between the two countries. Instead, there developed serious cross-border tensions and territorial disputes, particularly over Kashmir. This laid the foundations for India and Pakistan to develop an obsession with one another; and invoked a consciousness among the post-independence Indian leadership that as one of the largest and most populated countries in the world, with great human and material potential, India could not allow Pakistan to interrupt the evolution of the regional role that India had played under the British. Second, it prompted the Nehru leadership not to count too much for support for India's development and regional-global position on either Britain or the United States – particularly the latter (since the former was in any case a declining world power). Rather, India deemed it necessary, despite the common ideals and values that it shared with the West, to seek to build a foreign policy posture which could be seen as indigenous, and could help it to strengthen and maintain an independent central position in the region.

These considerations proved instrumental in shaping what Nehru instituted as India's nonaligned foreign policy, based on what he called the *Panchsheel* principles of mutual respect for the territorial integrity and sovereignty of states, mutual non-aggression, mutual non-interference in each others' internal affairs, equality and mutual benefit, and peaceful coexistence. This policy, which had its genesis in Nehru's pre-independence thought, was initially considered as most suitable for India, permitting it to develop friendly relations with all countries. However, to Nehru nonalignment did not imply neutrality in the sense of 'passivity'. In fact, he was very clear about this from the start. He claimed that it essentially meant that India remained

> uncommitted to military blocs; but the important fact is that we are committed to various policies, various urges, various objectives, and various principles; very much so . . .[3]

He further noted:

> If there is a big war, there is no particular reason why we should jump into it. Nevertheless, it is a little difficult nowadays in world

wars to be neutral . . . We are not going to join a war if we can help it; and we are going to join the side which is to our interest when the choice comes to it.[4]

Although originally this foreign policy posture was presented as limited in scope, with prime emphasis on India's disposition only as a peaceful and conciliatory actor, this soon began to change. The emphasis of the policy rapidly shifted towards escalating India's role as a central regional actor and seeking ways and means to prompt other regional countries, above all Pakistan, to recognise this role. It was effectively deployed to remove India somewhat from what Nehru had called, just before the partition, 'the Anglo-American group'[5] and to widen its foreign policy options in the direction of developing close friendship with other powers, most importantly the USSR. Despite all its police-state characteristics, which were diametrically opposed to most of the values for which Nehru and his close associates stood, the USSR was quickly embraced as a new and important friend. The underlying motive was not just to help India's national development, but to enforce the country's position as a pivotal actor in the region, without any degree of dependence on the West of a kind which could keep India vulnerable, particularly to American dictates.

The Indo–Soviet friendship began in 1955 with not only the commencement of a generous programme of Soviet economic and military aid to India, but also strong Soviet support for the country in its dispute with Pakistan. Of course, the Soviets had their own motives, as they clearly wanted to neutralise or counter-balance the post-War American penetration of the Southwest Asian region south of Soviet borders, where Pakistan, Iran and Turkey had rapidly drifted into the American camp as frontline states against Soviet communism. This development rapidly locked India and Pakistan into hostile and competitive relations, more or less along the same pattern as those of the American-Soviet rivalry, conflating their disputes with the rival US-Soviet interests at the global level and imperiling the chances for an early resolution of them on a bilateral basis. This also widened India's foreign policy dimensions, and its parameters of regional security and interests, as well as the needs and potentials for achieving greater regional capability. It was in this context that from the mid-1950s, India embarked on a road to achieve a military capability whereby it could not only strengthen its status in relation to its immediate South Asian neighbours, but also negotiate its wider interests beyond this region from a position of relative strength. The three subsequent wars that it fought – one with China over a border dispute in 1962 and two with Pakistan, in 1965 and 1971 – only strengthened the resolve of Nehru's successors, in particular his daughter, Indira Gandhi, and the latter's son, Rajiv, who together ruled India for most of the post-Nehru period from 1964 to 1989.[6]

II SOUTHWEST ASIAN REGIONAL IMPLICATIONS

These developments, which in the wake of the Sino–Indian war were also used by New Delhi to safeguard itself against China, had an alarming affect on Pakistan. The deeply suspicious and distrustful Pakistani leaders interpreted them as clearly anti-Pakistan, particularly in view of two additional factors. The first was that by the early 1960s it had become obvious that from the start Washington had intended its security ties with Pakistan, Iran and Turkey more to help the United States in its anti-Soviet global strategy than its allies in their regional disputes – in the case of Pakistan, with India. This was painfully underlined to Pakistan when in its 1965 war with India the United States (and for that matter CENTO as a whole) failed to provide any direct military assistance.[7] With the exception of the Shah of Iran, who provided some unilateral support for Pakistan, the same story was repeated during the Indo–Pakistan war of 1971. In fact, in the wake of this war, the United States went even as far as to place an arms embargo on both combatants – an embargo which remained in force against Pakistan until the Soviet invasion of Afghanistan in late December 1979. These developments had incrementally disillusioned many Pakistani leaders with both CENTO and the alliance with the United States. They saw that in contrast to Washington, Moscow had firmly supported India's position in both wars and had even signed a Treaty of Friendship and Cooperation with India shortly before it inflicted in the second war a crushing military defeat on Pakistan, causing the latter's eastern wing to break away and form the independent state of Bangladesh.

The second factor concerned the development of close ties between Afghanistan and the Soviet Union, and Afghanistan and India. Since the time of the independence of the Indian subcontinent from Britain, Afghanistan and India had developed a common anti-Pakistan position. Like India, Afghanistan had become embroiled in a simmering border dispute with Pakistan. It had its origins in the unilateral British demarcation in 1893 of the border between Afghanistan and

British India along an arbitrary line determined by Sir Mortimer Durand. Upon the partition of the subcontinent, while Pakistan declined to discuss the border issue with Afghanistan on the ground that it was not an issue as far as Pakistan was concerned, New Delhi strongly encouraged and backed the Afghans on their border claim as part of an anti-Pakistan regional campaign. When in the 1950s the border dispute led to a series of border skirmishes and to Kabul's support of secessionist movements in Pakistan's Northwest Frontier and Baluchistan Provinces, intent on creating from them an independent entity called 'Pushtunistan', Kabul deemed it necessary not only to accelerate its process of domestic modernisation, but also to strengthen its defences. Prompted by the United States' refusal to provide Afghanistan with military aid and help it to settle its border dispute with Pakistan unless that country joined CENTO – something which the Afghan rulers refused to do on account of a traditional policy of neutrality in world politics – Kabul turned to Moscow for economic and military aid.[8]

Along similar lines to its response to New Delhi's request for aid, Moscow commenced in 1955 a substantial programme of economic and military assistance to Afghanistan, and backed it in its claims against Pakistan. By 1961, according to Oleg Penkovskiy, discussions had even canvassed 'the possibility of sending Soviet troops into Afghanistan for joint operations against Pakistan'.[9] These developments resulted in the growth of close friendship between Kabul and Moscow, and between Kabul and New Delhi, which also found themselves in strong partnership within the emergent Nonaligned Movement. Of course, Afghanistan never engaged Pakistan in a full military confrontation and with the help of the mediation of the Shah of Iran, the two sides' disputes de-escalated from the early 1960s in favour of the development of reasonable neighbourly ties. An important factor from Kabul's point of view in seeking better relations was Afghanistan's dependence for vital transit on Pakistan, given its landlocked status. The improvement in relations persisted after the change of regime in Afghanistan in 1973 from monarchy to republic under the leadership of the former Afghan king's rival cousin and brother-in-law, Mohammad Daoud, who during his prime ministership (1953–1963) had been the architect of Afghanistan's 'Pushtunistan' policy. Nor did Afghanistan ever join India in any military action against Pakistan, for no Afghan government was prepared to endorse New Delhi's claim over Kashmir, given the Islamic bond between the Afghans and Kashmiris, and the implications of endorsement of India's position on Kashmir for Afghanistan's ties with the Islamic world. In fact, during both Indo–Pakistan wars, Kabul privately informed Islamabad that it had no intention of helping India in its war efforts by opening an eastern front against Pakistan.[10] Nonetheless, successive Pakistani leaders felt constantly fearful of what they perceived as a Moscow–Kabul–New Delhi axis, and of the danger that such an axis could produce for Pakistan in the event of a wider regional conflict.

These factors of disillusionment with the United States and regional alliances, as well as constant feelings of vulnerability to Pakistan's eastern and western neighbours and through them to the Soviet Union, provided Pakistani leaders from about the mid-1960s with ample ground to diversify and expand their sources of international support. The immediate option open to Pakistan was not only to exploit the growing Sino–Soviet and Sino–Indian disputes and forge close ties with China – which resulted in the development of an important strategic dimension in their relations – but also to look to Iran and Arab states for greater Islamic ties and support. Pakistan could always count on Iran under the Shah. In view of the decline of CENTO as a regional military organisation, Pakistan readily joined Iran and Turkey in setting up in 1964 the Regional Cooperation for Development (RCD) as an offshoot of CENTO for more effective economic cooperation. Initially the RCD worked more in favour of Iran. But with the emergence of Iran in the early 1970s as a major oil producer and consequently a significant economic and military power, Pakistan found Iran to be a very valuable partner. This, together with the Shah's anti-Soviet stance, resulted in growing economic cooperation between Pakistan and Iran, and a commitment on the part of the Shah to oppose any threat to Pakistan's sovereignty and integrity.[11]

While maintaining good working relationships with Kabul and New Delhi and a mediatory role from the early 1960s to help Pakistan settle its disputes peacefully with its neighbours, the Shah gradually but firmly shifted Iran's weight behind Pakistan in those disputes. Whereas in the 1965 Indo–Pakistan war the Shah supported Pakistan's 'just' claim over Kashmir with only limited logistical but considerable relief support, in the late 1960s he transferred to Pakistan a number of Sabre fighters (which were reportedly used against India in the war of 1971). He also provided some combat support to Pakistan during the war itself.[12] Moreover, in the aftermath of the 1971 war, he declared that Iran would not tolerate any further disintegration of Pakistan after the creation of Bangladesh; and he promised to help Zulfiqar Ali Bhutto's government to suppress Pushtun and Baluchi secessionist activities – something which he did through the supply of a number of helicopters.[13] Indeed, these developments, which were also in support of the Shah's drive to transform Iran into a regional superpower by the mid-1980s, with a naval capability to project Iranian power well beyond the Persian Gulf in the direction of the Indian Ocean, could not but be disconcerting, particularly for India. New Delhi's response was in four forms: it criticised the Shah's military buildup and accelerated the expansion of its own military capability; it rejected the Shah's proposal for a regional security arrangement; it made greater efforts to take advantage of the Shah's offer of economic aid, especially cheap oil, in support of the monarch's mediation efforts, and thus expanded its economic ties with Iran, in part to neutralise the dynamics of Iran–Pakistan relations; and it kept up its close ties with Afghanistan.[14]

Meanwhile, to strengthen its regional position further, the Bhutto government in the early 1970s declared Pakistan to be a nonaligned country, withdrew the country formally from the regional pacts, and emphasised its Islamic orientation. Despite the historically troubled relations between Iran and the Arab states and the latter's fear of the Shah's military buildup, Pakistan concurrently used its Islamic credentials and indeed the very underlying reasons for competition between Iran and the Arabs, to expand its ties with the oil-rich Arab states. When in the 1970s a massive amount of capital was transferred to these states, enabling their leaderships to embark on grand processes of social and economic modernisation and military expansion, Pakistan was in a position to cut a slice of this wealth. It used its surplus of skilled and unskilled labour as well as its technological and military capacity to supply much labour and many professionals and technicians to the oil-rich states. More importantly, it provided military trainers and even special units to guard some of their leaderships.[15]

Pakistan's customers included, most importantly Saudi Arabia, Kuwait and the United Arab Emirates, as well as Libya – at least until the turn of the 1980s, when the relationship between Pakistan's military ruler General Zia ul-Haq (1977-1988) and Colonel Mu'mmar al-Qaddafi turned sour in the wake of Zia's execution of Bhutto, who had forged a close relationship with the Libyan leader. In return, substantial Arab funds, in the form of both direct aid and remittances, found their way into Pakistan, bringing a higher level of economic activity and stability, and enabling General Zia to boost military spending. Libya even provided finance for Pakistan to develop a nuclear capacity and an 'Islamic bomb',[16] the programme for which began following the Indian detonation in 1974 of what it called a 'nuclear device for peaceful purposes'. The result of this development has been the contentious issue of a nuclear race between India and Pakistan, with both now reportedly having achieved a nuclear capability in the face of moves to establish a nuclear non-proliferation regime.

In response to these developments, India attempted to weaken Pakistan's position by seeking to strengthen its ties with the Gulf states. No doubt it has had some success in terms of expanding its trade and exporting some technological know-how into the region. It has done this while maintaining a consistent position in support of the right of the Palestinian people to free self-determination and a homeland of their own, to the point of recognising the recently-declared state of Palestine by the Palestine Liberation Organisation (PLO) and inviting the latter to open an embassy in New Delhi. However, its efforts were not so successful as to weaken Pakistan's Islamic credentials with the Gulf Arab states or neutralise the dynamics of Pakistan's economic and military ties in the region.[17]

The pattern of competition which developed between India and Pakistan in the Southwest Asian region in the 1970s was not much altered by the two dramatic events in the region which brought the decade to a close. These were the seizure of power in Kabul in the coup of April 1978 by the pro-Soviet People's Democratic Party of Afghanistan (PDPA) and the invasion of Afghanistan by the Soviet Union eighteen months later; and the fall of the Shah and rise of Ayatullah Khomeini's Islamic regime in Iran in early 1979. If anything these events, notwithstanding all their consequences, changed the regional equation only to the extent of strengthening rather than weakening the India–Pakistan rivalry in the region.

The Iranian revolution brought about a number of developments which could be manipulated by both India and Pakistan against one another. Those changes included the plunging of Iran into a lengthy period of post-revolutionary turmoil; the Khomeini regime's formal denunciation of the Shah's pro-Western goals of social-economic modernisation and military buildup; the regime's open hostility towards the United States and Islamic aversion to communism; and its claim of religious superiority over Iran's Arab neighbours. This rigourous assertion of the religious primacy contributed to Baghdad's decision to start in 1980 the Iran–Iraq war, which lasted for eight years, at very high costs for both sides. These changes certainly resulted in the weakening of Iran's capability to play as major a role in regional affairs as it had under the Shah; and by the same token it could no longer be a major source of support for Pakistan. This could only please India.

On the other hand, the Khomeini regime's 'Islamic militancy' set alarm bells ringing in New Delhi. The Indian leadership, especially under Mrs Indira Gandhi (whose Congress (I) party resumed power in January 1980 after being out of office for three years) seemingly perceived a potential link between this and Zia ul-Haq's assertive Islamic policies; and displayed growing concern about the direct and indirect implications of such a link for India. In tapping a common cord with the Soviets and many Western actors, New Delhi highlighted the serious threat that the growth of what it called 'Islamic fundamentalism' could pose not only to major power interests in the region but also to India's secularist democracy. It noted that if the spread of this phenomenon were not checked, it could inspire and radicalise Indian Muslims towards greater political agitation and inter-communal disturbances in India. Of course, this Indian position, which continues to govern New Delhi's approach to the issue of Islamic resurgence in the region to the present day, was in many ways misconceived. It failed to take into account the substantial differences which existed between the nature and characteristics of Shi'ite Islam – the dominant sect in Iran – and Sunni Islam, which commands majority followings in Afghanistan and Pakistan; and between the national conditions in these countries. Nonetheless, while finding it politically expedient to maintain reasonable working relations with the Khomeini regime, New Delhi could not approve of the Islamic character of the regime, in particular its call for radicalisation of Muslims in the region. It combined this disapproval with its traditional hostility towards Pakistan and sought to substantiate its stance against 'Islamic militancy' in the context of the growing Afghanistan crisis, which provided Pakistan and India with a sufficient bone of contention to allow them to pursue their rivalry unabated.

The responses that Pakistan, Iran and India provided to the Afghan crisis were quickly formulated, not so much in terms of the needs and aspirations of the Afghan people, but rather of the conflicting interests of these states. Pakistan opposed the PDPA takeover in Kabul from the outset and chose to pursue active opposition to the Soviet invasion; the Iranian Islamic regime, while disapproving of the PDPA rule and condemning the Soviet invasion, took a somewhat lower profile; and

India maintained close ties with the PDPA regime and made no public condemnation of the invasion.

Islamabad's opposition stemmed from the long-standing threat that it had perceived from Soviet communism and what it viewed as a Moscow–Kabul–New Delhi axis against Pakistan. The Soviet invasion and Islamabad's declaration of Islamic solidarity with the Afghan people and active support for the Afghan Islamic resistance forces, the *Mujahideen,* confirmed the position of Pakistan as a vital frontline state and dramatically raised the country's value to those regional and international forces which shared with the Pakistan leaders the widespread conviction at the time that the Soviet action may have marked the beginning of the USSR's long-cherished desire for regional domination. These forces, most importantly, included the United States, China and the conservative and moderate Arab states, led by Saudi Arabia. The result was the renewal of American military aid to Pakistan on an unprecedented scale and of US–Pakistan strategic ties; the strengthening of Sino–Pakistan relations, particularly in their military dimension; and the inflow of increasing Arab financial assistance to Pakistan.[18]

Indeed there was no more than a nominal connection between the Pakistani and Iranian responses, for these responses differed substantially in their character and scope. The Iranian stance was very much determined by the Khomeini regime's religious sectarian character and dire post-revolutionary situation. As a consequence, while condemning the Soviet invasion, Tehran could provide only limited help to the Afghan resistance, even then mainly to its pro-Iranian Shi'ite components, representing part of the 15 to 20 per cent Shia population of Afghanistan. By the same token, this limited the scope of Islamic cooperation between Iran and the Sunni-dominated Pakistan against the Soviets and their surrogates in Afghanistan.[19]

New Delhi swiftly capitalised on these occurrences to develop the thesis of a growing regional shift against India's interests. While ignoring the fact that Pakistan accepted the proffered American aid package only sixteen months after the Soviet invasion, in part because of New Delhi's continued failure to condemn the Soviet invasion publicly, India adopted a self-serving approach to the Afghanistan crisis. It continued to be the only democracy to repeat the Soviet version of events leading to the Soviet invasion, and it provided increasing political, economic and logistic support for the post-invasion regime of Babrak Karmal. Meanwhile, in order to maintain its credentials as a leading force in the nonaligned movement, it combined this with occasional perfunctory expressions of concern about the suffering and dislocation of the Afghan people, augmented by the admission of some Afghans to take up refuge in India, as well as periodic calls for the 'withdrawal of all foreign troops' from Afghanistan – a formulation conforming with the Soviet propaganda claim that Pakistani and American personnel were involved in combat operations in support of the Afghan resistance.[20]

The Soviet Union's withdrawal of its combat troops by 15 February 1989 did not alter the Indian position. As the Soviets sought to sustain the PDPA regime through massive non-combat support, India increased its efforts to aid the Soviets in whatever way feasible to boost the position of the regime. Following the Soviet announcement of the start of its troop withdrawal from mid-May 1988 under the terms of the flawed Afghan Geneva Accords of a month earlier (which did not provide for a political settlement of the Afghan problem on the basis of the right of the Afghan people to free self-determination), Prime Minister Rajiv Gandhi once again denounced the *Mujahideen* as 'Islamic fanatics'.[21] He invited Afghan President Najibullah to make an official visit to New Delhi – his first outside Warsaw Pact countries – to assure him of India's continued support and to determine the role that New Delhi could play in the nonaligned movement in boosting the international credibility of his government. Reportedly, despite India's public denials, there has since the Soviet withdrawal been a substantial increase in India's economic and military-logistic support for the Kabul regime; and this has come to include the introduction of Indian military 'observers' and 'personnel'.[22] Consequently, the *Mujahideen* have grown very resentful of India. It comes as no surprise that with the resurgence of troubles in Jammu and Kashmir in early 1990, while the Kabul regime supported India's position, the Pakistan-based *Mujahideen* leaders adopted a common position with Islamabad in firmly backing the Islamic-nationalist struggle of the Kashmiri separatists for independence. In whatever way one looks at the Pakistani and Indian role in the Afghan crisis, one fact cannot be escaped: that so far, the two antagonists have in a sense been involved in a war by proxy in Afghanistan.

III   THE FUTURE OF INDIA'S REGIONAL POSITION

Of course, there have recently been important trends in both international and regional arenas, as well as a change of government in India, which may create fresh opportunities and give rise to a degree of optimism about a change in India's Southwest Asia posture in the direction of lessening tensions in the region. To evaluate this, it is first of all important to outline these changes; and then to see the extent to which they are likely to affect India.

At the international level, there is no denying that Mikhail Gorbachev's domestic and foreign policy reforms have already produced immense impetus for change in the post-World War international order. Among many things, they have exposed the bankruptcy of communist ideology and the limits within which the USSR can operate as a global power. Whereas in the past, Soviet economic and military aid was channelled to many Third World countries for both ideological and pragmatic reasons, so as to generate and maintain effective anti-Western actors and alliances around the world, this may not be the case any longer.

This is not to suggest that, under the impulse of urgent domestic economic needs and global political relaxation, the Soviet Union from now on can be expected to be a passive force, unwilling to pursue its perceived interests in world politics. What it does intimate is that it would need to exercise greater pragmatism in the choice of the countries where it would like to make economic and military investment. Moscow could be expected to accelerate this process in order to lessen the burden on the USSR of those friendly states whose strategic value, especially in global terms, is at serious risk of diminishing as further changes in the international climate entrench the shift from confrontation to cooperation between the superpowers. In this context, a degree of rationalisation in India's foreign relations, particularly with the superpowers, is not beyond the realm of possibility. Moscow may find it necessary to put Soviet relations with India on a more mutually economically rewarding footing than has hitherto been the case. One of the outcomes of such a development would be a greater need on the part of India to find alternative sources of aid – most importantly the United States – to compensate for shortfalls from the Soviet Union. A greater balance in Indo–American relations could serve as a moderating factor, helping to improve Indo– Pakistan and India-China relations, with positive implications for India's broader Southwest Asian posture.

Meanwhile, the Southwest Asian region has entered a state of greater flexibility than was the case for most of the 1980s as far as the foreign policy position of its individual constituent states is concerned. This is mainly due to three factors. The first stems from a growing desire on the part of the Iranian Islamic regime, particularly since the death of Ayatullah Khomeini on 4 June 1989, to seek an end to its regional and international isolation. Although the Iranian leaders are still domestically constrained to agree on a common approach to foreign policy issues, the pragmatic forces among them seem to be gradually gaining ground. President Hashemi Rafsanjani, the most consummate politician in the Iranian leadership, has persistently made it clear that the best way to ease Iran out of its isolation is for the country to rationalise its Islamic militant image and conduct its foreign relations more in practical than ideological terms. In this respect, whereas in August 1990 Baghdad conceded all the demands of Iran in order to make peace with that country in the wake of Iraq's invasion of Kuwait and the consequent regional crisis, Rafsanjani has sought urgently an improvement in Iran's foreign relations, at both regional and international levels. This means that, if Rafsanjani had his way, he would like to dilute what India has made out to be a 'threat' of Islamic fundamentalism in the region, removing one of the major factors on which India has drawn to adopt a forward security posture in Southwest Asia.

The second factor is related to changes that Pakistan has experienced since the death on 17 August 1988 of General Zia ul-Haq. Although the military still commands a strong influence in Pakistani politics, the change to civilian rule has meant the creation of an opportunity for the injection of a degree of flexibility in the foreign policy posture that General Zia had promoted. Given Pakistan's immense national economic and social problems, no civilian ruler in Pakistan would be keen to spend almost half of the national budget on the military, as had grown to be the case under General Zia. However, for such a government to reduce expenditure in this sector without causing a backlash from the politically ambitious elements within the armed forces, it would need a reduction in the level of perceived outside threat to Pakistan's security, and a stable regional environment. It was in pursuit of these imperatives that the government of Benazir Bhutto, which was elected in November 1988 but dismissed twenty months later by Pakistan's President, Ghulam Ishaq Khan, on charges of 'corruption and incompetence', initially showed a strong willingness to reach some understanding with New Delhi over Indo–Pakistan differences. Her two meetings with Rajiv Gandhi in 1989, and the resumption of ministerial discussions, were potentially important steps in the right direction, although the good they did has been largely undone by the recent disturbances in Jammu and Kashmir.

The third factor concerns the Afghanistan conflict. The Soviet troop withdrawal, and the stalemate which has grown between the Kabul government and the *Mujahideen,* have helped to reduce dramatically the salience of the Afghanistan crisis in world politics. In the climate of growing detente between the superpowers, this has rapidly shifted the focus of both international and regional players in this conflict from a military solution to a political settlement. Should a settlement of this kind eventuate and result in the creation of a government of national unity with the backing of the Soviet Union then both Pakistan and India would have fewer grounds for pursuing their activities in Afghanistan in the way they have so far. Similarly, the need for superpower involvement in the region – which has only helped to widen the gap between the security perceptions and parameters of Pakistan and India and to fuel an arms race between the two sides – would be reduced, creating new grounds for the regional antagonists to seek a resolution of their problems without conflation of their interests with those of the major powers.

These developments are potential incentives for a change in the direction of Indian foreign policy in general, and towards Southwest Asia in particular. However, such a change may still not eventuate in the near future. There are a number of imperatives which may decisively prompt New Delhi, irrespective of who is in power, to manipulate regional and international developments in pursuit of maintaining India's position as a central actor in regional affairs and influential player in world politics, rather than amending the country's external behaviour to the extent necessary to promote the cause of stability and order in Southwest Asia on the basis of equality of states and the principle of non-interference. The most important of these imperatives are the following four.

First, India's foreign policy posture has had such roots in the country's domestic conditions that any substantial change in the external posture can only be validated if there is a shift in the domestic basis. For example, India's perception of a threat from Pakistan and regional 'Islamic fundamentalism' has been based not on a premise that these forces have, at any stage, either actively sought or achieved the necessary capacity to destroy India's sovereignty and independence, for India has always had more human and military resources than necessary to defend itself decisively against Pakistan (as it did in the wars of 1965 and 1971) or any other force from Southwest Asia. Rather it has emanated mainly from India's internal impoverished economic conditions and divided social structure. This has led many

Indian leaders to believe, and rightly, that if India fails to be sufficiently outward-looking and self-assertive, some of the country's separatist groups could become more inward-looking and domestically volatile and too vulnerable to negative outside influences and manipulations. It is this consideration rather than anything else that has caused New Delhi to do everything possible to ensure that no effective links are established between India's separatist movements and sympathetic and irredentist regional forces – in the case of this discussion, between Pakistan, and the Kashmiri and Sikh separatists.

Second, the regional imperatives have developed in such a way that India cannot easily disengage itself as an assertive actor from them in the short run. Whether India likes it or not, Pakistan's links with the Islamic world and the West are well entrenched; and nothing short of a viable settlement of the Kashmir problem and the Afghanistan conflict as well as India's recognition of Pakistan as an equal regional actor can change this. On the question of Kashmir, it must be noted that just as the Kashmir issue is deeply rooted in Indian domestic politics in the sense that its independence would not only radicalise other Indian Muslims but also encourage other separatist movements in India, it is also a very significant matter for Pakistan. It is so closely related to the national identity of Pakistan that no Pakistani political leader could refrain from backing the Kashmiri separatist cause and survive politically. Therefore, a resolution of the Kashmir problem is not easily attainable unless India respects the demand of the Kashmir people for free self-determination.

The crisis in Afghanistan is even more difficult to resolve than the Kashmir problem. The continued Soviet efforts to maintain the PDPA (lately renamed as *Watan* or 'Homeland') as an effective force in Afghan politics – which runs contrary to the new Soviet foreign policy approach at the global level – and the Soviets' political, economic and social destructuring of Afghanistan have ensured the prolongation of turmoil and misery in that country. Even if the superpowers agree on a settlement formula, it is most unlikely to bring peace and stability to Afghanistan in the foreseeable future. The Afghan resistance forces are so divided, partly because of the heterogeneous nature of Afghan society and partly because of the ambitions of certain selfish leaders, that they have become increasingly vulnerable to manipulation by both the Kabul government and regional forces. No regional actor has developed as much a stake in the Afghan crisis as Pakistan, which has provided haven for more than three million Afghan refugees as well as important logistic support for the *Mujahideen*. In the wake of the

Soviet troop withdrawal, it has also become increasingly clear that the Pakistan military establishment at least wants to secure substantial benefits in return. It not only wants a pro-Pakistan government in Kabul, but also a government to be headed by its favourite *Mujahideen* leader, Gulbuddin Hekmatyar. The latter, an Islamic extremist and a long-standing client of Pakistan's Inter-Services Intelligence Directorate (ISI), is intensely disliked by other elements in the Afghan resistance. He has also been the most prominent *Mujahideen* figure, on whose position New Delhi has dwelt to maintain its rage about the 'threat of Islamic fundamentalism'. Indeed the position that Pakistan has so far pursued on Afghanistan, bankrolled partly by Saudi Arabia, is unlikely to further the cause of a viable settlement of the Afghan conflict or to leave much room for India to reduce its involvement in the conflict. Consequently, with the continuation of the Afghan crisis ensured for the foreseeable future, the short-term prospects for India and Pakistan to reach some understanding on the issue look very grim.

Third, at the international level, the changing situation also does not hold out much promise for an early change in the Cold War pattern of major power involvement in Southwest Asia. With the Soviet Union remaining committed to the PDPA and lending support only to a settlement of the Afghanistan conflict which would maintain Soviet influence in the country, and with the Soviet–American and Soviet–Chinese relations still full of uncertainties, a considerable restructuring of Moscow's attitudes towards either the Afghan conflict or India does not seem to be on the cards in the near future. Moscow continues to find its friendship with New Delhi of immense strategic importance in both regional and global terms. While a rationalisation of this friendship in some degrees is very likely, it may not be of the extent to change the regional strategic picture so as to put sufficient pressure on India to modify its policies towards Southwest Asia. Similarly, there do not appear to be sufficient incentives for the United States to change the general thrust of its policy of the last decade towards Southwest Asia either. No doubt the Soviet troop withdrawal from Afghanistan, particularly in the context of a growing need for the United States to channel as much of its foreign aid to other areas as possible, has put mounting pressure on Washington to reduce drastically or cut off its aid to the *Mujahideen* and scale down its military assistance to Pakistan. A substantial drop in American aid to the *Mujahideen* has already been registered, and similar measures have also been adopted against Pakistan.

However, Pakistan has now assumed too much significance in American regional considerations to warrant withdrawal of US aid to the country, for two important reasons. The first is that Washington does not want to add anything which could alienate Pakistan's military leadership and prompt it to frustrate the post-Zia process of demo-cratisation in the country. The second is that Pakistan's relationship with the regional pro-Western Arab states, especially Saudi Arabia, is now so entrenched that Washington cannot afford to take any measure against Pakistan which could in any way undermine its relations with these states. Whereas in the 1970s Washington had relied on strategic relationships with Saudi Arabia and Iran to maintain a solid infrastructure of influence in the region, in the wake of the Shah's fall Pakistan replaced, to an appreciable extent, Iran in this relation-ship. Pakistan's support for the United States during the 1990 crisis in the Gulf is an illustration of this point. This of course does not mean that Washington has not been interested in improving relations with India. In fact, the Indo–American ties in the last few years have taken a steady turn for the better, as Washington has not been able to ignore the position of India as the world's largest democracy and a powerful regional actor and as New Delhi has found it beneficial to expand India's commercial and technological ties with the United States. This may remain the case in the future. However, what it does suggest is that ultimately the United States' wider regional considerations, in the context of its strategic ties with Saudi Arabia and Pakistan and India's continued drive to strengthen its regional military capability, would set the limit on how far Indo–American ties can develop. This would be particularly so if there were no marked progress in Indo–Pakistan relations.

Fourth, while both the Singh government and its successor showed some willingness to be less self-centred than their Congress predeces-sor, the way India's foreign policy is rooted in domestic imperatives and the way regional issues have taken shape may not allow any government to redirect the country's foreign policy priorities in neglect of its traditional goal of regional centrality. No matter what govern-ment is in power in New Delhi, it cannot be expected rapidly to undertake such foreign policy redirection and survive at the same time. This proved to be especially the case with the Singh government, which was made up of a fairly loose alliance of several political parties, ranging from liberals to extreme Hindu militants. It is largely due to this factor that, despite all of India's economic and social problems, the Singh government announced a huge increase of 21 per cent in

India's defence spending for 1990–1991.[23] While Singh claimed this to be a result of 'the situation on our borders' – that is troubles with Pakistan – the increase is most likely to invite a similar response from Islamabad. It can only strengthen the hands of Pakistan's military leadership to demand greater military spending at the expense of improving the economic situation and strengthening the process of democratisation. It is also likely to cause much concern for other regional countries and the United States, making them become more wary of India's increased military buildup. This can neither help the currently tense regional situation nor endear India to Chinese and Western circles.

There is no doubt that in its foreign policy priorities and actions, in particular towards Southwest Asia, India has historically grown to project an image of itself among the regional states not so much as the balancer and peace-maker, which its stance as a leading nonaligned force might ideally dictate, but rather as an actor which has consistently sought to build its position as central in the region. Its difficulty from the start in embracing Pakistan's existence as an Islamic and equal sovereign neighbour has not only caused it to be looked upon with a degree of suspicion in the region and prompted Pakistan to link up more and more with the United States and Islamic forces in Southwest Asia, but also has induced it to engage in wider activities which have only accentuated the perception of India as an actor consumed with its own interests. Its opposition to 'Islamic fundamentalism'- based more on India's interests than on the reality of such Islamic resurgence since the Iranian revolution and the Soviet invasion of Afghanistan – together with its support for the Soviet-installed PDPA government in Kabul, has ultimately given regional states little basis for embracing India as a stabilising and peace-promoting force in Southwest Asia. Similarly, in the cobweb of major power involvement at regional and global levels, this has done little to steer India towards developing balanced relationships with the superpowers, enabling the country to attract as much support from the United States as it has from the Soviet Union.

A resolution of India's disputes with Pakistan and an injection of balance in its relations with the superpowers would cut down the need for the degree of military buildup that it has undertaken and would be necessary for ameliorating its mass poverty. By the same token, it would be helpful to Pakistan to cut down its high military expenditures in favour of strengthening the process of democratisation and instituting substantial economic reforms which the country needs so badly. Moreover, a more cooperative relationship could only help an early resolution of the conflict in Afghanistan. All this, in turn, could help to improve India's regional standing and result in the possible widening of the country's economic ties with the Arab states and hence improve its domestic situation. While there have been some favourable international and global changes, these changes are unlikely to benefit India or to enhance regional stability unless the new Indian government takes urgent steps not to manipulate them in support of India's drive for regional supremacy, but to make effective use of them to settle peacefully its regional disputes and promote the cause of greater regional order and stability.

NOTES

1. Jawaharlal Nehru, *Points of View*, The Information Service of India, New York, 1941, p. 20.
2. For the text see B. N. Pandey (Ed.), *The Indian Nationalist Movement, 1885–1947: Selected Documents*, Macmillan, Hong Kong, 1979, pp. 243–4.
3. Jawaharlal Nehru, *India's Foreign Policy: Selected Speeches, September 1946–April 1961*, New Delhi, n.p., 1961, p. 86.
4. Jawaharlal Nehru's speech in the Constituent Assembly (Legislative) Debates, 4 December, 1947, *Constituent Assembly of India (Legislative) Debates*, vol. II, no. 5, Con. 14, 11, 5.47/904, p. 1260.
5. For the text see Pandey (Ed.), *op. cit.*, pp. 204–5.
6. For details of these developments, see A. Appadorai and M.S. Rajan, *India's Foreign Policy and Relations*, South Asian Publishers Private Ltd, New Delhi, 1985, Chapters 1–6.
7. For details see S.K. Asopa, *Military Alliance and Regional Cooperation in West Asia: A Study of the Politics of Northern Tier*, Meenakshi Prakashan, Meerut, 1971, Chapters 5–6.
8. See Henry S. Bradsher, *Afghanistan and the Soviet Union*, Duke University Press, Durham, 1985, pp. 21–8.
9. Oleg Penlcovskiy, *The Penkovskiy Papers* Doubleday, New York, 1965, p. 87.
10. Confidential sources.
11. See Amin Saikal, *The Rise and Fall of the Shah*, Princeton University Press, Princeton, 1980, pp. 171–4.
12. Shirin Tahir-Kheli, 'Iran and Pakistan: Cooperation in an Area of Conflict', *Asian Survey*, vol.17, May, 1977, p. 484.
13. Saikal, *op. cit.*, pp. 173–4
14. *Ibid.*, p. 175.

15. See Hermann Frederick Eilts, 'Saudi Arabian Foreign Policy Toward the Gulf States and Southwest Asia', in Hafeez Malik (Ed.), *International Security in Southwest Asia*, Praeger, New York, 1984, pp. 100–106; Shirin Tahir-Kheli and William O. Staudenmaier, 'The Saudi–Pakistani Military Relationship: Implications for U.S. Policy', *Orbis*, vol.26, Spring 1982, pp. 155–71.

16. Confidential sources. For a discussion of this point, see also Raju G.C. Thomas, *Indian Security Policy*, Princeton University Press, Princeton, 1986, p. 46.

17. For a detailed discussion of India's interests in, and trade with, the Persian Gulf see Robert G. Wirsing, 'India and the Gulf', in Malik (Ed.), *op. cit.*, pp. 107–139.

18. See Amin Saikal, 'The Regional Politics of the Afghan Crisis', in Amin Saikal and William Maley (Eds.), *The Soviet Withdrawal from Afghanistan*, Cambridge University Press, Cambridge, 1989, pp. 53–5 and 59.

19. *Ibid.*, pp. 57–8.

20. See Thomas Perry Thornton, 'India and Afghanistan', in Theodore Eliot Jr. and Robert L. Pfaltzgraff Jr. (Eds.), *The Red Army on Pakistan's Border: Policy Implications for the United States*, Pergamon Brasseys, Washington D.C., 1986, pp. 44–70.

21. Elaine Sciolino, 'Gandhi Faults Islamic Rule for Kabul', *The New York Times*, 11 June, 1988.

22. See Yossef Bodansky, 'New Pressures on key Indian borderlands', *Jane's Defence Weekly, 30* April, 1988, pp. 840–4.

23. *The Australian Financial Review*, 21 March, 1990.

8 Soviet Perspectives on India's Developing Security Posture

Gregory Austin

The visit by Gorbachev to New Delhi in 1986 had all the hallmarks of the old-style USSR/India relationship. During the visit, Gorbachev remarked that the USSR shared India's concern for the strengthening of its defences.[1] In the wake of Gorbachev's visit, the normal manifestations of the relationship, such as soft term loans and military sales, continued. Yet even in 1986, a new trend in the Soviet relationship with India was foreshadowed, a trend that is directly attributable to the new directions in Soviet foreign policy launched by Gorbachev.

During his visit, Gorbachev reminded India 'to resist the tendencies that lead to a nuclear catastrophe', to find an accommodation with Pakistan to avoid a situation with 'unpredictable consequences', and to note the 'burden of launching military programs . . . on the social processes' in the countries of the Asia–Pacific region.[2] He hoped for a continued improvement in relations between China, India and the USSR so that 'no-one will have to take sides'.[3]

In the 1990s, the trend in India–USSR relations foreshadowed by Gorbachev is likely to intensify. The physical manifestations of old-style Soviet globalism – economic assistance, naval deployments, military equipment sales, support for anti-Western, militaristic regimes, and a utopian, globalist ideology – will fade, just as the manifestations of China's short-lived globalism disappeared in the late 1970s and 1980s. The decline of Soviet global ambitions is inevitable regardless of the outcome of political reform in the USSR. The future of Soviet politics is discussed in more detail later but, in general terms, there are two broad outcomes. On the one hand, if Gorbachev's reforms are consolidated, the USSR will surrender the old globalist foreign policy willingly. On the other hand, if Gorbachev's reformist agenda is replaced by a more conservative agenda, the economic and social problems that exist now in the USSR will be aggravated to such an extent that the national will for global prestige will evaporate and the economic basis for any sort of aspiring globalism simply will cease to exist.

It is the aim of the Gorbachev reformers to replace the Soviet globalism of the 1970s and 1980s in the 1990s with a new 'universalist' approach which will owe more to Einstein, Da Vinci, Toffler, and Western Marxists than to Lenin or Soviet 'Marxism'.[4] The foreign policy of a reformist Soviet leadership in the 1990s will be radical in its conception compared with the *status quo* conceptions of international relations that the major Western powers adhere to. The invocation of moral concepts derived from Christian tradition as a guide to foreign policy, as suggested in one Soviet source,[5] would provide a stark contrast to the amoralism of the foreign policies of most Western countries.

In the USSR's geopolitical schema of the 1970s, India provided a number of opportunities. It was China's opponent, the rejected suitor of the United States, and a leader of the nonaligned movement. In these respects, India was a useful ally in the USSR's anti-containment policies. As Robert Donaldson summarised it, the USSR has regarded India as 'an essential participant in its efforts to limit Chinese and American presence and influence' in the context of global and regional competition.[6] This old geopolitical schema will no longer apply to the three-way relationship. The reason – Soviet geopolitics of the 1970s has little in common with current and prospective Soviet geopolitics. For example, a recent Soviet article on regional conflicts observed: 'The theory of a zero-sum game . . . can no longer be considered as a theoretical basis for action'.[7]

The Soviet interest in India will be – and has been in part already – redefined by the adjustments that the United States and China make in their foreign policy in response to changed Soviet foreign policy. If the United States and China are being less hostile towards – or less intimidated – by the USSR, then the USSR's need for India in geopolitical terms will be reduced. The common interests that once bound the USSR to India are in decline.

In addition, there are new areas of potential disagreement. India's doctrine of regional hegemony[8] in South Asia has more in common with the Brezhnev doctrine than Soviet new thinking. The apparent arrogance in India's posture, where all of India's security problems are seen as the fault of other countries,[9] is at variance with the USSR's willingness to accept that its own posture contributed significantly to its uncomfortable security environment since the Second World War.

Similarly, the USSR now opposes nuclear proliferation and arms racing more than it did previously. The USSR has not so far taken an overly critical approach on India's obvious capability to move rapidly towards nuclear weapons capability. It is attempting to address the problem in the broader, and somewhat radical framework of global security and the need for the superpowers to move away from vertical proliferation. In this respect, the USSR is at present in close agreement with India. As one Soviet commentator noted:

> It is common to encounter the proposition that the resolution of the question about whether India will go nuclear or not depends principally on the conduct of its principal opponent, Pakistan, or even on China. However, this is only one of the factors influencing India's position. A decisive role is played by the nuclear arms race between the United States and the USSR.[10]

It is more than likely, however, that a reformist leadership in the USSR would oppose any move by India to actually acquire nuclear weapons. In fact, the Soviet newspaper *Izvestiia* has criticised India for not signing the Nuclear Non-Proliferation Treaty.

Even if the USSR were to maintain a normal level of interest in political relations with India in the 1990s, it is difficult to see a long term constituency in the USSR for a continuation of an especially close relationship based on a strategic calculation, such as opposing China or opposing the United States. There are few political points to be scored in the USSR in backing India in its bid to become a world power. Who in Soviet ruling circles – especially in a democratically elected Supreme Soviet, the newly appointed Presidential Council, or a newly constituted Presidium of the Communist Party – is likely to care about India. India, as a major Asian power, will of course continue to be the object of Soviet diplomacy and trade interest, much as it is the object of French or West German diplomacy and trade interest. As Gorbachev or his successor seeks to re-cast Soviet foreign policy in the mould of a more benign and internationally responsible power, India will remain politically important to the Soviet Union as an important Third World country. There may also be a lingering strategic interest, based perhaps on common perceptions and concerns about resurgent Islam in Southwest Asia. Such concerns may be reflected in a renewal in 1991 of the twenty-year Treaty of Peace, Friendship and Cooperation. Any renewal of this treaty, however, is likely to be on broader, less security oriented terms than the existing treaty.

The Soviet General Staff has little expertise on the Indian military. Very few articles on the Indian armed forces have appeared in Soviet military periodicals. There has been no real requirement to date. The focus of Soviet military interest in India so far has been the provision of military training, the sale of military equipment and technology, or the possibility of naval basing. All of this was undertaken on the basis of the old foreign policy objectives of the USSR. None of those activities is likely to significantly occupy the attention of the Soviet top brass in the 1990s given the immense preoccupations faced by the Soviet armed forces closer to home.

The area of the Soviet bureaucracy previously responsible for the overall coordination of Soviet policy towards India on the basis of its strategic importance to the USSR was the International Department of the Communist Party. This Party department is currently being removed from any real involvement in Soviet foreign policy formulation. It is difficult to see a situation where the International Department might be resurrected even if the USSR reverts to a more authoritarian system.

Soviet strategic priorities in the 1990s will involve internal security and political measures to enhance the USSR's security *vis-à-vis* Germany, the United States, Japan and China. It is unlikely that the USSR will see India as a useful political counterweight to China in the 1990s. In the 1970s and 1980s, India was an important part of the USSR's policy of encirclement of China at a time when China and the United States were developing closer relations to oppose Soviet 'hegemony'. Now that the USSR has adopted a completely different strategic approach to China – based on normalisation of relations and demilitarisation of the border – the policy of encirclement is no longer necessary. In addition, the old Sino–Soviet rivalry for Third World leadership is dead and no longer offers a reason for Soviet strategic engagement of India. The changed nature of the US–Soviet relationship has also undermined the rationale for Soviet strategic engagement of India.

The need for the USSR to consider India as geopolitical counterweight to China was always more inspired by global politics than geography; China was and will remain the USSR's principal geopolitical preoccupation in Asia and India offers little in terms of counterweight to China; the military conflict between India and China offers few real opportunities for the USSR to feel more secure because of it; it is simply not significant enough in China's scale of military preoccupations.

To the commentators who wish to emphasise the enduring nature of the geographical circumstances of a state and therefore of its geopolitics, I would offer the following observation by the grandfather of the study of Soviet strategy:

> Geography is sometimes regarded as a relatively unchanging factor, but in fact is one dimension of a single dynamically changing world. Space, terrain, natural resources, ecology and virtually all other aspects of geography assume ever new significance as new political, economic, technological, military, and other developments take place.[11]

Even if the USSR itself were not losing interest in India, there is going to be sufficient competition for the USSR in India from other sources, such as the United States, Japan and the EC, in the next decade to suggest that the halcyon days of the India-USSR strategic engagement will within a few years be a thing of the past.

The Soviet position in India's trade has not in recent years been a particularly strong one compared with OECD countries. The European Community (EC) has been India's largest and fastest growing source of imports for a number of years (33.6 per cent of India's imports in 1987–88).[12] Within the EC, the Federal Republic of Germany took the largest single share in 1987–88 at 9.7 per cent of India's total imports in that year. After this, Japan and the United States came next with 9.5 per cent and 9 per cent respectively in the same year. The United Kingdom accounted for 8.1 per cent in that year. The share for Eastern Europe was 8 per cent and for the USSR it was 5.7 per cent. Australia's share was 2.2 per cent.[13]

The trend in India/USSR trade shows a declining Soviet share relative to other major countries: the Soviet share of India's exports dropped from 18.4 per cent in 1985-86 to 12.5 per cent in 1987–88; while the Soviet share of India's imports dropped from 8.5 per cent to 5.7 per cent in the same period, with a low of 5 per cent in 1986-87.[14] Share of Soviet trade taken by developing countries has fallen in the 1980s from 15 per cent to 11 per cent.[15] The Soviet share of developing country trade is now less than 4 per cent.[16]

The level of Soviet military and economic aid to India is declining from its high levels in 1988: US$2.5 billion military aid and US$1.3 billion economic aid. There will almost certainly be increasing Soviet pressure on India to accept harder terms.[17] Some Indian military officials have expressed concern that if Soviet arms sales were put on a proper commercial basis, then India's hardware procurement plans would be stopped in their tracks. The very favourable terms offered in the past by the USSR have allowed the extensive military modernisation of the past few years. Any change to the terms would be a major set-back to that program.[18]

There has been a marked improvement in United States relations with India. This has involved a tacit recognition by the United States of India's regional pre-eminence. During his term in office, President Reagan described India as making a 'valuable contribution to regional stability'.[19] As another United States official put it:

It doesn't make sense for the US not to have congenial relations with the largest democracy and the dominant military power in the sub-continent and with a country that will clearly take its place on the world stage in the 21st century.[20]

High level visits in both directions have become more frequent and the United States has begun to transfer high technology to India, including some military technology. The United States has sold India a super-computer previously denied to it on security grounds, and has also offered to participate in an Indian project for the development of a light combat aircraft. The aim of the United States policy is to help India become self-sufficient in defence technology and less dependent on the USSR – still its major single source of defence equipment. The long term prospect is that the USSR and India will become competitors courting Japan and the US rather than partners.

The preceding analysis is based largely on the premise of consolidation of the reformist trends in Soviet domestic and foreign policy. The question must be asked whether the conclusions would be significantly different if political trends in the USSR in the 1990s took a different direction. The main option to be considered in this respect is a reversion in domestic politics to authoritarian rule. Several possible outcomes for Soviet foreign policy in such a situation have been outlined by Professor Graeme Gill:

a) As living standards continue to drop, popular unrest will increase, with the country as a whole becoming virtually ungovernable. The centre will have recourse to virulent Russian nationalism in an attempt to maintain its sense of authority, but this will only serve to exacerbate the drive of the non-Russian nationalities for

independence . . . Instead of the USSR, there will be a predominantly Russian state surrounded by a string of newly independent,
almost invariably antagonistic, states . . .
b) the gradual slide towards chaos in the USSR . . . prompts the
emergence in Moscow of a government which seeks to maintain
central control through the application of forceful measures . . .
the emergence of such a militaristic government signals a return to
the worst years of Stalin's rule . . . The country turns in on itself
under the force of international condemnation . . .
c) little improvement will occur in the economy, but . . . through a
combination of concessions and force the centre will be able to
keep the disputatious forces in the society under control. As a
result, the system will muddle on, . . . but without major changes
to its domestic position or international position.[21]

While Gill sees a return to Cold War conditions, including a
globalist policy of challenging the West's position, as conceivable
only under the second of these three scenarios, it is difficult to see a
major role for India in the USSR's strategic calculations under any of
them given that the current government of China, which is likely to be
in place for a number of years at least, would be a willing ally of a
more authoritarian USSR. If China were to begin interfering in the
USSR's nationalities problem, the USSR might see considerable
benefit in returning to a policy of pressure on China by encirclement. It is more likely, however, that an authoritarian China, unloved
by the international community, would respond to the re-emergence of
an authoritarian USSR (or Russia) by seeking to rekindle the great
alliance of the 1950s.

All outcomes really seem to suggest either a much more inward
looking Soviet strategic policy and security posture on the one hand,
or a severely constrained if still pugnacious, anti-Western globalist
strategy. If the USSR reverts to a more pugnacious international
policy, its main strategic preoccupations will be on its borders –
especially in Europe, Muslim West Asia, and Japan (including a
United States military presence of sorts). In that environment, China
will present itself as one of the few available strategic opportunities.

A more pugnacious USSR, groaning under the weight of internal
disorder, will therefore almost certainly not see much benefit from
strategic engagement of India.

The conclusion must be that the odds favour a situation in the 1990s
where the USSR will come to regard India with less interest. It will

almost certainly cease to subsidise India's military development to the extent that it has done to date. The USSR will probably oppose any move by India to acquire nuclear weapons. There is some prospect for tension between a reformist USSR and India over India's tendency to domination of its smaller neighbours. An authoritarian Soviet regime, should one return to power, will probably be indifferent – from the point of view of strategic gain – to India's efforts to build-up its military forces. The USSR would face strong competing priorities back home.

NOTES

1. Interview given to Indian journalists, 21 November, 1986, *Security in the Asia Pacific Region; The Soviet Approach (Documents and Materials)*, Novosti, Moscow, 1988, p. 79.
2. Speech to Activists of the Indo–Soviet Cultural Society, 27 November, 1986, *Security in the Asia Pacific Region*, pp. 84–85; and Joint News Conference of Mikhail Gorbachev and Rajiv Gandhi, 28 November, 1986, *loc. cit*, p. 101.
3. *Ibid.*, p. 101.
4. V. Kubalkova and A. Cruickshank, *Thinking New about Soviet 'New Thinking'* Institute of International Studies, University of California, Berkeley, 1989, pp. 26–49.
5. Fedor Burlatskii, *Novoe myshlenie* 2nd edition revised Politizdat, Moscow, 1989, pp. 34–35.
6. Robert H. Donaldson, 'The USSR, the Sub-Continent, and the Indian Ocean: Naval Power and Political Influence' in Lawrence Ziring (Ed.), *The Subcontinent in World Politics*, Praeger, New York, NY, 1978, p. 168.
7. A. Kislov, 'Novoe politicheskoe myshlenie i regional'nye konflikty', *Mirovaia ekonomika i mazhdunarodnye otnosheniia*, 1988(8), p. 46.
8. According to Air Commodore Jasjit Singh, India has always been the pre-eminent power, 'militarily and otherwise', in the subcontinent. He says this is often forgotten by Western strategic literature when referring to India's emergence as a regional power. *Regional and Security Perspectives of India*, Institute for Defence Studies and Analyses, New Delhi, 1989, p. 5.
9. K. C. Pant, the former Defence Minister, described the 'dissonance between India and the countries around her' as one of the four major factors affecting India's security perceptions. Speech at the Massachussets Institute of Technology, 1 July, 1989.
10. V. Gol'danskii and V. Davydov, 'O predotvraschchenii gorizontal'nogo rasprostraneniia iadernogo oruzhiia', *Mezhdunarodnaia ekonomika i mezhdunarodnye otnosheniia*, 1988(8), p. 33.

11.   R. L. Garthoff, *Soviet Military Policy*, Faber and Faber, London, 1966, p. 98.
12.   *Government of India Economic Survey 1988–89*, p. 109.
13.   *Ibid*, p. S77.
14.   *Government of India Economic Survey 1988–89*, unnumbered pages between pp. 106–107, and 110–111.
15.   L. Zevin, 'Nekotorye voprosy ekonomicheskogo sotrudnichestva SSSR s razvivaiushchimisia stranami', *Mirovaia ekonomika i mezhdunarodnye otnosheniia*, 1988(3), p. 45.
16.   *Ibid*.
17.   Vietnam has already encountered this problem. As one Vietnamese official noted: 'We used to receive three parts aid to one part trade. Now it is one-to-one trade'. *Far Eastern Economic Review*, 1 March, 1990, p. 19.
18.   As one observer noted: 'After a decade of growth, India's ambitious defence plans have come to a dangerous pass . . . there is just no money to pay for the plans'. *India Today*, 28 February, 1989, pp. 42–3.
19.   *Time*, 3 April, 1989, p. 15.
20.   *Ibid*.
21.   Senate Standing Committee on Foreign Affairs, Defence and Trade, Perestroika inquiry, *Hansard*, 1 December, 1989, pp. 70–71.

9 India's Strategic Development: Issues for the Western Powers

Ross Babbage

THE INDIAN OCEAN IN WESTERN SECURITY PRIORITIES

The Indian Ocean region has rarely been the central focus of Western security attention. The primary strategic interests of the United States and most of the Western allies have long been, and are likely to continue to be, concentrated elsewhere, particularly in Europe, Northeast Asia and the Middle East. Hence while the United States and the other Western powers do have some significant concerns in the Indian Ocean, especially unfettered access to Persian Gulf oil, their strategic perceptions of this region and their activities within it are driven primarily by broader global priorities.

From Washington's perspective, the Indian Ocean is, first and foremost, a great connector between the Western Pacific on the one hand and the Mediterranean and Atlantic theatres on the other. Full access to and through this region permits not only unrestricted transit of commercial shipping and aircraft but also the flexible transfer of United States naval and air units between the primary theatres. The value of the 'west-about' route from the western United States through the Indian Ocean into the 'back door' of the Middle East was underlined in a most dramatic fashion during the 1973 Middle East War, when United States trans-Atlantic resupply flights to Israel were denied staging and overflight rights by several Western European allies and others.[1] Access via the 'west-about' route became even more pressing following the fall of the Shah in Iran, the American hostage crisis, the outbreak of the Iran-Iraq war and the Soviet invasion of Afghanistan. The United States and many of the Western allies felt impelled to respond to these events by deploying forces to the region and much of this response flowed from the Pacific rather than the Atlantic theatre.

154

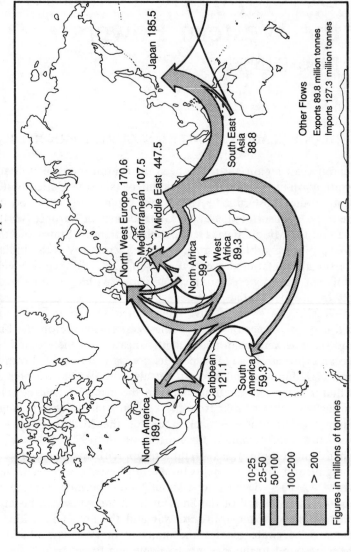

Figure 9.1 International shipping trade in oil

Japan 185.5

South East
Asia
88.8

North West Europe 170.6
Mediterranean 107.5
Middle East 447.5

North Africa
99.4

West
Africa
89.3

Caribbean
121.1

South
America
59.3

North America
189.7

Other Flows

Exports 89.8 million tonnes
Imports 127.3 million tonnes

10-25
25-50
50-100
100-200
> 200

Figures in millions of tonnes

Source: Dr A. K. L. Beresord, H. W. Dobson and C. Holmes (eds), *Lloyd's Maritime Atlas of World Ports and Shipping Places:* , Lloyd's of London Press, London, 1988, p. 10.

The rapid progression of events in the northwest corner of the Indian Ocean in 1979-80 was interpreted in most Western capitals as posing a serious potential threat to the free flow of Persian Gulf oil. As can be seen from Figure 9.1, oil supplies from this region are critically important to many Western economies. In the mid-1970s Japan drew no less than 79 per cent of its oil from the Middle East, Western Europe 69 per cent but the United States only 5 percent.[2] Nevertheless, alliance interests, recognition of the interdependency of the economies of the major Western states and a powerful geo-strategic desire to ensure that the Soviet Union did not steal a march in this theatre combined to stimulate a strong and sustained United States and broader Western response.

At the heart of Western concerns in the Gulf was a realisation that the Soviet Union held substantial ground and air forces in Afghanistan and adjacent to the northern Iranian border. Consequently, in the event that Moscow was tempted to intervene in a disunited or disintegrating Iran, the United States and its close allies would be hard-pressed to respond with sufficient timeliness and force to prevent Soviet seizure of important oil facilities on the Gulf.

President Carter took one early step in deterring such Soviet adventurism when he warned Moscow, during his January 1980 State of the Union address, that the United States would resist, with force if necessary, any Soviet attack on the area.[3] The United States naval force in the Persian Gulf (MIDEASTFOR) was strengthened from three to five ships and the frequency of naval battle group deployments to the western Indian Ocean rose to provide a strong continuous presence. In October 1979 President Carter announced the creation of a Rapid Deployment Joint Task Force, trained and equipped specifically for speedy commitment to crisis areas in the Middle East-Southwest Asian region. By January 1983 the forces earmarked for this role included 4.5 army divisions, 1.5 Marine amphibious forces, seven tactical fighter wings, two strategic bomber squadrons, three carrier battle groups and five maritime patrol squadrons.[4] It was commanded by a new separate unified headquarters, US Central Command, which was given responsibility for planning contingent operations from Pakistan and Afghanistan in the north, through Egypt and Sudan in the west, to Kenya in the south.

In order to facilitate rapid force insertion in a crisis, the heavy equipment of three marine brigades was pre-positioned on chartered ships, which were then deployed to the Indian Ocean, mostly in the vicinity of Diego Garcia. Priority was also given to strengthening civil and military airlift support capabilities. During the course of 1980 the United States concluded agreements with Oman, Kenya and Somalia to permit American air and sea access in future crises and for selected airfield and port facilities in those countries to be upgraded for such purposes.[5] Expanding the facilities on Diego Garcia was also accelerated greatly during this period to permit the atoll to provide shelter, fuel and logistic support for an entire aircraft carrier battle group and up to 18 pre-positioned ships. In addition, the airfield was expanded to handle large transport aircraft and B-52 bombers.

These and related developments were by far the most dramatic manifestations of Western military activity in the Indian Ocean since the Second World War. They were clearly driven by concerns about the potential for Soviet adventurism and the need to maintain the flow of oil to Western and other economies. Ten years later, the Iraqi invasion of Kuwait generated similar concerns about the security of Saudi Arabia, the minor Gulf states and the free flow of oil. This crisis also stimulated large scale western military deployments to the region. But it is of particular significance to this discussion that these major western military concentrations had nothing at all to do with events on, or perceptions of, India and other parts of the subcontinent.

Indeed, beyond the Persian Gulf and Afghanistan, United States and broader Western interests in the northern arc of the Indian Ocean are limited. Pakistani-Western relations have played a significant but varying role over the last forty years. Western, especially United States, interest has been partly founded on Pakistan's strategic location close to the mouth of the Persian Gulf, partly by what the Western allies have perceived as the anti-Soviet orientation of nearly all Pakistani governments since independence and partly, through the 1950s and 1960s in particular, by Pakistan's membership of the CENTO alliance. The Pakistanis have, however, always been aware of the broader nature of United States and Western interests. This was clearly apparent in the United States strong support for India during its border war with China in 1962 and its embargo on arms transfers to both sides during the 1965 Indo–Pakistani War.[6] Even when Washington ordered the USS Enterprise battle group into the Bay of Bengal during the 1971 war, Islamabad appreciated that this was designed as much to bolster the emerging United States relationship with Beijing as to hinder the Indians.[7]

Following the Soviet invasion of Afghanistan, the United States recognised Pakistan as a 'front line state' and furnished it with a six year $3.2 billion aid package designed to strengthen its defences and resolve against Soviet intimidatory behaviour. However, even this was shrouded with mutual suspicions as Congress made aid payments conditional on annual Presidential assessments of Pakistan's non-nuclear status. Many in the United States also worried about the potential for the infusion of American weaponry to be used by Pakistan in other directions and to further disturb Washington's relations with New Delhi.

The United States' long-standing relationship with Pakistan has complicated the development of government-to-government ties with India. Nevertheless, successive American administrations have clearly admired India's success as a democracy and economic, technological and educational ties have grown substantially. Washington has a clear objective of doing what it can to reduce Indo–Pakistani tensions and avert a nuclear arms race on the subcontinent.

India's view of the United States is substantially different. American naval deployments, creation of the Rapid Deployment Joint Task Force, the construction of substantial defence facilities on Diego Garcia and economic and military aid to Pakistan are viewed with great suspicion and seen as a challenge to India's natural dominance of the region.[8]

The apparent inconsistencies and reactive nature of United States policies in the region are perceived in New Delhi as both confusing and worrying. Differences between the many executive, congressional and agency actors on subcontinent issues and the variability and, to some extent, unpredictability of United States policy outcomes has strengthened Indian disenchantment.[9] Indian perceptions of the United States are therefore something of a confused mixture of admiration and appreciation for American technology, economic cooperation and education and deep concern and resentment at what is widely seen as American inconsistencies, power-plays and overt interference in it's backyard.

In this situation suggestions of hidden motives for American policies and actions tend to gain a level of credence they rarely deserve. Several commentators have continued to suggest, for instance, that one reason for the American military buildup in the region is to support deployments of United States ballistic missile-firing submarines (SSBNs).[10] This is despite the fact that SSBN deployments to the Indian Ocean have generally been rare, that the American SSBN force has been withdrawn from its most proximate base at Guam, and that developments in American ballistic missile technologies make stationing in the Indian Ocean unattractive. Moreover, the prospects of

American SSBN deployments into the Indian Ocean are likely to decline even further if, as seems likely, a START agreement is concluded by the superpowers in the early 1990s.

In a similar manner, a great deal has been made of the suggestion that the United States might conduct operations against satellites belonging to the Soviet Union and perhaps other countries from its facilities at Diego Garcia.[11] While it is certainly the case that some Soviet satellites of strategic significance fly over the southern hemisphere at relatively low (and hence comparatively vulnerable) altitudes, Indian commentators appear to have overlooked the fact that Diego Garcia is only seven degrees south of the equator and that the most important space 'gateway' through which launches from the three major Soviet launch sites (Plesetsk, Tyunatam and Kasputin Yar) must pass in their first orbit is not over the Indian Ocean at all but over the Southeastern Pacific Ocean.[12] Moreover, the F-15-launched miniature homing vehicle anti-satellite system that it has been suggested might operate from Diego Garcia has been cancelled.

In a dynamic democratic state such as India individuals representing various interest groups and points of view can be expected to enter debates on matters of international security concern. This is obviously welcome and unsurprising. However, in preparing this chapter I have been struck by the rarity with which prominent Indian commentators acknowledge the foundations of American policy in the region, whether they agree with them or not. Several external analysts of the regional situation have similarly noted an apparent insensitivity on the part of many Indian policy makers and others regarding the security concerns of other regional actors.[13] Such gaps in international perceptions can sow the seeds of future misunderstandings, tensions and even conflicts.

France is the external state with the second most powerful forces in the region. Its security concerns relate primarily to the defence of the remaining French possessions in the western Indian Ocean, to its close security cooperation with several littoral and island states and its general concern for the security of Persian Gulf oil and the free flow of associated shipping. France maintains an Indian Ocean squadron, normally comprising three frigates, four patrol craft, one amphibious ship and three support vessels including La Charente, a replenishment tanker with extensive command and control facilities. These vessels operate routinely from the French possessions in the western Indian Ocean. French forces also maintain port and airfield access at Djibouti, near the mouth of the Red Sea. At Mayotte and La Reunion there are, in addition, three marine infantry regiments, a Foreign Legion company and an air transport unit.[14]

British concerns in the Indian Ocean and Persian Gulf largely parallel those of the United States but because of Britain's diverse historical and economic ties in the region it is well placed to play an independent and sometimes influential diplomatic role. The Royal Navy maintains what it calls the Armilla Patrol in the Persian Gulf. This force normally comprises three frigates or destroyers and a support ship. On the British Indian Ocean Territory of Diego Garcia there is a small naval party and a marine detachment.[15] Most Indian commentators have tended to view the French and British force commitments to the region as colonial relics.

Australia is in the unusual situation of being both a close Western ally and an Indian Ocean littoral state. Australia maintains a national as well as an alliance interest in unhindered access to Persian Gulf oil and in the free flow of international shipping through the region. Because of its proximinity and its possession of significant Indian Ocean island territories, Australia maintains an enduring interest in strategic developments in the region, especially in its more immediate Eastern Indian Ocean approaches. Australian P-3 Orion long range maritime patrol aircraft operate routinely from west coast bases, the Cocos Islands and Butterworth airfield in Malaysia on Indian Ocean patrols. By the late 1990s close to half of the Royal Australian Navy will be based on the Australian west coast. Australian naval units conduct frequent patrols in Southeast Asian waters and periodically also visit central and western Indian Ocean waters.[16]

ISSUES FOR THE FUTURE

Adapting to multipolarity

The 1990s and the early part of the twenty-first century will see a substantially different pattern of global power emerge with profound implications for relations in the Indian Ocean region.

At the end of the Second World War, the United States' and the Soviet Union's economic, military and political influence dominated the agenda. In the late 1940s the United States economy alone accounted for close to half of global gross national product.[17]

However by 1990 the relative influence of both superpowers had declined with the United States share of global gross national product more than halved to about 22 percent.[18] By contrast, the economies of

Western Europe, Japan, China, South Korea, Taiwan and, in the Indian Ocean, India, Pakistan and a few of the Middle Eastern states had grown substantially, giving them the status of major regional actors and, for some, significant global players.

This diffusion of economic power has been paralleled by a spreading of military power and influence. In nuclear strategic forces, the two superpowers remain in a class of their own. But conventional military capabilities have proliferated, providing many regional powers with formidable capabilities to deter external power interference. Illustrative of this trend is the fact that Iraq now deploys more main battle tanks than Germany and more than the United States has deployed in Europe.[19] India, for its part, has more than twice the number of main battle tanks as Britain and almost twice the number of destroyers and frigates as Germany.[20]

But while the relative power and influence of the major Western countries has declined, that of the Soviet Union and its Warsaw Pact allies has fallen even further. The Soviet-style centrally planned economic model is now viewed almost universally as an anachronism, even within the Soviet Union itself. The growing independence of the Eastern European countries and the reform and opening of their economies, together with the restructuring challenge facing Moscow, portend a substantially different and probably less tense European environment. Provided Gorbachev remains in power, tensions between the superpowers will probably not return to the severity of the Cold War.

These trends would appear to have several important implications for relations between India and the major Western powers.

First, the dramatic reductions in inter-bloc tensions in Europe and the strong prospects for substantial early progress in arms control have generated irresistable pressures for heavy cuts in defence spending in Washington and most of the Western European capitals. Once the Iraq-Kuwait crisis is resolved and baring the emergence of a further major crisis in the Persian Gulf or elsewhere in the region, the effects of this so-called 'peace dividend' are likely to be seen in a significantly reduced Western military presence in the Indian Ocean through the 1990s. This, in turn, may help to facilitate the development of more harmonious Indian relations with the major Western powers.

A second consequence of the emerging multi-polar world is that as the security attention of the United States and most of the Western powers on central Europe declines, they are likely to show significantly increased concern about the possibility of coercive activities and military operations by the new range of major regional powers. This means that in the Indian Ocean context, United States and broader Western policies will be driven far more directly by regional factors than by the bi-polar global influences of the past. Particular sensitivities will continue to be in the Persian Gulf region, which will supply a significantly greater proportion of the West's oil by the end of the 1990s.[21] Were there to be serious domestic disturbances in Saudia Arabia, renewed hostilities between Iran and Iraq or other problems, large Western force deployments could again be made to the region. In these circumstances India would have a direct and parallel interest with the major Western allies because 33 per cent of its oil imports flow from the Gulf region.[22] Nevertheless, New Delhi would almost certainly be concerned to limit United States and external major power involvement in the theatre.

In the event of serious renewed tensions and even hostilities between India and Pakistan, the United States and most of the Western allies stances would most likely be driven far more than in the past by their direct interests in this region. Most Western countries would probably prefer to stand aloof.

The prospect of the United States and other Western allies directly challenging Indian military operations in its immediate region seems remote in the period ahead. While many elements of the Western media have portrayed India's military buildup in a dramatic and sometimes alarmist fashion, most Western goverments have responded cautiously and in measured terms. Few seem particularly disturbed by most aspects of India's developing conventional military capabilities. (Concerns about India's nuclear capabilities are discussed later.)

This has not always been the case. There were certainly concerns, following India's conclusion of its Treaty of Peace, Friendship and Cooperation with the Soviet Union in 1971, that Moscow would gain undue influence in New Delhi. India maintains cooperative activities with the Soviets in numerous fields and sees advantage in purchasing many durable but comparatively inexpensive Soviet military systems. However, India's approach to the Soviet Union is essentially pragmatic. Soviet forces do not have bases in India or automatic rights of access to Indian facilities, nor is there any evidence that these two countries coordinate operational planning. India has, in fact, gone to great lengths to diversity its sources of military supply, purchasing many items in Western Europe, often at considerable expense.[23]

There have also been few Western concerns in recent years about the employment of India's armed forces. The United States and most

Western allies expressed understanding of, and even support for, India's use of it's armed forces to suppress the 1988 abortive coup in the Maldives.[24] Similarly Western official comments on India's military involvement in Sri Lanka have been moderate and cautious.

Western governments expect India's security concerns to continue to be focused heavily in its border regions and in its immediate approaches. For instance, while there have been regional expressions of concern about India's development of naval and air facilities at Port Blair in the Andaman Islands, at the western end of the Straits of Malacca,[25] the interest of the major Western powers in this development has been muted. Indian facilities at this location will certainly facilitate surveillance of shipping in these straits and, more generally, in India's eastern approaches but they do not pose a serious constraint on Western passage of the Indonesian archipelago, not least because of the numerous alternative passages that are available.

Overall then, the 1990s are likely to see some limited development of India's conventional military capabilities and possibly their further periodic employment in India's immediate approaches. Provided this military power is wielded with some caution and regional sensitivity, the prospect of it stimulating a direct confrontation with the West is very small. However, were India to accelerate its military development program beyond that currently planned and commence the construction of substantial capabilities for long range sea, air and missile force projection, broader Western security concerns would arise. Enhanced capabilities of these kinds would raise fundamental questions about New Delhi's motivations, could stimulate competitive buildups (arms races) by other regional powers and might encourage some littoral countries to invite strengthened external power presences as a balance.

A more likely trend in the coming decade is that the military strategic elements of Indian-Western relations will gradually fade into the background as a variety of Western countries play stronger roles in India's economic development. The domestic economic crises of the Soviet Union and the Eastern Bloc states have underlined their poor capacity to assist rapidly developing economies, such as India's. Economic, technical, educational and political ties may well be reinforced with a range of Western states during the 1990s. Moreover, if India wishes to sustain its high rates of real economic growth throughout the twenty-first century, it may need to provide more flexible opportunities for infusions of foreign capital and technologies in at least some industrial sectors. Movement in these directions would provide a basis for the further development of Indian economic strength, accelerated growth of India's middle class and a gradual rise in the average standard of living.

Nuclear weapon and ballistic missile proliferation

One issue that will continue to complicate Western relations with both India and Pakistan is the acquisition by both countries of the technologies and the components required to build nuclear weapons and ballistic missile delivery vehicles.

Western countries have long been concerned about the potential of nuclear power and research facilities in these countries to be diverted into nuclear weapons programs and, in consequence, all foreign-supplied facilities operate under international safeguards. However, in addition to these facilities, both countries operate unsafeguarded plants. In the case of India there are presently two unsafeguarded power plants with a further six planned to come on-stream during the 1990s. India also has two unsafeguarded reprocessing plants.[26] Assessments suggest that India could produce enough plutonium to build twelve to eighteen small nuclear bombs annually.[27] Pakistan has a single unsafeguarded nuclear facility at Kahuta containing a uranium enrichment plant capable of producing enough weapons-grade uranium to build one-to-two nuclear weapons each year.[28]

Both countries have come under severe pressure from Western countries to place all their nuclear facilities under international safeguards. While this has not been achieved, India did announce in the late 1970s that it would not conduct a second nuclear test and it has frequently stated that it would not build nuclear weapons.[29] Pakistan responded by promising not to test a nuclear explosive device, not to manufacture nuclear weapons, not to enrich uranium to weapons grade and not to acquire nuclear technology illegally from the United States.[30] Only some of these Pakistani commitments appear to have been kept as it struggles to catch up with the much larger and more mature Indian programme.

While both countries now appear to have the wherewithall to build nuclear weapons, neither has announced that it intends to do so and this degree of restraint and ambiguity could work to both sides' advantage. The primary motivation for the Indian nuclear programme is undoubtedly deterrence of China.[31] New Delhi has no interest in spurring Islamabad into a nuclear arms race, not least because Pakistani nuclear weapons could pose a threat to India's heartland that is inconceivable by conventional means.

The nuclear programme in Pakistan sprang from defeat in the 1971 war and was accelerated following India's 'peaceful nuclear explosion' in 1974. As the late Prime Minister Ali Bhutto said, 'Pakistan would eat grass' if necessary to acquire its own nuclear deterrent.[32] Nevertheless, publicising an indigenous nuclear arsenal would stimulate an open and much more powerful response from India and aggravate severely its relations with the United States and others, probably triggering substantial cuts in international aid.

Both countries already possess extensive capabilities for delivering nuclear weapons by air. India's Jaguar, Mig 27, Mig 23 and Canberra aircraft are likely nuclear delivery candidates and Pakistan's F-16, Mirage 5 and Mirage III aircraft would also be able to perform the task.[33]

In addition, both countries are actively engaged in ballistic missile development programmes. India used a domestically-built SLV-3 rocket to launch a satellite into orbit in 1980.[34] A broader range of large rockets has been developed since. These span from *Prithvi*, a 250 km range missile with a payload of about 1000 kg recently put into production for the Indian Army, to a geostationary satellite launch vehicle planned to lift 3000 kg payloads to 36000 km orbits by the late 1990s.[35] This latter system could provide the basis for an Indian intercontinental ballistic missile programme. On 22 May 1989 India successfully tested a demonstration medium range ballistic missile called *Agni*, with a range of up to 2500 km and a payload up to 1000 kg.[36] The director of the responsible research institute has claimed that production of this system could begin as early as 1995.[37]

Pakistan's capability for indigenously producing ballistic missiles is much weaker than India's but in April 1988 it announced that it had tested two types of ballistic missile. One system, named *Haft* I, is believed to have a range of about 80 km and the other, named *Haft* II, about 300 km.[38] In 1985 Pakistan announced the establishment of a ten year space launch programme.[39] In addition to these domestic initiatives, Pakistan could possibly be given access to intermediate range ballistic missile technologies and components by China or Saudi Arabia.

The United States and other Western countries have made clear to both countries, especially Pakistan, the serious consequences that would flow from acquiring a nuclear weapons capability. They have also encouraged both sides to explore actively diplomatic solutions and, in particular, the arms control proposals that New Delhi and Islamabad have mooted in recent years.[40]

Recent trends suggest that the nuclear ambiguity of both sides may be sustained indefinitely, or at least diluted only gradually, as in the case of Israel. There are, nevertheless, many dangers accompanying even this gradualist approach. History suggests that the possession of nuclear weapons is unlikely to prevent cross-border and other limited hostilities. In these types of situations nuclear capabilities add a new level of unpredictability to regional relationships and an additional source of serious tension. There may also be scope in the future for national nuclear potentials to be manipulated for domestic purposes, possibly by religious fanatics on either side.

A broader danger is the prospect that countries in the Middle East, Southeast or East Asia may feel compelled to follow suit and initiate their own nuclear weapons programs. Iraqi, Iranian, Saudi Arabian or Indonesian nuclear weapons programs would have the potential to accelerate the pace of nuclear proliferation and dramatically exascerbate regional and global security instabilities.

Developments of these or related kinds are unlikely to be welcomed by any of the Western powers. However, the capacity of the West to influence developments in this theatre, especially in India, is declining. The power and international prestige of these countries is rising and nuclear weapons and associated delivery capabilities offer substantial reinforcement of these trends as well as practical means of deterring major regional and external power interference.

The most likely prospect therefore is that in the 1990s both India and Pakistan will continue to actively develop their nuclear weapon, ballistic missile and related programs but that these will continue to be shrouded by a degree of ambiguity for at least several years. By the turn of the century both countries can, nevertheless, be expected to be reaping the prestige, influence and strategic deterrence benefits of medium-sized nuclear weapon states.

OUTLOOK

A primary conclusion of this analysis is that by the mid-1990s, the Indian Ocean region will have changed substantially. For the United States and the other major external Western powers the reduction in superpower tensions, new arms control agreements and concurrent cuts in defence budgets will probably force substantially reduced military presences. The Western powers will certainly remain capable of deploying formidable forces into the theatre but this is only likely in the event of a serious regional crisis, most credibly in the Persian Gulf. Barring the remote possibility of radical change in New Delhi or Islamabad, fundamental Western interests are unlikely to be challenged by developments on the subcontinent during the coming decade, and the prospect of a direct confrontation between India and the major Western allies is remote and probably receeding.

A reduced Western military presence in the Indian Ocean would go some way towards removing a significant irritant in relations with India. This may help, in turn, to facilitate a larger and more extensive range of economic technological, educational and political cooperation which, from an Indian perspective, will probably become increasingly desirable in order to maintain high rates of economic growth.

Nevertheless, the West will remain very uncomfortable with the gradual unravelling of the nuclear non-proliferation regime on the subcontinent and these concerns will be exacerbated if India chooses to accelerate the expansion of its medium and long range force projection capabilities. An important policy challenge for the major Wetern powers will be managing this situation while simultaneously coming to terms with their reduced relative power and influence in this region.

For the leading Western countries these problems will be viewed in the context of a much more complex global regime. The mid-late 1990s are likely to confirm the serious decline of the Soviet Union and its increasingly independent but economically troubled neighbours in Eastern Europe. At the same time there will most probably be increased cohesion and prosperity in Western Europe. Japan's economic strength will continue to expand, possibly giving it a more independent and assertive political role. For China, the easing of superpower tensions and a probable continuation of domestic tensions will weaken its 'swing' position between the United States and the Soviet Union. China's current political and social system will increasingly be seen as an anachonism and there is a real possibility of further serious domestic disturbances.

In the context of these broader developments, India will be seen as comparable in population to China, with impressive economic growth, an indigenous space launch program, a developing IRBM and possibly ICBM force and, provided domestic problems do not proliferate, India will emerge as clearly the predominant power in the Indian Ocean.

India will claim major power status and involvement in central global deliberations comparable at least to that of China. For the United States and the other Western powers there would be advantage in not obstructing the gradual achievement of these Indian aspirations.

This is not only because they are largely inevitable but also because many of India's fundamental values and interests are broadly compatible with those of the West. India's deeply entrenched democratic heritage, its successful market economy, its open culture and English language and its role as a rising, strong but essentially *status quo* power provide a basis for enhanced relationships. There would appear to be scope for an expanded range of cooperative activities, not only with the United States, France and Britain but also with Japan, Western Europe, Australia and others.

In the coming quarter century the most dynamic focus of international activity will be the West Pacific. There, economic growth rates will be high, political power will expand and military capabilities will also develop substantially. But while the Indian Ocean, and especially India's role there, is unlikely to be the primary focus of global attention, it will deserve to be a much higher priority for the major Western countries than it has been in the past. India's potential is very substantial and by the middle of the next century it is likely to emerge as a major global power.

NOTES

1. The rapid growth in United States interests in the Indian Ocean in the mid and late 1970s is discussed in Walter K. Anderson 'Emerging Security Issues in the Indian Ocean' in Selig S. Harrison and K. Subrahmanyam (Eds.) *Superpower Rivalry in the Indian Ocean: Indian and American Perspectives*, Oxford University Press, Oxford, 1989, pp. 22–3.

2. Calculated from figures in *Oil and Security*, A Stockholm International Peace Research Institute Monograph, Stockholm, 1974, pp. 69, 71.

3. The sequence of United States measures in Southwest Asia during this period is detailed at greater length by Walter K. Anderson in 'Emerging Security Issues in the Indian Ocean' in Selig S. Harrison and K. Subrahmanyam *op. cit.*, pp. 27–36.

4. *Ibid* pp. 30–1.

5. *Ibid* pp. 33–4.

6. For details see Pervaiz Iqbal Cheema 'American Policy in South Asia: Interests and Objectives' Stephen Philip Cohen (Ed.) *The Security of South Asia: American and Asian Perspectives*, University of Illinois Press, Chicago, 1987, pp. 123–4.

7. This point is made by several analysts including William J. Barnds 'The United States and South Asia: Policy and Process' in Stephen Philip

Cohen (Ed.) *The Security of South Asia*, p. 155. and Pervaiz Iqbal Cheema 'American Policy in South Asia: Interests and Objectives' also in Stephen Philip Cohen, p. 125.

8. This sentiment is expressed by K. Subrahmanyam 'Prospects for Security and Stability in South Asia' in Stephen Philip Cohen, *op. cit.*, p. 211 and Selig S. Harrison 'India, the United States and Superpower Rivalry in the Indian Ocean' in Selig S. Harrison and K. Subrahmanyam, *op. cit.*, pp. 246–7.

9. See comments by Pervaiz Iqbal Cheema 'American Policy in South Asia: Interests and Objectives' in Stephen Philip Cohen, *op. cit.*, p. 119 and R. R. Subramanian 'US Policy and South Asia: The Decision-Making Dimension', pp. 146–7.

10. The debate on this point is addressed by Walter K. Anderson 'Emerging Security Issues in the Indian Ocean: An American Perspective' in Selig S. Harrison and K. Subrahmanyam, *op. cit.*, pp. 16–18.

11. See, for instance, Jasjit Singh 'Indian Ocean and Indian Security' Satish Kumar (Ed.) *Yearbook on India's Foreign Policy 1987–1988*, Sage Publications, New Delhi, 1988, p. 128; K. Subrahmanyam *Strategic Developments in the Indian and South Pacific Ocean Regions* (A paper presented to a seminar on Australia and the Indian Ocean, Fremantle, Australia, March 1988), p. 18; and Michael McKinley 'Indian Naval Developments and Australian Strategy in the Indian Ocean' in Robert H. Bruce (Ed.) *The Modern Indian Navy and the Indian Ocean: Developments and Implications*, Centre for Indian Ocean Regional Studies, Studies in Indian Ocean Maritime Affairs, Number 2, Curtin University of Technology, Perth, 1989, p. 146.

12. For details see Aadu Karemaa 'What Would Mahan Say About Space Power?' *US Naval Institute Proceedings*, vol. 114/4/1022, April, 1985, pp. 30–50.

13. See, for example, Robert H. Bruce 'Implications for International Security: Observations on the Security Dilemma and the Nature of Concerns Provoked by Indian Naval Expansion' in Robert H. Bruce, *op. cit.*, p. 115, and Ashley J. Tellis 'Securing the Barrack: The Logic, Structure and Objectives of India's Naval Expansion' also in Robert H. Bruce, *op. cit.*, pp. 44–5.

14. For details of the French military presence in the Indian Ocean see: *The Military Balance 1989–1990*, The International Institute for Strategic Studies, London, 1989, p. 62

15. *Ibid*, p. 82.

16. For details see Department of Defence *Defence Report 1987–88*, Australian Government Publishing Service, Canberra, 1989, pp. 60–62.

17. For details of these and related comparisons see: *Japan 1987: An International Comparison*, Keizai Koho Centre, Tokyo, 1987, p. 9.

18. *Ibid.*

19. *The Military Balance 1989–1990*, pp. 101 and 63.

20. *Ibid*, pp. 63, 79 and 159.

21. Western dependence on Persian Gulf oil is expected to rise from 30 per cent in 1990 to 40 per cent in 2000. See the statement by William Webster, Director of the Central Intelligence Agency, to the Senate

Armed Services Committee *Asia and Pacific Wireless File*, 23 January, 1990, pp. 26–30.

22. *The Statistical Outline of India* 1988–89, Tata Services Ltd., Bombay, 1988, p. 67.

23. These factors are discussed in the Department of Defence *Submission to the Senate Standing Committee on Foreign Affairs, Defence and Trade: Inquiry Into Australia's Relations with India*, Parliament of Australia, Canberra, 1988, pp. 4–6.

24. Dr A. D. Gordon has noted that when President Gayoom of the Maldives approached Washington for assistance at the time of the coup, the United States Government referred him to India. See A. Gordon *Nation Neighbourhood and Region: India in the 1990s*, Work in progress seminar paper, Strategic and Defence Studies Centre, Australian National University, October 1989, p. 20.

25. Indonesian concerns are discussed in Michael Byrnes 'Silent Superpower on our Doorstep,' *Australian Financial Review*, 3 December, 1988, p. 10.

26. Peter Galbraith *Nuclear Proliferation in South Asia: Containing the Threat*, A Staff Report to the Committee on Foreign Relations, United States Senate, United States Government Printing Office, Washington, 1988, p. VIII.

27. *Ibid.*

28. *Ibid.*

29. *Ibid.*

30. *Ibid.*

31. *Ibid.*, p. 2.

32. *Ibid*, pp. 2–3.

33. *The Military Balance 1989–1990*, pp. 160 and 171.

34. The evolution of India's space launch and large rocket booster programmes is detailed in *SIPRI Yearbook 1989: World Armaments and Disarmaments*, Oxford University Press, Oxford, 1989, pp. 296–7.

35. *Ibid.*

36. 'Missile Test Firing Declared a Success' *The Sydney Morning Herald*, 23 May, 1989, p. 11.

37. Amarnath K. Menon 'We Can Design Any Missile' *India Today*, 15 June, 1989, p. 31.

38. *The Military Balance 1989–1990*, p. 150.

39. *SIPRI Yearbook 1989*, p. 304.

40. For details of the arms control proposals made by India and Pakistan see Peter Galbraith *Nuclear Proliferation in South Asia*, pp. 20–26 and the testimony of Robert Peck, Former Deputy Assistant Secretary of State, Near East and South Asian Affairs in the *Hearing Before the Subcommittees on Asian and Pacific Affairs and on International Economic Policy and Trade of the Committee on Foreign Affairs of the House of Representatives*, United States Congress, 17 February 1988, pp. 6–13.

10 Conclusion

Sandy Gordon

South Asia has inherited a volatile ethnic, religious and social mix that generates powerful cross-currents of tension between the states of the region. These cross-currents are intensified by the new forces of the mass media and democracy, which help to create new ethnic and religious consciousness or re-awaken old rivalries. Population growth pushes agricultural and urban systems to the limit and the security environment becomes ever more difficult to manage.

In India, the order imposed by the Congress system once seemed immutable. Now, however, governments are frequently voted out of office by a frustrated, even angry electorate. It is a system riven by conflict between centre and region, country and city, caste and caste and religion and religion. It is a system in which the attitudes of the English-educated and secular-inclined elite are coming under increasing attack by those espousing a 'home-grown' interpretation of India and its role in the region, one that is more openly Hindu in outlook and, some would say, more chauvinistic. It is also a system in the throes of an intense debate about the traditional role of the state at the 'commanding heights' of the economy, a debate which has developed in the context of the near collapse of socialism in Europe and the stagnation of the large and growing government sector in India itself.

It is within this context of growing domestic and regional turbulence that India during the past decade has put its cards openly on the table in its quest for great power status. It appears to aspire to the status of a power like China. Its quest is underwritten by the presence of a large and wealthy middle class, an increasingly open and vibrant economy and a 'military-industrial' complex which stretches deep into the bureaucratic structure of the nation.

Because of the complexity and difficulty of the South Asian environment, however, India's attention has been focused more on the problems associated with its immediate neighbourhood and on nation-building than those of the Indian Ocean region, let alone the world. This fact is not without irony. While it is the problems of the neighbourhood that have largely driven India's military buildup, it is also those very problems that continue to limit its strategic reach.

170

This combination of a drive for great power status and intensifying regional and national problems poses a number of questions. Can the Indian system sustain the current rate of growth in military power? Will India remain an essentially subcontinental power, or will it have the capability and will to exercise power further afield, for example in the Persian Gulf or Straits of Malacca? And will it remain an essentially *status quo* power?

The papers collected in this volume present a variety of views on these questions. There are, however, a number of points in common that may usefully be drawn from them.

To begin with, the authors have few doubts that India is an emergent power in Asia. Recent years have witnessed a steady growth in India's power based upon comparatively strong economic performance. According to the World Bank, India's *per capita* income is now higher than China's,[1] and some reports put its rate of economic growth above China's in real terms.[2] This increase in the underlying growth of the economy is what has underwritten India's substantial growth in conventional military power. In documenting India's military growth, Thomas points out that by default India could acquire what he calls a 'maximalist' position that would enable it to have a strategic reach throughout the Indian Ocean.

Furthermore, with the prospect of a declining role for the superpowers in the region, India's growth in military capability is likely to leave it stronger in relative as well as absolute terms. The Soviet Union is no longer a major factor in the Indian Ocean and the 'peace dividend' in world politics may eventually lead to a reduced presence on the part of the United States. However, in exploring the theme of India's relative rise to power *vis-à-vis* the superpowers, Babbage notes that the lure of Gulf oil will remain strong for the West throughout the 1990s and that this will in turn ensure a continuing presence on the part of the United States, a point that has been underlined by the August 1990 crisis in the Persian Gulf.

While India's emerging role is fully acknowledged in the papers collected in this volume, another theme which runs through a number of contributions is that there are clear limitations both upon the current extent of India's power and upon the rate at which that power will accrue. With India, it is very much a question of 'watch this space'.

Some of these limitations to power are explored by Manoj Joshi. He identifies the failure to implement an adequate system of military planning, current limitations in availability of foreign exchange, which restrict force modernisation plans, and the general sense of caution that has resulted from India's intervention in Sri Lanka. Another limiting factor is the slow pace of India's indigenous weapons programme, a theme covered by Gordon as well as Joshi. Added to this, India faces continuing problems from irridentist forces at home, problems that in turn have become linked with and reinforce the competition between India and its neighbours, especially Pakistan.

It is this competition between India on the one hand and Pakistan and China on the other that poses the major restraint on India's strategic reach. While quite clearly the leading military power on the subcontinent, as both Saikal and Habib point out India is not yet accepted as the paramount power, especially by Pakistan. Indeed, Thomas argues that India does not yet have clear superiority in the event of a combined attack by Pakistan and China, a point borne out by the situation on the border with Pakistan, where because of demands on Indian forces elsewhere, Pakistan is still able to match India almost division for division. One could even argue the case that Pakistan has never been in a stronger position militarily *vis-à-vis* India, with that position set to strengthen further should the acquisition of sixty additional F-16 aircraft from the United States proceed as scheduled.[3] Neither Saikal in his study of India's prospects in Southwest Asia nor Klintworth in his account of the relationship with China foresees an early end to the competition between India and its two most powerful neighbours. As Klintworth notes with respect to China, however, in the post-Tiananmen environment relations between the two Asian giants are as positive as they have been for some considerable time as China seeks to win friends from whatever quarter it can. It is more in the long term that he sees the competition for Asian leadership between the two unfolding. From Beijing's perspective the current thaw might be more tactical in its intent than strategic.

Given the continuation of this troubled environment in South Asia, India will be restrained for some time to come from casting its strategic net further throughout the Indian Ocean, even should it wish to do so.

Both Thomas and Gordon, however, are of the view that in the longer term India will continue to grow as a military power, a growth that will be underwritten by continuing economic growth and increasing technological sophistication. Over the longer term, India's centrality in the Indian Ocean is likely to be a salient feature on the strategic map of the region. It becomes pertinent to ask, therefore, where its primary interests are likely to lie.

India's goal of quarantining the subcontinent from what it would regard as outside interference will remain the fundamental concern of security policy. But within such a framework, Thomas notes the propensity for India progressively to define its security interests somewhat further afield than South Asia.

One such area of growing concern to New Delhi is the Persian Gulf. India's dependence on imported oil has recently been increasing rapidly[4] and its economic links with Gulf states, including remittances from guest workers and a growing number of project-related activities, are important to it. But surpassing even these interests is the concern on the part of India that the linkages between Pakistan and wealthy Gulf states such as Saudi Arabia could upset the strategic balance on the subcontinent itself. New Delhi's concerns about such linkages have been reinforced recently by Pakistan's efforts to cast India in a negative light over the Kashmir issue and by the transfer of intermediate-range ballistic missiles from China to Saudi Arabia.[5]

New Delhi's concerns about the Gulf are, however, likely to continue to be expressed in a muted fashion. While concerned over the longer term to build forces capable of intervening in the region, India will be equally concerned not to appear to be doing so. In the context of India's competition with Pakistan, the last thing New Delhi would want would be for Gulf states to perceive India as a military threat. On the contrary, New Delhi's diplomacy to date has been heavily weighted towards countering attempts by Pakistan to cast it in such a light. India's low key response to the 1990 Gulf crisis should be seen not just in terms of the strength of its relationship with an Iraq that it perceived to be a secular force in the Gulf (Saikal), but also in the context of its ongoing diplomatic competition with Pakistan in Southwest Asia (Gordon).

Some have speculated that India may also wish to bring the Straits of Malacca and possibly some of the nations of Southeast Asia into this wider security framework. ASEAN leaders such as the Malaysian Minister for Defence and the Prime Minister of Singapore have expressed concern about India's naval buildup.[6]

Seen in this light, the views of Habib are particularly pertinent. He identifies no strong impetus on the part of India to be involved with the nations of Southeast Asia in the security context. He also is of the view that the growth of India's military power is directed primarily towards China and Pakistan. He is therefore apparently unconcerned about the motivation for India's development of its military facilities in the Andaman and Nicobar Islands, which will in any case be secondary to those on the western side of peninsula India. Perhaps it is worth noting at this point the possibility that India's plans to develop a naval–air base on Great Nicobar Island, situated only 160 km from Sumatra, may have been shelved because of expressions of concern on the part of Indonesia.[7] If this was indeed the case, it says something about India's sensitivity to the views of ASEAN nations, a sensitivity that would derive both from the growing trading interest in that part of the world and the perception that Southeast Asia could emerge as an important meeting ground for the interests of China and India. India would thus appear to see any competition with China in Southeast Asia as being conducted more in the diplomatic and economic spheres than the military arena.

But should China seek to assert more strongly its territorial claims in the South China Sea – claims that, if realised, would take its territory to within 80 km of Malaysia – then India could see a need further to develop its military capability in the Bay of Bengal. The Straits of Malacca could potentially become a venue for naval competition between India and China. Should such a situation begin to develop, those ASEAN countries most affected might come to feel sufficiently squeezed that they would be forced to choose between India and China, or even build up their own forces further in response. As in the case of Singapore, they might also take more active steps to encourage the presence of a balancing third force such as the United States. But we would do well to note that at least in the early stages of such a development, ASEAN member states might have different perceptions, depending on their histories, as to whether the real threat were to lie more from China than India. Moreover, given the requirements of regional diplomacy, their expressions concerning the direction of the perceived threat may well be ambiguous, if not misleading.

But with China currently going out of its way to improve relations with India, with growing tension between India and Pakistan over Kashmir, with the highly unstable situation in the Persian Gulf and with continuing strong Indian support for the Soviet-backed regime in Kabul, the Western and Northern theatres are likely to command the major part of India's attention and resources for some considerable time to come.

Indeed, as a number of authors speculate, the deteriorating relationship between Hindus and Muslims in India could cause some Islamic nations to 'gang up' on India. But should such an event occur, any reaction by Islamic nations would be more likely to emanate from Southwest Asia than Southeast Asia. This is because the countries to the West of India have been more closely involved in South Asian issues and particularly in the Pakistan–India dispute. An additional factor is that the elites of predominantly Muslim ASEAN nations have been traditionally concerned to ensure that Islam is subsumed into the wider goal of development of the nation state.

Another element in the India–Pakistan equation that will have increasing effect over the long term is the 'nuclear brinkmanship' (to use Thomas' terms) that has developed with respect to nuclear weapons. Both Saikal and Thomas observe that India and Pakistan have already developed some of the features of nuclear competitor states, including the fighting of proxy wars, with India lending support to Pakistan's opponents in Afghanistan and dissident elements in the Pakistani province of Sind, and with Pakistan supporting dissidents in Indian Punjab and Jammu and Kashmir.

As noted by both Babbage and Thomas, India's major concerns in the nuclear sphere are with China rather than Pakistan. Therefore, any declaration by India that it possessed nuclear weapons would probably mean that it would move quickly to acquire near parity with China, rapidly overtaking Pakistan in the process. If, on the other hand, it chooses to maintain its current ambiguous stance, this would probably involve the maintenance of a lesser stockpile directed more at countering Pakistan than China.

A 'nuclear' India would thus relatively quickly emerge as the only major regional nuclear power in the Indian Ocean. While recognising the severe limitations on the negotiability of the nuclear currency of power as demonstrated by the superpower example, it needs also to be recognised that in circumstances in which the superpowers might be forced or choose to play a lesser role in the Indian Ocean, there would exist no restraining strategic balance on India. This is not to say that India would necessarily choose to use any nuclear capability in a threatening way, but rather that the perceptions of other regional states about India's role and status in the region would alter radically, and that such a shift in perception would be bound to affect India's currency of power in the region. More worrying still, such a development might also lend support to those elements in regional countries advocating development of a nuclear deterrent.

In respect of the superpowers, the receding of the tide of Cold War should facilitate a more measured approach on the part of all regional countries. On its part, New Delhi is likely to assess that India's future security and status will be built as much on the development of a sophisticated economy from which it can derive effective dual-use technologies as from the importation of complete or near complete weapon systems. The United States and other OECD nations will be best placed to assist India in developing sophisticated technologies throughout the 1990s. Furthermore, as Austin also points out, the Soviet Union will be less well placed to provide the concessional arms transfers that were such an important feature of the relationship in the past, even should it desire to maintain its strategic involvement in South Asia, which he feels it will not. In his view, in whatever way events unfold in the Soviet Union, Moscow will be too tied up with its own problems to be able to maintain its former strategic role in South Asia. According to Joshi, even now there is a growing tacit acceptance in New Delhi that the US presence in the Indian Ocean has more to do with wider concerns on the part of Washington than any desire to interfere in the affairs of India or its neighbours; a point that Babbage notes has not been the case in the past.

But perhaps it is worth introducing a note of caution into the discussion about India's future relations with the superpowers. Although we have seen over a number of years a greater balance in relations between India and the superpowers, a number of factors may cause India to proceed slowly and cautiously in its drift towards the West.

Saikal believes that there will be little early change in the dynamics of the relationships between the Soviet Union, Afghanistan, Pakistan and India, and that this will limit the movement of New Delhi away from Moscow. Afganistan is important to India strategically in the context of its competition with Pakistan, an importance that pre-dates the Soviet invasion of that unfortunate country and that is certainly not diminished by the Soviet withdrawal. The fall of Benazir Bhutto, moreover, may well see the reassertion of Pakistan's support for Islamic fundamentalist groups within the Afghan *Mujahideen*, an event that could delay a settlement and add fuel to the flames of the 'proxy' war in Afghanistan. As Gordon points out, another factor that may act as a sea anchor on New Delhi's drift from Moscow is the important residual arms relationship.[8] Moreover, Austin notes that both Moscow and New Delhi also have a common interest in attempting to limit the role of radical Islam in Southern Asia and in supporting secular forces.

The 1980s commenced with considerable tension between the superpowers, tension that spilled over into the South Asian region of which India is a part. It was a decade also that saw India play a more prominent role as it sought to project power to maintain the *status quo* in the subcontinent. Many of the issues that were at the forefront of the agenda during the 1980s have not yet been resolved. These include the conflict in Afghanistan, the civil war in Sri Lanka and the competition between India and Pakistan over Kashmir. Such issues will continue to be played out during the 1990s, but the backdrop against which they will unfold is likely to be somewhat different. The superpowers are unlikely to seek to be so closely involved, thus leaving India's role even more prominently exposed to view. As technologies advance, the nuclear ambiguity is likely to provide a more ominous backdrop to events, even should the protagonists not choose an overt nuclear position. The relationship between India and China will be central, not just from the nuclear point of view, but also because it will shape India's attitude towards and disposition of forces within the Northeast of the Indian Ocean. Increasingly, India's role is likely to be important not only in South Asia, but also further afield, for instance in the Gulf. While final acquisition of true Indian Ocean-wide great power status by India is likely to be an issue for the twenty-first rather than the twentieth century, regional states and superpowers alike will eventually have to recognise the fact of India's new-found status in the region.

NOTES

1. World Bank, *World Development Report 1989*, Table I, pp. 164–5.
2. See 'Key Economic Indicators', *Asiaweek*, 6 July, 1990, p. 6.
3. Unlike the situation at the time of the 1965 and 1971 wars, Pakistan would not have to fight India with its forces divided between eastern and western wings in any renewed bout. India, on the other hand, is currently struggling with its own serious internal problems.
4. See 'Petrol: The Coming Crunch', *India Today*, 15 June, 1990.
5. See Leonard S. Spector, *The Undeclared Bomb: The Spread of Nuclear Weapons, 1987–88*, Carnegie Endowment (Ballinger), Cambridge, Mass., p. 15.
6. See Michael Richardson, 'Southeast Asia Wary', *Pacific Defence Reporter*, vol. XVI, no. 8, February, 1990, p. 42.
7. See Mohammed Ayoob, *India and Southeast Asia: Indian Perceptions and Policies*, Routledge, London, 1990, pp. 42–3; and Mohan Ram, 'Ruling the Waves', in *Far Eastern Economic Review*, 15 May, 1986.
8. We can even now see signs of the durability of the arms relationship with the recent Soviet offer radically to upgrade the MiG 21 aircraft currently manufactured in India, including with the provision of MiG 29 engines. See *Pacific Defence Reporter*, May, 1990, p. 31. India is, however, holding out for a deal on joint production of the MiG 29.

Index